ISBN 978-1-330-33669-4
PIBN 10031902

This book is a reproduction of an important historical work. Forgotten Books uses
state-of-the-art technology to digitally reconstruct the work, preserving the original format
whilst repairing imperfections present in the aged copy. In rare cases, an imperfection in
the original, such as a blemish or missing page, may be replicated in our edition. We do,
however, repair the vast majority of imperfections successfully; any imperfections that
remain are intentionally left to preserve the state of such historical works.

1 MONTH OF
FREE
READING

at

www.ForgottenBooks.com

By purchasing this book you are eligible for one month membership to ForgottenBooks.com, giving you unlimited access to our entire collection of over 700,000 titles via our web site and mobile apps.

To claim your free month visit:

www.forgottenbooks.com/free31902

English
Français
Deutsche
Italiano
Español
Português

www.forgottenbooks.com

Mythology Photography **Fiction**
Fishing Christianity **Art** Cooking
Essays Buddhism Freemasonry
Medicine **Biology** Music **Ancient
Egypt** Evolution Carpentry Physics
Dance Geology **Mathematics** Fitness
Shakespeare **Folklore** Yoga Marketing
Confidence Immortality Biographies
Poetry **Psychology** Witchcraft
Electronics Chemistry History **Law**
Accounting **Philosophy** Anthropology
Alchemy Drama Quantum Mechanics
Atheism Sexual Health **Ancient History**
Entrepreneurship Languages Sport
Paleontology Needlework Islam
Metaphysics Investment Archaeology
Parenting Statistics Criminology
Motivational

FRAGMENTS AND SCRAPS

HISTORY.

VOL. I.

LONDON:
WILLIAM CLOWES, 14, CHARING CROSS.

1834.

FRAGMENTS AND SCRAPS

OF

HISTORY.

b

HISTORIA EST TESTIS TEMPORUM, LUX VERITATIS, VITÆ
MEMORIA, MAGISTER VITÆ, NUNCIA VETUSTATIS.

CIC. DE ORATORE, lib. ii. c. 9.

NOTE.—The extracts of the Greek and Latin passages, which are referred
to as authorities throughout these fragments, are wholly omitted, for two
reasons: 1st, Because they are so numerous that they would extend this
work to an inconvenient length; and, 2dly, That they would much enhance
the expense of it. Wherever references are made to writers of antiquity, Greek
or Latin, the fidelity of the citations in this their ENGLISH dress may be perfectly relied upon.

b 2

PREFACE AND DEDICATION.

It may be satisfactory, if not even due, to those few friends for whom the private perusal of these pages is designed, to explain the reasons why this heterogeneous mass of Fragments and Scraps is presented to them instead of some continuous history, of which, from what follows, it would seem there were abundant powers of selection. The fact is of easy, if not of satisfactory explanation. With the exception of a few passages in the original text, and in the notes, these Fragments are the growth of considerably more than thirty years. It will be seen that about thirty years ago (and about two years before I quitted my PROFESSIONAL occupation, and accepted the invitation to undertake the duties, and to encounter the arduous and incessant labours of the OFFICIAL station which I filled for more than twenty years, and which, I can venture to say with truth, I never neglected,) I had entertained a very comprehensive design for a HISTORY of BRITAIN, which, however, was soon abandoned, from the conviction that a *long* life of *leisure* would scarcely suffice for its completion, and that it would have been utterly inconsistent *even* with my less laborious *professional* pursuits, and when my time was more than afterwards at *my own* disposal; but from the moment of my acceptance of OFFICIAL station, my time became exclusively the PROPERTY of the PUBLIC. From that moment there was an end at once of history as a STUDY,—it became the PLAY-THING of an *occasional* hour of leisure and relaxation, from the toil of my OFFICIAL avocations. The periods of excessive and incessant labour were of very *long*—the occasional hours of leisure and relaxation were few, rare, and of very *short* duration. The STUDY of HISTORY had ever been with me a favourite pursuit. These Fragments and Scraps are, therefore, the hasty productions of the very few hours of relaxation which occasionally before, but very rarely afterwards, occurred. Some historical subject happened, in one of those hours, to excite my interest in its perusal,—my thoughts were committed (as was always my custom) to paper,—the subject was pursued with eagerness,—and proceeded, until interrupted by the urgent and necessitous calls of OFFICIAL business, which continued so *long*, that, at the expiration of them, the interest which had been originally excited was worn out or weakened; the subject had been thrown aside, and was never resumed. Again and again, the perusal of some other historical works originally excited similar interests,—were followed by similar pursuits — similar interruptions — and at length similar terminations ensued. The subjects were never resumed. In this manner have these Fragments and Scraps grown up and accumulated. The state of my health has been, and still is, such as scarcely to enable me even to revise what I have written, still less to complete the unfinished Fragments; but such as they are, and with all their imperfections on their heads, I unhesitatingly, but with diffidence, consign them to a PRIVATE tribunal of partial affection, and dedicate them to MY DEAR SON, whose expressed wishes for their EARLY publication may, probably, be gratified in my lifetime,

ON

THE USE AND STUDY

OF

HISTORY.

THE USE AND STUDY

HISTORY.

—————

As one of the great schools of instruction in the practical philosophy of life — the regulation of human conduct — HISTORY holds forth the EXAMPLES of ages PAST, as the most impressive lessons for the moral instruction of ages PRESENT and TO COME.

We shall soon see that this sentiment has been illustrated, and the use of HISTORY, as a STUDY, has been, by energetic and incessant precept and argument, urged upon the attention and inculcated for the observance of mankind by almost every HISTORIAN of antiquity, in those ANNALS or writings which recorded the transactions and events in the ages which preceded them; but which have unfortunately perished, and been swallowed up in the insatiable gulf of TIME. When we consider, however, that in those ages copies were not multiplied, as at the present day, by the art of printing, we ought to be thankful even for that scanty portion of the works of ANCIENT authors which have been handed down to us, even in a mutilated state, and which we now possess.

But although their writings have perished, the fact of the advice which they inculcated has been ascertained and certified to us, upon the testimony of another celebrated historian of antiquity, *Polybius*(1), whose history has unhappily been only partially preserved to us, from the sacrilegious ravages of this ruthless, indiscriminating, unsparing destroyer. *Polybius*, in the outset of his history, observes, that it is unnecessary for him to begin his work in advising mankind to apply themselves with earnestness to the STUDY of HISTORY, since the knowledge of PAST EVENTS affords the BEST INSTRUCTIONS for the regulation and good conduct of human life; and he assigns as the reason for his omission, that the greater part, or rather all, of the historians employed *before* him in relating the transactions of former times, have taken every occasion to declare (repeating it, as may be said, from one end of their writings to the other) that HISTORY supplies the only proper discipline to train and exercise the minds of those who are inclined to enter into PUBLIC affairs; and that the evil accidents which are there recorded to have befallen other men, contain the wisest and most effectual lessons for enabling us to support our own misfortunes with dignity and

(1) See Note A. The edition of *Polybius* here referred to is that of *Gronovius*. Much use has been made of Mr. Hampton's elegant translation.

courage; and as this is the fact, "there is surely little need,"
says he, "to repeat again what *others* have *so often* urged
with eloquence and force *."

In his second book, de Oratore, *Cicero* introduces a dialogue
between *Catulus* (2) and *Antonius* (3) (the grandfather of
Marc Antony, the triumvir, at whose instigation *Cicero* was
afterwards assassinated), in which he gives the following account, as to the style and manner of HISTORICAL composition in
use amongst the very early GREEK and also LATIN historians.
Antonius is made to inquire, what style of writing and what
talents are requisite to constitute an HISTORIAN; to which
Catulus replied—"That to write after the manner of the
GREEKS would require the highest style of oratory, but to write
as a ROMAN there was no occasion for eloquence—to *adhere
to the* TRUTH *was all that was requisite.*" *Antonius* dissents
from this proposition, observing that "the GREEKS themselves
at first wrote in the same style with *Cato* (4), *Pictor* (5), and
Piso (6). HISTORY was *then* only an annual chronicle of
events. It was the custom for the *Pontifex Maximus* to
write down the transactions of each year from the foundation
of ROME up to the time of the *Pontifex*, Q. Mutius Scævola (7),
for the sake of retaining the recollection of events. These
chronicles were fixed upon a tablet for the information of the

---

* Polyh. lib. i. c. 1.   (2) See Note B.
(3) See Note C.   (4) See Note D.
(5) See Note E.   (6) See Note F.
(7) See Note G.

public, and were called the GREAT ANNALS.   Many imitated
this mode of writing HISTORY, and left behind them mere naked
unembellished chronicles of dates—of men—of places—and
events.   Such amongst the GREEKS were *Pherecydes* (8), *Helanicus* (9), *Acusilaus* (10), and many others.   Such amongst
the ROMANS were *Cato, Pictor,* and *Piso,* who were wholly
unacquainted with the art of embellishment, and, provided
the narrative was intelligible, considered BREVITY the only
excellence in HISTORICAL composition."   *Antony* then proceeds to discuss the merits and excellencies in point of composition of the GREEK HISTORIANS, but with this preliminary
observation descriptive of an important distinction between
the ROMAN and GREEK historians :—" It is no wonder," he
observes, " if HISTORY makes no figure in the language of the
former, for no ROMAN ever studied eloquence with any other
view than to shine at the bar; whereas the most eloquent
among the GREEKS, removed from forensic pleading, devoted
themselves, amongst other high pursuits, principally to the
writing of HISTORY *."

In ancient times the *Pontifex Maximus* used to draw up
a short account of the public transactions of every year in a
book, and to expose this Register in an open place at his
house, where the people might come and read it,—which
continued to be done to the time of Mutius Scævola, who was

(8) See Note H.   (9) See Note I.
(10) See Note K.   * Cicero de Orat.

slain in the bloody proscriptions and massacres of *Marius*(11) and *Cinna*(12). These records were called in the time of *Cicero* ANNALES Maximi*, as having been composed by the *Pontifex Maximus*. The annals composed by the *Pontifices* before ROME was taken by the GAULS, called also *Commentarii*, perished most of them with the city †. After the time of *Sylla*(13) the *Pontifices* seem to have dropped the custom of compiling annals ‡.

My Lord *Bolinbroke* § remarks, that " it is worth while to observe the progress that the ROMANS and the GREEKS made towards HISTORY. The ROMANS had journalists, or *annalists*, from the very beginning of their state. In the sixth century of the Republic, or very near it at the soonest, they began to have antiquaries, and some attempts were made towards writing of HISTORY." He calls " these first *historical* productions attempts only, or essays—and they were no more, neither among the ROMANS nor among the GREEKS; as they wanted style and skill to write in such a manner as might answer all the ends of HISTORY, so they wanted materials. *Pherecydes* wrote something about *Iphigenia*, and the Festivals of *Bacchus*. *Helanicus* was a poetical historian, and *Acusilaus* graved genealogies on plates of brass.

---

(11) See Note L.   (12) See Note M.
* Cic. Orat. ii. c. 12 ; Gell. iv. c. 5.   † Livy, vi. 1.
(13) See Note N.   ‡ Adams's Roman Antiquities, p. 282.
§ On the Study of History, vol. iii. p. 412.

Pictor, who is called by *Livy*, ' *Scriptorum antiquis-simus*,' published, I think, some short *Annals* of his own time.   Neither he nor *Piso* could have sufficient materials for the HISTORY of ROME, nor *Cato*, I presume, even for the antiquities of ITALY.   The ROMANS, with the other people of that country, were then just rising out of barbarity, and growing acquainted with letters.   These *Annals* could contain nothing more than short minutes or memorandums hung up in a table at the Pontiff's house, like the rules of the game in a billiard-room, and much such HISTORY as we have in the epitomes prefixed to the books of *Livy*, or of any other historian in lapidary inscriptions, or in some modern almanacks.   Materials they were for HISTORY, no doubt, but scanty and insufficient, such as those ages could produce when writing and reading were accomplishments uncommon.   In those nations that preserve their dominion long and grow up to manhood, the elegant as well as the necessary arts and sciences are improved to some degree of perfection; and HISTORY, that was at first intended only to record the names, or perhaps the general characters of some famous men, and to transmit in gross the remarkable events of every age to posterity, is raised to answer another and a nobler end."

Sir *William Jones*, with reference to the dialogue in *Cicero* between *Catulus* and *Antonius*, observes, that " HISTORY in its original state was probably nothing more than the BARE RELATION of public events, which were digested in the form of ANNALS, like the Life of *Tully*, by *Fabricius*.   We are

assured that this was the case in old ROME: and *it seems, indeed, in all ages to be the wisest, as well as the most useful method of writing* HISTORY, *unless the facts were more diligently examined and more fairly represented than they appear to be in most productions of this nature.*"
" Among the GREEKS—*Pherecydes, Helanicus,* and *Epimenides*(14), and among the LATINS—*Cato, Pictor,* and *Piso,* are said to have written without affecting any ornament or arriving at any other merit than that of a nervous brevity."

Thucydides(15) (who was born 471 years before the birth of our Saviour) is quoted by *Dionysius* of *Halicarnassus* as defining HISTORY to be " PHILOSOPHY teaching by EXAMPLES."

Of the HISTORIANS now extant who have treated of the use of HISTORY as a STUDY, *Polybius* follows next to *Thucydides* in order of time:

————" Longo sed proximus intervallo."

Upon *Polybius* two eminent writers of the age which has just gone by, have bestowed the palm of a well-merited eulogium and of a just commendation :—" Accuracy and probity " (says Mr. Gibbon *) " shine in his writings : he was a soldier, a statesman, and a philosopher." In drawing

(14) See Note O.　　　　(15) See Note P.
* Miscel. vol. ii. pp. 177, 183.

a comparison between *Polybius* and *Livy*, as to the TRUTH
of their respective narrations of the passage of *Hannibal*
across the *Alps*, and in his preference of that of the *former*
over that of the *latter*, he observes, that "in *Polybius* we
meet with nothing but unadorned simplicity and plain
reason.   A justness of thinking, rare in his age and country,
united with a sterility of fancy still more rare, made him
prefer the TRUTH which he thoroughly knew, to ornaments
which he was perhaps the more inclined to despise because
he felt himself incapable of attaining them."

After an enumeration and very concise criticism of *Herodotus* (16), *Thucydides*, and *Xenophon* (17), Sir *William
Jones* observes, that " of all the GREEK historians *Polybius*
was perhaps the gravest, the wisest, and the most faithful."

An adherence to TRUTH is a universal, essential, and
FUNDAMENTAL requisite in the composition of HISTORY.   If
this indispensable quality be disregarded HISTORY would
become to all intents and purposes an idle tale, without the
attainment of the object for which it was designed—in short
a NOVEL.

Let us now see in what particulars *Polybius* considers the
excellence and use of HISTORY as a STUDY to consist.   In
support of the various propositions which he advances, either

(16) See Note Q.   (17) See Note R.

as to the *falsehood* of the narration or the want of a due observance of the EXAMPLES presented by HISTORY, *Polybius,* for the most part, adduces the instances, and contends that by a proper STUDY and attention to these EXAMPLES the unfortunate results which occurred might have been either wholly or partially avoided.

Speaking of the proper office and duties of an HISTORIAN, and of the absolute necessity for an undeviating adherence to TRUTH, *Polybius* observes, that " it is in part the character of a good man to love his country and his friends, and to hate the enemies of both. But the HISTORIAN must divest himself of those affections, and be ready on many occasions to speak largely in the praises of an enemy when his conduct deserves applause, nor scruple to condemn his most esteemed and dearest friends as often as their actions call for censure."

" TRUTH," he observes, " is the eye of HISTORY. If we take away TRUTH from HISTORY, what remains will be nothing but a useless tale. Now, if we pay a proper regard to TRUTH, we shall find it necessary, not only to condemn our friends on some occasions, and to commend our enemies, but also to commend and condemn the same person as circumstances may require. An HISTORIAN, in all that he relates, should take care to be directed in his judgment by the genuine and *real* circumstances of every action, without regarding the *actors* *

* Polyh. lib. i. c. 1.

in it;" and he proceeds to illustrate this proposition by
EXAMPLES.

He adduces, as an instance of the first, *Philinus,* who wrote
an account of the affairs of SICILY; and *Polybius* distinctly
states, that the facts are *false* which are first affirmed, and that
the ROMANS were victorious in the two engagements in which
they are represented by this historian to have been defeated.
The same mistakes are to be found in almost every part of
his performance. Nor is the history of *Fabius*(18) in this
respect more accurate.

In speaking of the conduct and fate of *Regulus*(19), he
observes, " How wide a field of reflection is opened to us by
this event; and what admirable lessons does it contain for
the good conduct of human life. In the fate of *Regulus* we
may discern how little confidence should be reposed in *Fortune,* especially when she flatters with the fairest hopes. Let
the reader take care to reap some profit from EXAMPLE, and
apply it to the improvement of his life and manners : for
since there are two sources only from whence any real benefit
can be derived—our own misfortunes, and those that have
happened to other men,—and since the first of these, though
generally perhaps the most effectual, is far more dangerous
and painful than the other, it will always be the part of prudence to prefer the latter, which will alone enable us at all

(18) See Note E.   (19) See Note S.

times to discern what is fit and useful without any hazard or disquiet,—and hence appears the genuine excellence of HIS-TORY; which, without the labour or the cost of suffering, instructs us how to form our actions upon the truest models, and to direct our judgment right in all the different circumstances of life *."

Upon this subject *Diodorus Siculus* makes the following judicious and appropriate remarks :—" The ROMANS transplanted a great army into AFRICA, under the command of *Regulus* the *Consul*. They first prevailed over the CARTHAGINIANS, and took many of their towns and castles, and destroyed great numbers of their soldiers; but as soon as *Xantippus*(20), the SPARTAN, whom they had hired to be their general, came out of GREECE, the CARTHAGINIANS totally routed the ROMANS, and destroyed a numerous army. Afterwards they fought several battles by sea, wherein the ROMANS lost many ships, and abundance of men, to the number of a hundred thousand†. Who can but utterly condemn the pride, folly, madness, and insolence of *Regulus?* who, not able to bear the weight of his prosperous fortune, both lost his own reputation, and brought many great mischiefs and calamities upon his country : for when he might have concluded a peace with the CARTHAGINIANS, honourable and advantageous to the ROMANS, but base and dishonourable

* Polyh. lib. i. c. 3.

(20) See Note T.   † Diod. Sic. Fragm. lib. xxiii. No. 12.

to the other, and his name might have been for ever renowned
among all men for his clemency and humanity, he had no
regard to any of these things; but proudly insulting the distresses of the afflicted, stood upon such terms as not only
provoked the gods to anger, but forced the conquered, by
reason of these unreasonable conditions, to stand it out reso-
lutely to the utmost extremity: so that the face of affairs was
suddenly changed, insomuch that the CARTHAGINIANS, who
but a little before were in great terror and amazement on
account of their late rout, and despaired of any relief,
gathered courage, and cut off and routed their enemy's army.
And upon this misfortune, such was the distress and amazement of the city of ROME, that they who were before esteemed
the best soldiers in the world, durst not engage the enemy in
that kind any more; and, therefore, this is the longest war
we read of in former times: and the matter was now to be
decided by sea-fights, in which a vast number of ships, both
of the ROMANS and their confederates, were destroyed; and
a hundred thousand men perished in these battles. And it
is easy to conceive how vast a treasure must be expended,
sufficient to maintain so great a fleet for the continuance of a
war for fifteen years.   But he who was the author and occasion of so many miseries had himself no small share in the
calamity, since his present dishonour and disgrace far over-
balanced his former glory and reputation,—and *by his misfortune others are taught not to be proud in prosperity.*
And that which was most cutting and grievous was, that he

was now forced to endure the scoffs and scorns of those over whom he had before exulted in the time of their calamity, having entirely debarred himself from that pity and commiseration which is usually shown to those who are in affliction. But as for *Xantippus,* he not only delivered the CARTHAGINIANS from the present evils which hung over them, but altogether changed the face of affairs; for he utterly routed the ROMANS, who were but just now conquerors, and after a prodigious slaughter, raised the CARTHAGINIANS to such a height of prosperity, who were expecting their last doom, that for the future they slighted and contemned their enemy. The report of this famous action being circulated over almost the whole world, every one admired the valour of this general. For it appeared like a miracle to every one, that there should be such a sudden change of affairs, by one man only joining with the CARTHAGINIANS, and that they who were but lately so closely besieged, should on a sudden besiege the enemy; and that they who, by their valour, were a little before lords both of sea and land, should be now cooped up in a small town, expecting every day to become a prey to their enemies; but it is not to be wondered at, since the prudence and wisdom of the general overcame all difficulties*."

Upon this conduct and fate of *Regulus,* my Lord *Bolinbroke,* after quoting *Polybius,* observes, that " *Regulus* had seen at Rome many EXAMPLES of magnanimity—of frugality

* Diod. Sic. lib. xxiii. Fragm. 1 : Booth's Translation.

D

—of the contempt of riches—and of other virtues—and these virtues he practised. But he had not learned—*nor had opportunity of learning another*, which the EXAMPLES re· corded in HISTORY inculcate frequently—the *lesson of mode-ration*. An insatiable thirst of military fame—an uncon-fined ambition of extending their empire—an extravagant confidence in their own courage and force—an insolent con-tempt of their enemies—and an *impetuous overbearing spirit* with which they pursued all their enterprises, composed, in his days, the *distinguishing characte*r of a ROMAN. What-ever the senate and people resolved, to the members of that commonwealth appeared both practicable and just. Neither difficulties nor dangers could check them, and their sages had not yet discovered, that *virtues in excess degenerate into vices.* Notwithstanding the beautiful rant which Horace(21) puts into his mouth, I make no doubt that *Regulus* learned at CARTHAGE those *lessons of moderation,* which he *had not learned* at ROME; but he learned them by EXPERIENCE, and the FRUITS of this EXPERIENCE came TOO LATE, and cost TOO DEAR; for they cost the total defeat of the ROMAN army— the prolongation of a calamitous war, which might have been finished by a glorious peace—the loss of liberty to thousands of ROMAN citizens and to *Regulus* himself—the loss of life in the midst of torments, if we are entirely to credit what is perhaps exaggerated in the Roman authors *."

But to return to *Polybius.* " Let us consider," says he, " what is the genuine and proper character, and what the peculiar use of HISTORY ? An historian, then, instead of endeavouring, like writers of tragedy, to strike the reader with terror, instead of dressing up probable speeches, and enumerating all the circumstances that might possibly have followed after every accident, should be satisfied with giving a bare relation of such facts and discourses as really happened, though perhaps they may contain nothing great or elevated. For the nature and design of tragedy are very different from those of HISTORY : the business of the former is to strike and captivate the minds of the hearers, for the present moment, by such representations as are barely probable ; whereas HISTORY professes to give lessons of improvement even to future times, by relating such discourses and events as are strictly TRUE. In the one, therefore, the probable, though false, may be sufficient to conduct us to the end in view, which is amusement and delight ; but the other, whose proper work is to convey instruction, must be always built on TRUTH *."

In illustration of this proposition, *Polybius* adduces the instance of *Philarchus,* the historian, and censures him for a want of talents and capacity. " His relations, too," he says, " are fabulous and false, and do not possess that credit which ought only to be paid to those that are genuine and

* Polyh. lib. ii. c. 4.

D 2

true.   He has shown abundant proofs of haste, inaccuracy, want of judgment and discernment." *Polybius* concludes his criticism of *Philarchus*, by stating, that "there is no need to use many words to explode a kind of writing so mean and womanish."

" It is true, indeed," says *Polybius*, " that a distinct and close survey of past events, though it might yield some entertainment to the curious, would, however, be of little use, if mankind were able of themselves, without the assistance of EXAMPLE, to repel effectually every stroke of fortune, and obviate the evils that are incident to life.   But such is human nature, that this can by no means be affirmed either of public societies or of single men; since the most fair and flourishing condition is so subject to decay and change that we can build no lasting expectations on it.   And it is on this account that the knowledge of *past* transactions ought to be esteemed, not a mere amusement only, but rather an instructive and a necessary STUDY;   for unless we have made due reflection upon the conduct of men in former times, how shall we learn the arts of gaining allies and friends when any danger threatens our country or *ourselves*.   In the accounts of former ages the facts themselves disclose to us the real views and genuine dispositions of the actors.   And from thence we are enabled to discern, in various circumstances, from whom we may reasonably expect good offices, favour, assistance, or the contrary ;   or to know, with perfect certainty, what kind of persons may be induced to compassionate our distresses, defend our cause with zeal, or join us in avenging any injuries to which we may have been exposed,—a knowledge surely of the greatest use and benefit, both in the administration of *public* affairs and in the conduct also of *private* life *." But in order to gain this end, it will be necessary that both the author and the reader, instead of being satisfied with a bare relation of events, should carefully consider all that passed both before and after, as well as at the time of the transaction. If we take from HISTORY the *motives* to which every action owed its birth—the manner in which it was carried into *execution*—the *end* that was proposed—and whether the *event* was answerable to the first design,—what remains is a mere exercise fit for schools, and not a work of science; and, though it may afford perhaps some *transient amusement* to the mind, is not capable of yielding any sound instruction or lasting service; for the most useful part of HISTORY is the knowledge of what passed before and after every great *event*, and especially of the *causes* that produced it †.

He observes, that "a knowledge of PAST transactions, which may afford a sure recourse in dangerous conjunctures, and which is supplied by HISTORY, may always be gained, with

* Polyh. lib. iii. c. 3. † Ibid.

not less pleasure than advantage, even in the shade of a safe and honourable repose*."

Polybius further observes, that "those written memoirs which record events, however faulty they may be in style and disposition, and however defective in some necessary properties, yet, if the FACTS be TRUE which are related, deserve to be called a HISTORY; but if these be FALSE, they are utterly unworthy of that name. For my part, I am ready to acknowledge that TRUTH should be considered as the principal and most essential part in all such composition. There are two kinds of falsehood; one which proceeds from ignorance, and the other from design. And as those writers may be excused who offend against TRUTH through ignorance; so those, on the contrary, who pervert it with design, ought never to be pardoned †."

He observes, that "the knowledge acquired by reading is gained without any danger or any kind of toil. But the knowledge which is drawn from personal examination and inquiry is attended with great fatigue and great expense. It is *this*, however, which is the most important, and which gives, indeed, the chief value to HISTORY. HISTORIANS themselves are ready to acknowledge this truth. For thus

* Polyb. lib. v. c. 7.   † Polyh. lib. xii. Extract 3.

Ephorus says (22), that if it were possible for the writers of HISTORY to be present at all transactions, such knowledge would be preferable to any other.—It was said by *Plato* (23), that human affairs would be well administered when philosophers should be kings, or kings philosophers. In the same manner I would say, that HISTORY would be well composed if those who are engaged in great affairs would undertake to write it, not in a slight and negligent manner, like some of our present age, but regarding such a work as one of the noblest and most necessary of their duties, and pursuing it with unremitted application as the chief business of their lives; or if those, on the other hand, who attempt to write, would think it necessary to be also conversant in the practice of affairs. Till this shall happen, there will be no end of mistakes in HISTORY *."

Lastly, *Polybius* observes, that " in every thing which is offered to the eyes or ears the design should always be to convey either some utility or some pleasure. All *history* especially should be directed constantly to these two ends. An historian should be contented barely to relate what may serve for imitation, or may be heard with pleasure. An enlarged description of calamity which may exceed those bounds, may be proper indeed for tragedy, but not for *history*."

(22) See Note V. (23) See Note W.
* Polyh. lib. xii. Ex. 8.

Polybius illustrates this proposition by the fate of "*Aga-thocles*, who, when he had the fairest opportunity, upon the death of *Philopater*, to maintain himself in his exalted station, in a short time threw away, by the mere want of spirit and ability, both his power and his life: and he draws a distinction between *this Agathocles* from that other *Aga-thocles*, the tyrant of SICILY, who acquired a name by his ability and great exploits. This is a man, from whose actions an historian may take a fair occasion to stop his readers with reflections; to remind them of the power of fortune; to remark the course of human affairs; and, in a word, to inculcate many useful lessons. But others, like to the *Agathocles* whose fate he has described, are very unfit to be made subjects of such discourse."

About a century after the age of *Polybius*, but the next in order of time, a star of the first magnitude emerges from the horizon, and blazes upon us in the full lustre of literary splendour. To this authority, on the subject of HISTORY, almost every man will bow with reverence, and few men pos-sibly will be disposed to dispute it. We have seen that, some centuries before, Thucydides had defined HISTORY to be— " PHILOSOPHY teaching by EXAMPLES." In his amplification of this definition, CICERO, in his own definition, gives us a full and accurate description of the many admirable and valuable properties which are justly attributed to HISTORY, as a STUDY of mankind. This high authority is no less than that of by far the most eloquent and distinguished orator of all antiquity, and an eminently profound and learned writer on a variety of subjects :—" HISTORIA," says *Cicero* (24), *" est Testis Temporum,—Lux Veritatis,—Vitæ Memoria,—Magister Vitæ,—Nuncia Vetustatis* *."

At one period, it seems that *Cicero* meditated a HISTORY of ROME. He then established a set of rules for the conduct of his work, which he puts into the mouth of *Antonius,* in his treatise on the *accomplished orator*. He observes, that " the basis and groundwork of all HISTORY depend upon TWO primary laws ;" and that the edifice of HISTORY must be raised on their *foundation*. These are—TRUTH, and a total freedom from all fear of divulging the TRUTH, —and the avoidance of any just suspicion of partiality or resentment. The edifice, thus raised, consists of two parts—the relation of *things* or *facts,* and the *words* or *language* in which they are related. In the first the HISTORIAN should adhere to the order of time, and diversify his narrative with a description of countries. He proceeds, " Since in all the memorable transactions, *first,* the *counsels* are explained, then the *acts,* and lastly the *events,* the historian should pronounce his own judgment on the merit of the *counsels,* should show *what acts* ensued, and in *what manne*r they were *performed,* and unfold *the causes of all great events;* whether he imputes them to *chance,* or *wisdom,* or

(24) See Note X.   * De Orat. lib. ii. c. 9.

E

rashness. He should also describe not only the *actions*, but the *lives* and *characters* of all the persons who are eminently distinguished in his deeds: and as to the *words* or *language,* the *historian* should be master of a copious and expanded style, flowing along with ease and delicacy, without the roughness of forensic pleading or the affectation of pointed sentences."

Sir William Jones* observes, that " if we form our idea of a *complete* HISTORIAN from these rules, we shall presently perceive the reason why no writer, antient or modern, has been able to sustain the weight of so important a character, which includes in it the perfection of almost every virtue and every noble accomplishment—an unbiassed integrity, a comprehensive view of nature, an exact knowledge of men and manners, a mind stored with free and generous principles, a penetrating sagacity, a fine taste, and copious eloquence. A perfect HISTORIAN must know many languages, many arts, many sciences; and, that he may not be reduced to borrow his materials wholly from other men, he must have acquired a height of political wisdom by long experience in the great affairs of his country, both in peace and war. There never was perhaps any such character, and perhaps there never will be."

The learned translator of *Dionysius's* Antiquities (*Mr.*

* Vol. v. p. 538.

Spelman) refers to these directions laid down for the conduct of an historian; and he observes, that though they are conceived with all the power of thought, and expressed with all the power of language, these directions rather show what disposition of mind is required of an HISTORIAN than what rules he ought to pursue. I confess I do not altogether agree with Mr. Spelman in this observation.

" What man,' exclaims Cicero, " can be ignorant that the first law of HISTORY is, that he should not dare to set down a FALSEHOOD, nor be deterred by fear from divulging an interesting TRUTH; and that he should avoid any just suspicion of partiality or resentment. These are *fundamental* principles in the composition of HISTORY, and are, therefore, known to every body *."

Cicero inquires—" By what voice can HISTORY be consigned to immortality but by that of eloquence and oratory?" and he considers " a knowledge of HISTORY, and of the models or EXAMPLES of antiquity, as among the necessary qualifications of an orator;" and that " he should be well versed in HISTORY and the records of antiquity, particularly those of his own country; not neglecting, however, to peruse the records of other powerful nations and illustrious monarchs. To be unacquainted with what has passed in the world before we came into it ourselves, is to be always

* Lib. ii. 15.

children. For what is the age of a single mortal, unless it is connected, by the aid of history, with the times of our ancestors? Besides, the relation of past occurrences, and the producing pertinent and striking examples, is not only very entertaining, but adds a great deal of dignity and weight to what we say."

Next to *Cicero*, and contemporary with him, is DIODORUS SICULUS (25). He places in a very clear and forcible point of view the distinction between the EXAMPLES presented to us by HISTORY and the personal EXPERIENCE of any individual. He very successfully contrasts the advantages to be derived from the innumerable EXAMPLES presented to us by HISTORY, with the advantages which can, by any possibility, arise from the limited personal EXPERIENCE of any man, to whatever length his life may be protracted by *Providence*. But then these superior advantages are only to be acquired by the STUDY of HISTORY. He observes, in the *Preface* to his Universal History, that " all mankind are under great obligations of gratitude to those who have written universal histories; for as much as there has been an honourable contest amongst them by their labours and pains to be helpful to others, in the due conduct and management of the common affairs and concerns of this present life; for they usher in a sort of wholesome instruction *without any hazard* to the person. Knowledge gained by EXPERIENCE,

(25) See Note Y.

though it brings a man to an aptness to be quick in dis-
cerning what is most advisable in every particular case, yet
such knowledge is attended with many toils and hazards.
Knowledge of what was well or ill done by others, gained by
HISTORY, carries along with it instructions, freed from those
misfortunes that others have before experienced. HISTO-
RIANS, by committing to writing the common actions of men
through the whole world, as if they were the affairs of only
one city, represent their labours as one entire account, and a
common repertory and treasury of human transactions. For
it is a desirable thing to be in a capacity to make use of the
mistakes of others, the better to order the course of our own
lives, and in the various events and accidents that may befal
us, not be then at a loss, and seeking what is to be done, but
rather to be able to imitate what has been well done. And,
certainly, as to counsel and advice, all prefer antient men to
those that are young, because of their prudence gained by
long EXPERIENCE. But HISTORY goes as far beyond the
knowledge of old men as we are sure it does surmount all
their EXPERIENCE in multitude of EXAMPLES : so that any
man may justly look upon it as a thing most profitable and
advantageous, to make use of this upon all occasions and
accidents of this life. As for young men, it teaches them
the wisdom and prudence of the old; and increases and
improves the wisdom of the aged; it fits private men for
high stations; and stirs up princes (for the sake of honour
and glory) to those exploits that may immortalize their

commendation after their deaths; and, as a curb to the impious and profane, it restrains them in some measure upon the account of being noted to posterity with a perpetual brand of infamy and disgrace. It is most certain that HISTORY is the preserver of the virtues of worthy men in posterity; an eternal witness to the cowardice and impiety of others; and a general benefactor to all mankind. For if a fine-spun story, consisting merely of *fiction*, tends much to the promotion of piety and justice, how much more then may we conclude that HISTORY, the most noble assertrix of TRUTH, and the very metropolis, as it were, of all philosophy, may adorn the manners of men with principles of justice and honesty. Those who have signalised themselves by virtuous actions are made famous in every age, their praises being proclaimed, as it were, *by a divine voice from* HISTORY. HISTORY conduces much to make a man eloquent, than which nothing is more commendable. HISTORY comprehends what is both pleasant and practicable; for who cannot discern but that it persuades to justice, condemns the wicked, praises the good, and greatly improves the understanding of the readers?"

" To write the lives of persons in former ages, is indeed a difficult and troublesome task to the historian, but very profitable to others, for their direction in the course of their

lives. For this kind of HISTORY, by recording the good and
bad actions, graces the memory of the good, and fixes a
stain upon the name of the wicked, by sharing out praise
and disgrace to each of them according as they deserve it.
' For praise is a certain reward of virtue without cost; and
disgrace is the punishment of vice without a wound.' And
therefore it is very fit that every one should understand, that
according to the course of life men lead here, such will be
the account and remembrance of them afterwards when they
are dead; so that they need not employ all their thoughts.
upon marble monuments, which are set up only in a little
corner, and decayed and gone in process of time(26); but
rather apply their minds to learning and other virtuous qualifications, which would render their names famous all over
the world. For *time,* which consumes all other things, pre-
serves these to perpetual generations; and the older they
grow, the more fresh and flourishing it presents them. For
they that have gone long ago are still in every man's mouth,
as if they were now at this very day alive*."

" I look upon it," says he, " as the *duty* of an HISTORIAN
diligently to observe the stratagems and management of
affairs by generals on both sides; for by laying open and
criticising other men's faults, the like miscarriage may be
prevented in them that come after. And on the other side,

(26) See Note Z.   * Booth's Preface.

carnassus(27), an eminent historian and critic. "He came into ITALY" (as he tells us himself) "immediately after *Augustus Cæsar* had put an end to the civil war, in the middle of the 187th Olympiad; and, having from that time to this present, that is, twenty-two years, lived at ROME, learned the ROMAN language, and acquainted myself with their writings, I employed all that interval in preparing materials for this work."

He observes, that "those who write histories, which we look upon *as the repositories of* TRUTH,—the source of prudence and wisdom,—ought, first of all, to make choice of worthy and grand subjects, and such as are of great utility to their readers." He is convinced that these considerations are necessary, and ought first to be regarded by HISTORIANS. He says he has made choice of a subject, worthy, grand, and useful: and he takes credit to himself for "not having made choice of subjects, or proposed to relate trivial or obscure actions, but has undertaken the HISTORY both of the most illustrious state and of the most shining achievements that can possibly be treated of."

* Diod. Sic. lib. xxiii. Fragm. 1.   (27) See Note A 1.

He looks upon it as the greatest duty of an HISTORIAN, " not only to relate the military actions of illustrious generals, and the glorious and salutary institutions they have invented in favour of their commonwealth, but also to give an account of their *private* lives, when they have passed them with moderation and temperance, and a strict adherence to the customs and discipline of their country."

He considers that those who read HISTORY "do not receive a sufficient advantage by being informed *only* of the *events* of things: for every man desires to be made acquainted with the *causes* also, and the *manner,* of all transactions, and with the *views* of the *actors,* and the interposition of Heaven upon those occasions, and to hear *every circumstance* that usually attends those events." "And I observe," says he, " that the knowledge of these things is absolutely necessary for public ministers, to the end they may have EXAMPLES before them to make use of upon occasion *."

And speaking of the administration of *Lartius* (29), the first Dictator, and in what manner he adorned that magistracy, he observes, that " he looks upon these things to be of the greatest use to the readers, as they will open a large field of noble and profitable EXAMPLES, not only to legislators and patrons of the people, but also to all others who aspire at the magistracy and the administration of public affairs."

* Lib. v.   (29) See Note B 1.

F

an unadmired and mean commonwealth, or the counsels and actions of men unknown, and unworthy to be known, which might make our endeavours, if employed upon small and frivolous objects, to appear tedious and trifling; but he is treating of that commonwealth which prescribes rules of justice and honour to all mankind, and of those magistrates who have raised her to that dignity; which is a subject which philosophers may desire to know and statesmen approve of."

Dionysius divides his history into two parts, that is, into the *pragmatic* part, as he calls it, and the *language:* the former comprehends,

1st. The choice of the subject;

2nd. The knowledge where to begin, and where to end;

3rd. The discernment between such events as are to be related and such as are to be omitted;

4th. The placing every event in its proper order; and,

5th. The heart of the historian.

The *language* he divides into simple elementary words; both which are susceptible either of a proper or a figurative sense.

In his Treatise on the Composition of Words, he lays down such rules for this composition, supported throughout by examples drawn from the best GREEK writers, both poets and historians, that any man, by observing them, may acquire a smooth and harmonious style; and, notwithstanding these rules seem calculated for the GREEK language only, their influence will, upon a close examination, appear to be universal, and to govern every other language, both antient and modern.

Dionysius proceeds to a comparison of *Herodotus* with *Thucydides.* But as this comparison is foreign to the design of this essay, it will be omitted.

These are, however, the rules laid down by *Dionysius* for writing HISTORY; and by these rules he has examined the histories of *Herodotus, Thucydides, Xenophon, Philistus,* and *Theopompus.*

His translator considers that *Dionysius* has executed all these rules with fidelity in his own history.

As to the style of *Dionysius,* his translator considers, as amongst its many beauties, his *poetical* expressions. With these he has animated his style, particularly in his speeches, which, by these means, become elevated and pathetic, and insensibly persuade while they seem intended only to please. " His style," says Mr. Spelman, " is poetical, not poetry; and melodious, not melody *."

* Preface to his Translation.

one seriously and earnestly to apply his thoughts,—by what kind of men, and by what sort of conduct, in peace and war, the empire has been both acquired and extended; then, as discipline gradually declined, let him follow in his thoughts the structure of antient morals, until he arrives at the present times, when our vices have attained to such a height of enormity, that we can no longer endure either the burden of them or the remedies necessary to correct them. This," says he, " is the great advantage to be derived from the study of HISTORY; indeed the only one which can make it answer any profitable and salutary purpose: for, being abundantly furnished with clear and distinct EXAMPLES of every kind of conduct, we may select for ourselves, and for the state to which we belong, such as are worthy of imitation—and, carefully noting such as, being dishonourable in their principles, are equally so in their effects, learn to avoid them. Now, either partiality to the subject of my intended work misleads me, or there never was any state either greater, or of purer morals, or richer in good EXAMPLES."

Thus we perceive that *Polybius, Cicero, Diodorus Siculus,* and *Dionysius Halicarnassus,* have all of them laid down rules for the composition of HISTORY very different from those pursued by the dry ANNALISTS of the olden times.

(30) See Note C 1.

But in the study of these dry ANNALS of the olden times, as the student was not in any degree assisted or led by the historian's judgment, the study would be one requiring greater application, as he must of course have himself dis-covered the nature of the EXAMPLES which they presented to him, and endeavoured, by deep research, to ascertain in what manner a *different* train of action might have produced a *different* and a more successful and fortunate result than that which is presented by the EXAMPLE before him. Unless these dry ANNALS are STUDIED with the attention which alone can lead to this beneficial result, this great and legitimate purpose of HISTORY will not be obtained. It cannot be ob-tained by a bare recital, or naked chronicle of events and dates—a mere dry record of the past actions of men.

We have thus presented to us the expressed opinions of almost every eminent writer of *antiquity,* whose works have been preserved, on the excellence and use of HISTORY, as a STUDY of the innumerable EXAMPLES in *real* life, which it exhibits for the edification of mankind—the regulation of his conduct throughout life—and (if he reflects and studies for improvement) for his imitation in the performance of that which is good, and the avoidance of that which is evil. The mere personal, and necessarily limited, EXPERIENCE of the longest life can never attain these important objects. But they are readily to be acquired by a STUDY of the EXAMPLES which HISTORY affords.

portraits and individual EXAMPLES of the *real life* of the olden times, eminently useful and instructive to mankind, it becomes the province and duty of HISTORY, in the exercise of its philosophic and DIDACTIC functions, (while it records the events of nations, and the actions of the individuals through whose instrumentality they may, advisedly or unconsciously, have been brought about,) to endeavour to develope the efficient causes, both proximate and remote, to which those events and actions owe their birth. For it is by a due reflection upon those causes that nations and individuals, in the ages present and to come, may best be enabled to steer that prudent and judicious course, by which they may attain the same moral or political good, or shun the same moral or political evil, which history has laid before them as the result of the conduct of nations and of individuals in the ages which *are past*.

The *antient* writers whose histories we have quoted, and the *modern* writers whom we are about to quote, were all of them men eminent in literature, — renowned for their wisdom,—and distinguished for their intellectual attainments and their profound erudition and learning.

Let us now examine rigidly, but with candour, the writings of *Dionysius* and *Livy*, these two self-denominated, but miscalled HISTORIANS of ROME and its *antiquities* during the *early* periods of its assumed HISTORICAL existence. Let us try them by their own test—the test of TRUTH. " HISTORY," says *Dionysius,* " is the *repository of* TRUTH." " HISTORY," says Livy, " is abundantly furnished with EXAMPLES of every kind of conduct." We shall find that their practice, in the observance of HISTORIC truth, does not accord with the precept which *they* inculcate. On the contrary, it essentially differs from it. In my humble judgment, they have both of them violated the two fundamental laws of HISTORY :—they have dared to utter what they must have known, or ought to have known, to be FALSEHOODS; and have displayed a manifest *partiality,* for the purpose merely of gratifying ROMAN vanity.

Dionysius says himself, that during the twenty-two years he lived at ROME, " he acquainted himself with the ROMAN writings, and employed all that interval in preparing materials for this work; and some things he received from men of the greatest consideration among them for learning, whose conversation he used; and others he gathered from histories, written by the most approved ROMAN authors, such as *Porcius Cato, Fabius Maximus, Valerius Antius, Licinius Mace*r, the *Ælii, Gellii,* and the *Calpurnii,* and several others of good note. Supported by the authority of these historians, which are like the GREEK ANNALS, he undertook this work." *Livy* professes to have taken the facts of his story from *authentic* materials and records of HISTORY; we must, therefore, give them both full credit for an implicit (but, I must be allowed to say, a *blind* and *inconsiderate*) belief in all the events of early ROMAN STORY (I will not be guilty of a misnomer by denominating the narration of them HISTORY); and which they have both of them illustrated and commented upon in all the circumstantiality of detail, AS EVENTS of true and genuine HISTORY. I have adopted the terms "*blind and inconsiderate,*" because the events, upon the very face of them, have every appearance of being altogether PSEUDO-HISTORICAL, and to rest upon no solid basis or firm foundation of REALITY; and I cannot help thinking that a reflection upon them, not very deep, should have taught both him and *Livy* to have viewed them in the same light. Let us try the justice of this apparently harsh criticism (which somewhat differs from that of Niebuhr) by the test of historical *probabilities.*

We know, upon the authority of *Cicero,* that the *Annales Maximi,* or *Commentaries* (as they were sometimes called), consisted of nothing more than a mere *dry register* of events and dates, and of the names of the individuals concerned in them. We know, on the authority of *Livy* himself, that " whatever information might have been contained in the commentaries of the pontiffs, and other public or private records, it was almost entirely lost in the burning of the city by the GAULS." The knowledge of these events, throughout a period of 365 years, must therefore have been preserved by *recollection* merely. We know how treacherous the recollection

of man is; and it must be admitted that the recollection of
the numerous events which occurred within the long period
of 365 years, (and of which both *Dionysius* and *Livy* have
given us all the *circumstantial details,*) is an effort of memory beyond the powers of human achievement. But, we
may ask, where are all these *circumstantial details* to be
found? They *did not exist in these very records themselves.*
They can only be found in the gratuitous *invention* of later
times, or in their preservation as *legendary tales,* handed
down to posterity through the obscure and glimmering lights
and the dark and uncertain medium of *tradition.* Invention
is the mother of *absolute fiction*—and their preservation as
legendary tales, is a fact founded upon very dubious authority.

Mr. *Niebuhr* (31), with indefatigable and persevering
industry, and great critical acumen and solid powers of dis-
crimination, has, in part, detected the *fallacy* which has
pervaded the early periods of ROMAN STORY,—has in some
measure disunited and disengaged the impure dross from the
pure and genuine metal,—and has distinguished between the
FABLE and the TRUTH, and separated the one from the other.
But, still, upon this subject, he seems to me to be very obscure.
In so far as these incidents may, any of them, have been preserved as *legendary tales* by traditional transmission, they may
afford *some* foundation for a belief in them, and some justification for their introduction into *historical* composition, but

(31) See Note D 1.

G

they should always be accompanied by the observation that they are built upon traditionary legends or tales, and therefore are matters of *doubtful authenticity*. By both *Dionysius* and *Livy* they have been unhesitatingly adopted as facts in *true* and *genuine* HISTORY. The various INSTITUTIONS, the nature of which they explain, are unquestionably TRUE, because we find them in existence at a later period, and one of genuine HISTORY; but *when* many of them were founded, and by *whom*, is a question which we are unable to answer.

Niebuhr asserts that he has proved that the " STORY of Rome under the kings" (a period of 244 years out of the 365, which, according to *Dionysius* and *Livy*, is fabled to have elapsed between the foundation of the city and its capture by the GAULS) " was altogether without HISTORICAL foundation,"—an assertion which we shall hereafter see is expressed in terms of rather a doubtful or problematical meaning. He proceeds to say, that " he has sifted the *legends* which *pass for* HISTORY;—such fragments as lay scattered about he had collected for the sake of restoring the manifold forms they once bore; not, however, as though this could bring us nearer to HISTORICAL knowledge: for while the grandeur of the monarchy, the seat of which was on the Seven Hills, is attested by the monuments it left behind, the recollections of its history have been purposely destroyed; and, to fill up the void, the events of a narrow sphere, such as the pontiffs after the GALLIC irruption were familiar with, have been substituted in the room of the forgotten transactions of an incomparably wider empire*." He further observes that, " it is true, the copies of the censorian families must have flowed from transcripts of but a few (of these ' *annals* or *commentaries*') that had been preserved in the capitol, or in the neighbouring towns; but it was enough for their coming down in a genuine form to posterity, if a single one remained and was multiplied." " It admits of no doubt that these rolls were preserved for memorials in the *censorian* families,—so those who had the image of a *consul* among their ancestors kept *consular fasti,* wherein the memorable events, at least of the year they were interested in, were noted down; and many others also must have been in the possession of the like. These, now, were original *annals,* that arose independently of the pontiffs, and were drawn up by divers persons; not always contemporaneously, but, in their earliest parts, from the recollections of the writer himself, or of his neighbours, and sometimes, no doubt, from erroneous ones touching past events."

Trying this supposition of *Niebuhr's* by the test of HISTORICAL probabilities, I must confess that I cannot find a sufficient justification for it. *Livy* positively asserts, that " the commentaries of the pontiffs, and other public or *private* records, were almost entirely lost in the burning of the city †."

* Niebuhr's History of Rome, vol. ii. p. 1.
† Livy, lib. vi. 1.

might have perished at the destruction of ROME by the GAULS; and that they were replaced by *new* ones; and that they were not likely to have been preserved in the *capitol.* It was only the " *young* men who were fit to bear arms, and the abler part of the senate, who were to go up into the citadel and the capitol *." It is very improbable that the *young* men should carry any records, *public* or *private,* with them into the capitol; nor is it likely that the abler part of the senate, even if they possessed them, should regard the *annals* of past times, in the confusion and hurry of their retreat into the capitol. That every record which remained in the city was either burned in its conflagration, or destroyed by the barbarians in their occupation of it for six or eight months, there can be no question. Any ANNALS or commentaries of *private* censorian or consular families would most likely be of a similar description with the *public* ones; and it is very improbable that they should have been kept up in that regular and connected chain and series of illustration and comment on the events which happened, which are exhibited both in the antiquities of *Dionysius* and the HISTORY of *Livy.*

" It is impossible," says *Niebuhr,* " to pronounce whether any ' *annals* or *commentaries* ' were preserved or not, which begun any number of years before the insurrection of the

* Livy, lib. v. c. 39.

commonalty *." This insurrection of the commonalty took place soon after the supposed abolition of the *kingly* power. He observes, "that none of these ANNALS can have gone back so far as the *origin* of the *consulate,* is clear from the confusion in the *fasti* for the first years of the free republic, and from *all genuine* HISTORY *of this period having vanished without leaving a trace.*"

Dionysius commenced his second book of the Antiquities of ROME with the FABLE of the Death of *Remus* in a conflict with his brother *Romulus,* and of the foundation of ROME by the latter. He describes him, in all the grave solemnity of *true* and *genuine* HISTORY, to have been a man of great military accomplishments and personal bravery, and extremely capable of instituting the most perfect sort of government. " I shall relate," says he, " such of his civil and military actions as may be thought worthy of HISTORY." He describes minutely and circumstantially the form of government which he instituted,—the " TRIBES "—the "CURIÆ "—the distinction of the ranks of the people into PATRICIANS and PLEBEIANS— the PATRONS and their duties—the SENATE, denominated also " CONSCRIPT FATHERS."

Having made these regulations, he distinguished the honours and prerogatives which each class or rank should enjoy.

* History of Rome, vol. ii. p. 3, 4.

1st. Supremacy in all religious ceremonies and divine worship.

2nd. The guardianship of the laws and administration of justice.

3rd. To take cognizance of the greatest crimes; leaving to the senate the lesser, with the power of appeal to himself.

4th. To assemble both the senate and the people; and, after delivering his opinion, to pursue the resolutions of the majority.

5th. The absolute command in war.

Second. The particular functions and duties of the SENATE (32), and the CELERES their body-guard, and of the PEOPLE, are then most minutely described.

" By these institutions," says *Dionysius,* " *Romulus* sufficiently regulated, and properly disposed the city, both for peace and war. He admired these institutions of the man. *Romulus* established good government,—first, by seeking the favour of the gods, the enjoyment of which gives success to every enterprise,—next, temperance and justice, by which the citizens, being less disposed to injure one another, are more inclinable to unanimity, and make virtue, not shameful pleasures, the measure of their happiness,—and, lastly, mili-

(32) See Note E 1.

tary courage, which renders even the other virtues useful to their possessors. He was sensible that none of these advantages are the effects of chance; but that good laws, and the emulation of worthy pursuits, render a commonwealth pious, just, temperate, and warlike.

Upon what authority *Dionysius* gained an insight into all the movements, even the *mind*, of *Romulus*, at the distant period of 750 years, does not appear, except in so far as he has himself stated his authorities. But it seems he knew much more, even of the *unwritten* laws, than he felt it necessary to communicate; for he says, that *Romulus* " enacted many good and useful laws, the *greater part unwritten*, but some committed to writing; *all of which I do not think necessary to mention*, but shall only give a *short account* of those I chiefly admire, and look upon as proper to illustrate the tenor of his other laws, and to show how austere they were, how averse to vice, and how nearly resembling the lives of the heroes."

After enumerating, in very minute *detail*, an *infinity* of other institutions, established by this pretended lawgiver of ROME, *Dionysius* observes, " his other actions, both in war and peace, which deserve the notice of HISTORY, are as follows." He then, in HISTORICAL detail, proceeds to relate them.

a tyrant before his death; and that " those who write the *most probably* say that he was put to death by his own people." Not so the great HISTORIAN of ROME. " Unfortunately *Livy* has not treated the explanation of the disappearance of *Romulus* in the same manner, and hence it has taken deep root *." He describes the apparition and speech of *Romulus* to *Proculus Julius*, who was a person whose testimony, *we are told*, deserved respect in any case, even of the greatest importance. And he says, " it was wonderful how this story told by that man was credited." But the death of *Romulus* he gravely describes in the following terms: " As he was holding an assembly in the plain, on the borders of the lake of *Capra*, for the purpose of reviewing his army, a sudden storm arose, accompanied with violent thunder and lightning. The king was enveloped in a thick cloud, which hid him from the eyes of the assembly, and he was never more seen upon earth. The ROMAN youth were at length eased of their apprehensions by the return of calm and serene weather after such a turbulent day; but when they saw the royal seat empty, though they readily believed the senators who had stood nearest to him, that he had been carried up on high by the storm, yet they were struck with

* Niebuhr, vol. i. p. 233.

such dread at being thus left in a manner fatherless, that, for some time, they remained in mournful silence. At last, some few setting the example, the whole multitude saluted *Romulus* as ' a deity, the son of a deity, the king and parent of the city of Rome;' and implored his favour with prayers, that he would always be pleased propitiously to watch over the safety of his own offspring." Having gravely related this fact, *Livy* proceeds: " *Some,* I believe, were, at that time, harbouring silent suspicions that the king had been torn in pieces by the hands of the senators. *Such a report* was spread abroad, but it *was little credited,* both on account of the high admiration entertained of the man, and because the present consternation caused the *other* account to be *more generally* received. It is further mentioned, that a contrivance of one particular man procured additional credit to this representation of the matter *." " The principal transactions in peace and war," says *Livy,* " during the reign of *Romulus,* were none of them unsuitable to the belief of his divine origin, or to the rank of a divinity, which, after his death, he was supposed to have obtained †."

Not content with recording, in most minute and circumstantial HISTORICAL details, wise institutions, which were never framed and promulgated,—and public actions, by non-existent individuals, which were never performed, of course, (or existent only in fable or in idle legendary tales, entitled to no credit,)

* Livy, lib. i. c. 16.　　　　　† Id. lib. i. c. 15.

H

the motives, and the movements of mind which actuated the conduct of these individuals, as matter of *historical* notoriety and authenticity.

Livy has narrated almost all the *facts* stated by *Dionysius*, and although not in the same circumstantial details, yet in all the " pomp and circumstance " of HISTORY.

It results, therefore, as matter of certainty, that the foundation of ROME by *Romulus*, and his wise institutions—the rape of the Sabine virgins—the treason and death of *Tarpeia*—the association with him of Tatius, their king, as joint sovereigns of *Rome*—the death of Tatius—the UNHISTORICAL, clumsy, fabulous wars of the *Etruscans* before the death of of *Romulus*—the manner of his death—the interviews of *Numa Pompilius* with the goddess *Egeria*—the principles of justice, laws, and morals, upon which he founded *anew* the city, which had been originally founded by violence and arms—are absolute fables, utterly undeserving of any credit whatever, and therefore wholly destitute of any pretext for their adoption by the HISTORIAN, in true and genuine HISTORY.

" With regard to ROME, the story of her foundation," says *Niebuhr*, " is the very point we are most ignorant of. While I allow the heart and imagination their full claims, I

assert the right of reason to refuse to admit any thing as
HISTORICAL which cannot possibly be so." The story—the
old ROMAN legend, of the origin of ROME, was settled as an
article of popular belief*. "The account of the ETRUSCAN
wars, in the long period which intervened before the death of
Romulus," says he, "is unhistorical, clumsy, and fabulous
as the romances of chivalry."

He observes that, "with *Tullus Hostilius*, we reach the
beginning of a narrative resting on HISTORICAL grounds, of
a kind totally different from the story of the preceding period."
This would appear to contradict *Niebuhr's* general position,
that "the story of Rome *under the kings* was altogether
without HISTORICAL foundation," and, in any event, renders
his meaning obscure. Are we to understand by this, that
the story of *Tullus Hostilius*, and the succeeding narratives,
do "rest on HISTORICAL ground?" He observes, that as to
the period of the ROMAN kings, the chronology itself is a
forgery and a *fiction* throughout. There is no rational
ground to *doubt the personal existence* of *Tullus Hostilius:*
but most assuredly the combat of the *Horatii* and the
Curiatii, and the king's marvellous death, are more likely
to be HISTORICALLY true, than the dates assigned to his reign.
"No *national* annals," says he, "were left concerning the
times of the *kings;* neither did the family narratives reach
so far back†." Where, then, we may be permitted to

* Niebuhr, vol. i.   † Ibid. vol. i. 250.

of this period, which they adopt as TRUE and genuine HIS-TORY. Again, *Niebuh*r observes, that "the poems, out of which what *we cull* the HISTORY of the ROMAN kings, was resolved into a prose narrative, and were different from the *Neuia* in form, and of great extent." He places the dismal story of the brutal ravishment and heroic suicide of Lucretia, and the horrible patriotism and unnatural conduct of the elder Brutus in the murder of his two sons, and all the incidents throughout a period of 244 years, in the *same class* or description of events with the FABLES of *Romulus*, and the foundation of the city. It is an epopee of *Romulus*, and they are all of them together, equally with this FABLE, an epopee, which, in force and brilliancy of imagination, leaves every thing produced by the ROMANS in later times far behind it. According to *Niebuhr*, they are equally "LAYS," or LEGENDARY TALES.

"The 'LAY' of *Tullus Hostilius*," says he, "is followed by the narration of a course of events, without any marvellous circumstances or poetical colouring. By the founding of Ostia this narrative is connected with *real* HISTORY; but it is referred to a chronological computation, in which the tricks of elaborate *falsifiers* are most clearly apparent."

*Niebuh*r next describes what he calls "the LAY of L. *Tarquinius Priscus* and *Servius Tullius*." "Of the wars ascribed to L. *Tarquinius*," says he, " *Dionysius*, adopting the FORGERIES of very recent annalists, has given an intolerable newspaper account;"—for the purposes of this work, even *Livy's* dignified brevity goes too much into detail.

" The wars of *Tarquinius*," says *Niebuh*r, " are far the least important part of his actions. A successful one against the Veientines, of which L*ivy* makes only slight mention, is magnified by *Dionysius* into victories over the whole ETRUSCAN nation. Indeed the FORGERY has made way even into the *Fasti*, where the PRETENDED triumphs are recorded with the year and day of their occurrence."

The Alban wars under *Tullus Hostilius*,—the battle of the three *Horatii* and the three *Curatii* (33) (sisters' children),—and the horrifying and more improbable tale (unexampled for its barbarity) of the surviving victorious *Horatius*, in the inbuman murder of his *own sister*,—and the unparental, unnatural conduct of his father (which, however, are extolled by *Dionysius* as instances of *Roman* patriotism of the most exalted character), because she very naturally lamented the death and loss of her lover, one of the *Curiatii*, to whom she had, with her mother's consent, been betrothed,—the acquittal of *Horatius* by the voice of the people,—the treason and horrid death of *Mettius*, in being drawn asunder by four horses,—the total destruction of *Alba*,—the Sabine wars which fol-

(33) See Note F 1.

lowed,—the accession of *Ancus Marcius,*—the battles with the Latins,—the accession of *Tarquinius Priscus,*—his wife *Tanaquil,*—his wars,—his assassination by the two sons of *Ancus Marcius,*—the succession of *Servius Tullius,*—his wars with the *Veientians,* and afterwards with the *Etruscans,* —his institution of the *census,* and the plan of the *classes* and *centuries,*—his enlargement of the city,—his assassination by *Tarquinius Superbus,*—and the horrid barbarity of the con· duct of his impious daughter, *Tullia,* which, says *Dionysius,* is " not only dreadful to hear, but, at the same time, astonishing and incredible," and which, says *Livy,* " was inhuman and shocking,"—the succession of *Tarquinius Superbus,*—the ravishment, and affecting dagger-scene and suicide, of *Lucretia,*—the banishment of the *Tarquins,*—the abolition of the *regal* dignity,—and the unnatural conduct of the elder *Brutus,*—are all of them very gravely narrated, both by *Dionysius* and *Livy,* as events in true and genuine HISTORY.

*Niebuh*r asserts his proof, that " the story of ROME under the kings was *altogether* without HISTORICAL foundation;" and the fact, that " all genuine HISTORY of this period vanished without leaving a trace." But he asserts also, that " with *Tullus Hostilius,* we reach the beginning of a narrative *resting on* HISTORICAL grounds."

Are we therefore to believe that all these events, although

not resting " on HISTORICAL foundation," are *legendary tales*
handed down to posterity by tradition, and therefore entitled
to some degree of credit, as justifiable materials on which to
build the commencement of a HISTORY, although not resting
on genuine HISTORICAL foundation? or if not, which are we to
believe, and which are we to discredit? *Niebuhr* is by no
means clear upon this subject.

We must acquit both *Dionysius* and *Livy* of being
themselves the fabricators of many of the fables which
they too hastily adopted, and too easily incorporated with
their *grave* and serious works, as if they had any foundation
in REALITY, and were, therefore, subjects fitting and appropriate for introduction into that which professes to be a true
and genuine HISTORY. These fables were the base-born offspring of ROMAN pride and vanity—the spurious creatures of
ROMAN manufacture;—*Roman* pride and vanity originated
and continued the delusion (a contemptible and unworthy
delusion it was) as to their TRUTH.

But I cannot acquit them, as HISTORIANS professing deep
research and minute and particular inquiry into events, of a
criminal credulity in this respect, and of adopting them
without a due investigation as to their REALITY—an investigation which, in many instances, at least, must have satisfied
them of their FALSITY. The gratification of ROMAN pride
and vanity, in the indulgence of an absurd belief in the anti-

province, and sacred duties to posterity as HISTORIANS.

The injuries which they have done to HISTORY in this abandonment are without reparation. A zealous student of HISTORY, for instance, is actuated by the laudable design of obtaining ACCURATE information as to the events of the *early* periods of ROMAN HISTORY. He resorts, as a matter of course, to *Dionysius* and to *Livy* for this purpose ; and he places a firm and confident reliance on the TRUTH (as far as he perceives the TRUTH to be ascertainable), in their fidelity as HISTORIANS. He employs many hours in the perusal, perhaps in the study, of the events therein described, as EXAMPLES of REAL life, derived from true and genuine HISTORY, and presented to him for his imitation or avoidance in the regulation of his own conduct, either in public or private life, as it may happen. At length he finds, to his great vexation, that he has been misled and deceived by the very writers whom he supposed to be, and who themselves assumed the garb and all the exterior appearance, but without the *real* character of, sober and dignified HISTORIANS of the events which they describe. He finds, to his great mortification, that, with reference to his object of obtaining accurate information, his time has been wholly mispent and misapplied. He finds that, instead of perusing and studying a true and genuine HISTORY of the events of the olden times, he has, in fact, been employed only in the perusal of an interesting and beautifully-written NOVEL. He may possibly derive some *amusement* from the perusal of this beautiful narration;—the character with which *Dionysius* and *Livy* have clothed the primitive ROMANS (those ROMANS who are erroneously supposed to have lived in the days of these kings, and in the *early* ages of their commonwealth) for disinterested magnanimity, bravery, patriotism, frugality, and contempt of riches, is a character highly attractive, and worthy of admiration : but when the student learns that the whole of this interesting narrative, for upwards of 350 years, is composed of fiction or of legendary tales, handed down by the dim and uncertain lights of tradition, and is, therefore, for the most part, a fabric of ROMAN construction, almost wholly IDEAL, and almost wholly destitute of TRUTH, he will cease to admire these now flitting *phantoms* of visionary existence—these imaginary beings of unreal creation; but in ceasing to admire, he will not cease to lament that he has lost the benefit of the instruction which he might have derived from the study and contemplation of the events of these 350 years, had they really been what they falsely professed to be, EXAMPLES in the REAL life of genuine ROMAN history.

" In ROMAN history," says *Niebuhr,* " the range of pure fiction does not reach much lower than the PERSIAN war; although it appears again, from time to time, down to the

the war with *Pyrrhus,* when foreigners at least began to write it contemporaneously, is studied *alteration.*"

The preceding criticism of the author of these remarks applies *equally* to *Dionysius* and *Livy:* the following relates exclusively to *Livy.*

Livy states, that " such a subject must require a work of immense extent, as our researches must be carried back through a space of more than 700 years." The mere circumstance of so *long a retrospect* ought to have rendered the researches of *Livy* of more avail in seeking after the TRUTH, and made him more cautious in the admission of fables or legendary tales as true and genuine HISTORY. " As to the relations, which have been handed down, of events prior to the founding of the city, or to those transactions that gave occasion to its being founded, and which bear the semblance rather of poetic fiction than of *authentic* records of HISTORY— these I have no intention either to maintain or refute."

Does not this manifestly imply that all the relations of *Livy,* inclusive of and posterior to the foundation of the city, were established upon the firm basis of AUTHENTIC records of HISTORY? But we have seen, and we know, that the very reverse of this implication is the fact, and that *Livy,* in reality, did not possess any one " AUTHENTIC record of

HISTORY," as applicable to this early period, more than 700 years before his story commences. Mr. *Niebuhr* endeavours to palliate and excuse the heinous offences of *Livy*, as an HISTORIAN, in a manner unworthy of a man who had undertaken to relate the HISTORY (he must intend the TRUE and genuine HISTORY) of ROME; and I must be allowed to adopt the conclusion that, in the contemplation of the manly vigour and beauty, and classical elegance of *Livy's* style, Mr. *Niebuhr* has been blind to his violation of the " fundamental laws of HISTORY," and his neglect of the sacred duties which he owed to posterity as an HISTORIAN. " It is hardly too much to affirm," says he, " that L*ivy* first taught the Ro-MANS what a HISTORY they had. Their great actions and victories " (fabulous in the early period of them) " were now encircled by the graces of his bewitching style—with the noblest ornaments of republican and civic virtues,—height-ened, through his *wish* of beholding in the times of his ancestors the remains of the brazen age coming down almost to his own days, with a gravity and dignity which surpassed the great men of ATHENS, with their unconcealed human failings and weaknesses, and threw them into the shade as much as the conquest of vast empires and fierce nations did the passionate struggles between petty republics." I cannot refrain from inquiring how *Livy's* justification as an HISTO-RIAN can be found in any such gratuitous *wish* (wholly unsuited to the occasion), or in any " *gravity and dignity*," of his " bewitching," but unfaithful, narrative. I admire as much as *Niebuhr* can do the beauty of *Livy's* style of composition, and the highly interesting manner in which the various incidents and fabulous tales of his early STORY of ROME are related. But the more bewitching and fascinating these PSEUDO-HISTORICAL productions of his pen—the more elegant and classical his style of composition—the more dangerous and injurious are they to the interests of HISTORY, properly so called; for, from the beauty of his style, his composition will, of course, be perused with the greater eagerness; and the character of AUTHENTICITY with which they were stamped by this TALE-TELLER or PSEUDO-HISTORIAN himself, and by others, would seem to afford a justification for the unwarrantable credulity with which they will be perused, and to which, in REALITY, they are not entitled.

Niebuhr says, elsewhere, that *Livy* " tells the tales of these times *like a* HISTORY, *without meaning it for one;* his poetical feeling enabling him to comprehend *these ages* better than those in which HISTORICAL light was beginning to dawn *." If he did not " *mean it for* HISTORY," how is his assurance, in telling us that it is true and genuine HISTORY, to be justified? or how is the HISTORIAN (the professed guide of posterity) to be justified in the indulgence of his POETICAL feeling at the expense of TRUTH.

From all these sages of *antiquity*, we arrive at the period

* Vol. i. p. 225.

when men of a more modern date, but no less eminent for their talents and literary attainments, flourished. I allude to Lord *Bolinbroke*, Mr. *Gibbon*, and Sir *William Jones*.

But before I proceed to develope their sentiments upon this subject, I shall be excused for citing a testimonial, on the dignity and use of HISTORY, by an eminent, but an unfortunate and ill-fated personage, who made a distinguished figure in the annals of his country, and who came to an untimely and unjust end through the intrigues and machinations of his enemies, and the bitter, unrelenting, insatiable enmity and malice, and the indecent and iniquitous conduct of *James I.* A modern biographer of Sir *Walter Raleigh* (34) sums up his character in the following terms :—" He belongs to that class of great men who may be said rather to fashion, or create, than to reflect the character of their age. His individual story is indissolubly linked with the annals of his country ; and he who reads of the danger and the glory of ENGLAND during the reign of *Elizabeth*—of the humiliation of SPAIN—the independence of HOLLAND—the discovery and wonders of the New World—and the progress of our naval and commercial prosperity, must meet with his name in every part of the record. If required to describe in a few words the most prominent features in his mind, I should say they were his universality and originality. A warrior, both by sea and land ;—a statesman ;—a navigator and discoverer of

(34) See Note G 1.

elegant writer;—a sweet and true poet;—and a munificent patron of letters;—there is scarcely one of the aspects in which we view him where he does not shine with a remarkable brightness. In some of the pursuits, indeed, in which he attained distinction, he has been excelled by other eminent men of his time. But where do we find such a combination as in *Raleigh?* They were satisfied with the glory of being great in one department: he aimed at an almost universal excellence. They wisely concentrated their efforts on the cultivation of a single insulated branch of human knowledge: his discursive and vigorous mind was not contented till it had made an inroad, and achieved a triumph in them all; and it may be certainly affirmed, that upon every thing which he undertook he has left that stamp of power and originality which belongs to the man of genius*." The testimonial of *such* a man as Sir *Walter Raleigh* cannot fail to be acceptable.

" History," says Sir *Walter Raleigh,* " hath triumphed over time, which, besides it, nothing but eternity hath triumphed over; for it hath carried our knowledge over the vast and devouring space for so many thousands of years, and given to our mind such fair and piercing eyes, that we plainly behold living now, as if we had lived then, that great world, *Magni Dei sapiens opus*—' the wise work,' says *Hermes,*

---

* Tytler's Life of Sir *Walter Raleigh,* p. 427.

' of a great GOD, as it was then but new in itself.' But it is, I say, that we live in the very time when it was created. We behold how it was governed—how it was covered with waters, and again repeopled—how kings and kingdoms have flourished and fallen—and for what virtue and piety GOD made prosperous, and for what vice and deformity he made wretched, both the one and the other. And it is not the least debt which we owe unto HISTORY, that it hath made us acquainted with our dead ancestors, and out of the depth and darkness of the earth delivered us their memory and fame. In a word, we may gather out of HISTORY a policy no less wise than eternal, by the COMPARISON and APPLICATION of other men's fore-past miseries with our own like errors and ill-deservings *."

We now arrive at the period in which my Lord BOLINBROKE(35) "fretted his hour upon the stage." This noble and highly talented writer, but unwise, versatile, and inconsistent politician, and no very creditable actor, either in his public or in his private life, in his admirable Dissertation on the Use and Study of HISTORY, places the distinction between the superior *advantages* to be derived from a study of the EXAMPLES which HISTORY presents to us over those advantages which can possibly be derived from the limited EXPERIENCE of the longest life of man, in so clear and able a manner, that I trust I shall be excused in making copious extracts of the most

* Preface, p. iv. (35) See Note H 1.

highest degree, confirmatory of the sentiments of antient sages upon this subject.

I must premise, however, that I· do not by any means concur with the noble author in many of his sentiments and opinions on HISTORY, as connected with HOLY WRIT; and that I unhesitatingly adopt the pure and enlightened sentiments of Sir *William Jones* on this interesting subject, in preference, and as opposed, to those of my Lord *Bolinbroke*. It is, as the eulogist of the use and study of HISTORY *generally*, that I perfectly coincide in his opinions.

Lord *Bolinbroke* observes, " that the love of HISTORY seems inseparable from human nature, because it seems inseparable from self-love : the same principle carries us forward and backward—to future and to past ages. HISTORY, true or false, speaks to our *passions* always;—what a pity that the best should speak to our *understandings* so seldom." He considers (in perfect accordance with the sentiments of the wise men of antiquity whom we have before quoted) the study of HISTORY, as of all others, " the most proper to train us up to private and public virtue."

He adopts the sentiment of *Thucydides*, as quoted by *Dionysius*, that " HISTORY is philosophy teaching by EXAMPLES." " Instruction by EXAMPLE," he observes, " appeals not to our understanding alone, but to our passions likewise. EXAMPLE assuages these or animates them;—sets passion on the side of judgment, and makes the whole man of a piece; which is more than the strongest reasoning and the clearest demonstration can do; and thus, forming habits by repetition, EXAMPLE secures the observance of those precepts which EXAMPLE insinuated."

" The school of example is the world; and the masters of this school are HISTORY and EXPERIENCE."

" The study of HISTORY without EXPERIENCE is insufficient. Experience itself is so without GENIUS, which is preferable to the other two. A man will never shine with full lustre, or shed the full influence he is capable of, unless to his own experience he adds the EXPERIENCE of other men and other ages. Men having experience, without knowledge of the HISTORY of the world, are but half scholars in the science of mankind."

" HISTORY prepares us for EXPERIENCE, and guides us in it."

" HISTORY serves to purge the mind of those national partialities and prejudices that we are apt to contract in our education; and *that*, experience, for the most part, rather confirms than removes, because it is, for the most part, confined like our education. Though an early and proper

K

application to the study of HISTORY will contribute extremely to keep our minds free from a ridiculous partiality in favour of our own country, and a vicious prejudice against others, yet the same study will create in us a preference of affection to our own country."

" The EXAMPLES which we find in HISTORY, improved by the lively descriptions and the just applauses or censures of HISTORIANS, will have a better and more permanent effect than declamation or song, or the dry ethics of mere philosophy. In fine, to converse with HISTORIANS is to keep good company: many of them were excellent men, and those who were not such have taken care to appear such in their writings. It must, therefore, be of great use to prepare ourselves by this conversation for that of the world; and to receive our first impressions, and to acquire our first habits, in a scene where images of virtue and vice are continually represented to us in the colours which belong properly to them, before we enter on another scene, where virtue and vice are too often confounded, and what belongs to one is ascribed to the other."

" There is this farther advantage in the study of HISTORY, that we begin our acquaintance with mankind sooner, and with such a temper of mind as will enable us to make a better use of our EXPERIENCE. It has this farther advantage, that the improvement we make by it extends to more objects than is made at *the expense of other men;* whereas that improvement which is the effect of our own experience is confined to fewer objects, and is made at *our own expense*. To state the account fairly between these two improvements—though the latter be the more valuable, yet allowance being made on the one side for the much greater number of EXAMPLES that HISTORY presents to us, and deduction being made on the other of the price we often pay for our EXPERIENCE, the value of the former will rise in proportion."

" There is another advantage worthy of our observation that belongs to the study of HISTORY, namely, that the EXAMPLES which HISTORY presents to us, both of men and of events, are generally complete: the *whole* EXAMPLE is before us, and consequently the *whole* lesson; or sometimes the various lessons which philosophy proposes to teach us by this EXAMPLE."

" As to events that stand recorded in HISTORY, we see them all; we see them as they followed one another, or as they produced one or other of causes or effects immediate or remote. We are cast back, as it were, into former ages; we live with the men who lived before us, and we inhabit countries which we never saw. *P*lace is enlarged and time prolonged in this manner; so that the man who applies himself early to the study of HISTORY may acquire, in a few years, and before he sets his foot abroad in the world, not only a more extended knowledge of mankind, but the EXPERIENCE of more centuries than any of the patriarchs saw. The events we are witnesses of in the course of the longest life, appear to us very often original, unprepared, single, and unrelative,—in FRENCH, I would say, ' *isolés*.' We get over the present difficulty; we improve the momentary advantage as well as we can, and we look no further. EXPERIENCE can carry us no further; for EXPERIENCE can go a very little way back in discovering *causes;* and *effects* are not the objects of EXPERIENCE till they happen. From hence many errors in judgment, and, by consequence, in conduct, necessarily arise. And here, too, lies the difference we are speaking of between HISTORY and EXPERIENCE. The advantage on the side of the former is double. In antient HISTORY, as we have said already, the EXAMPLES are complete which are incomplete in the course of EXPERIENCE. The beginning, the progression, and the end appear not of particular reigns, much less of particular enterprises or systems of policy alone, but of government of nations, of empires, and of all the various systems that have succeeded one another in the course of their duration."

" In *modern* HISTORY the EXAMPLES may be, and sometimes are, incomplete; but they have this advantage when they are so, that they serve to render complete the EXAMPLES of our own time. EXPERIENCE is doubly defective: we are born too late to see the beginning, and we die too soon to see the end, of many things. HISTORY supplies both these defects.

Modern HISTORY shows the *causes,* when EXPERIENCE presents the *effects* alone.   And *antient* HISTORY enables us to guess at the *effects,* when EXPERIENCE presents the *causes* alone."

Lord *Bolinbroke* illustrates his meaning by two EXAMPLES; one *past,* and the other then actually *present.*

" When the revolution of 1688," says he, " happened, few men then alive, I suppose, went farther in their search after the *causes* of it, than the extravagant attempt of King *James* against the religion and liberty of his people. His former conduct, and the passages of King *Charles the Second's* reign, might rankle still in the hearts of some men, but could not be set to account among the *causes* of his deposition; since he had succeeded, notwithstanding them, peaceably to the throne; and the nation in general (even many of those who would have excluded him from it) were desirous, or at least willing, that he could continue in it. Now this EXAMPLE, thus stated, affords, no doubt, much good instruction to the kings and the people : but this instruction is not entire, because the EXAMPLE thus stated, and confined to the EXPERIENCE of *that age,* is imperfect. King *James's* maladministration rendered a revolution necessary and practicable; but his maladministration, as well as all his preceding conduct, was *caused* by his bigoted attachment to popery, and to the principles of arbitrary government, from which no warning could divert him.   His

royal family; this exile was *caused* by the usurpation of *Cromwell;* and *Cromwell's* usurpation was the *effect* of a former rebellion, begun, not without reason, on account of liberty, but without any valid pretence on account of religion. During this exile our princes caught the taint of popery and foreign politics. We made them unfit to govern us, and after that were forced to recall them, that they might rescue us out of anarchy. It was necessary, therefore, at the revolution, and it is more so now, to go back in history, at least as far as I have mentioned, and perhaps farther, even to the beginning of King *James the First's* reign, to render this event a complete EXAMPLE, and to develope all the wise, honest, and salutary precepts, with which it is pregnant, both to king and subject."

The other EXAMPLE Lord *Bolinbroke* takes from what succeeded the revolution. He here indulges his political feelings against the Whig administration of *William III.* " Few people," says he, " foresaw how the creation of funds and the multiplication of taxes would increase yearly the power of the crown, and bring our liberties, by a natural and necessary progression, into more real, though less apparent, danger, than they were in before the revolution. The ex-cessive ill husbandry practised from the very beginning of King *William's* reign, and which the foundations of all we feel, and of all we fear, was not the effect of ignorance, mistake, or what we call chance, but of design and scheme in those who had the sway at that time." But he acquits them of " intending to bring upon their country all the mischiefs that we, who came after them, experience and apprehend. No;—they saw the measures they took singly, and unrelatively, or relatively alone to some immediate object. A due reflection on the passages of former times," says the noble lord, " as they stand recorded in the history of our own and of other countries, would have deterred a free people from trusting the sole management of so great a revenue, and the sole nomination of those legions of officers employed in it, to their chief magistrate."

" It remains to observe the difference between the two manners in which HISTORY supplies the defects of our own EXPERIENCE. It shows us the causes as, in fact, they were laid, with their immediate effects, and it enables us to guess at future events. It can do no more in the nature of things."

" The study of HISTORY, far from making us wiser and more useful citizens, as well as better men, *may be* of no advantage whatever; it may serve to render us mere antiquaries and scholars; or it may help to make us forward coxcombs and prating pedants: but this is not the fault of HISTORY; and to convince us that it is not, we need only contrast the *true* use of HISTORY with the use that is made of it by such men as these."

" We ought always to keep in mind that HISTORY is ' PHILOSOPHY *teaching by* EXAMPLES,' in all the situations of PRIVATE and PUBLIC life; that, therefore, we must apply ourselves to it in a philosophical spirit and manner; that we must rise from *particular* to *general* knowledge; and that we must fit ourselves for the society and business of mankind by accustoming our minds to reflect and meditate on the characters we find described, and the course of events we find related there."

· "There are certain general principles and rules of life and conduct which always must be true, because they are conformable to the invariable nature of things. He who studies HISTORY as he would study PHILOSOPHY will soon distinguish and collect them, and by so doing will soon form to himself a general system of ethics and politics on the surest foundations—on the trial of these principles and rules in all ages, and on the confirmation of them by universal experience."

" By contemplating the vast variety of particular characters and events,—by examining the strange combinations of causes, different, remote, and seemingly opposite, that often concur in producing one effect; and the surprising fertility of one single and uniform cause in the producing the multi-tude of effects as different, as remote, and seemingly as oppo-site,—by tracing carefully all the minute and sometimes scarcely perceptible circumstances, either in the characters of actors, or in the course of actions, that HISTORY enables him to trace, and according to which the success of affairs, even the greatest, is mostly determined; by such methods as these a man of parts may improve the study of HISTORY to its proper and principal use; he may sharpen the penetra-tion—fix the attention of his mind—and strengthen his judgment; he may acquire the faculty and habit of discern-ing quicker and looking farther, and of exerting that flexibi-lity and steadiness which are necessary to be joined in the conduct of all affairs that depend on the conaurrence or opposition of other men."

" In this manner the study of HISTORY will prepare us for action and observation. HISTORY is the ANTIENT author. EXPERIENCE is the MODERN language. We form our taste on the first;—we translate the sense and reason;—we trans-fuse the spirit and force;—but we imitate only the particular graces of the original—we imitate them according to the idiom of our own tongue, that is, we substitute often equiva-lents in the lieu of them, and are far from affecting to copy them servilely."

" As EXPERIENCE is conversant about the *present,* and

the *present* enables us to guess at the *future,* so HISTORY is conversant about the *past;* and by knowing the things that *have been,* we become better able to judge of the things *that are.* The nature of man, and the constant course of human affairs, render it impossible that the first ages of any new nation which forms itself should afford authentic materials for HISTORY. We have none such concerning the originals of any of those nations that actually subsist: shall we expect to find them concerning the originals of nations dispersed or extinguished two or three thousand years ago? If a thread of dark and uncertain traditions therefore is made, as it commonly is, the introduction to history, we should touch it lightly and run swiftly over it. Such introductions are, at best, no more than fanciful preludes."

" Learned men, in learned and inquisitive ages, who possess many advantages that we have not, and among others, that of being placed so many centuries nearer the original proofs that are the objects of so much laborious search, despaired of finding them, and gave fair warning to posterity, if pos_terity would have taken it."

" Most certain it is, *Varro* looked on the true era when the *Olympic* games were instituted by *Iphitus,* as the break of day, or the beginning of the HISTORICAL age. He might do so the rather, perhaps, because he included by it the date (he likewise fixed, or, upon recollection, the elder *Cato* had fixed) of the foundation of ROME, within the period from which he supposed that HISTORICAL truth was to be found. But yet most certain it is, that the HISTORY and CHRONOLOGY of the ages that follow are as confused and uncertain as the HISTORY and CHRONOLOGY of those which immediately precede this era."

"Man is the subject of every HISTORY; and to know him well, we must see and consider him as HISTORY alone can present him to us in every age,—in every country,—in every state in life—and in death. HISTORY, therefore, of all kinds—of civilized and uncivilized—of antient and modern nations; in short, all history that descends to sufficient detail of human actions and characters is *useful* to bring us acquainted with our species, nay, with ourselves. To teach and to inculcate the general principles of virtue, and the general rules of wisdom and good policy, which result from such details of actions and characters, comes for the most part, and always should come, expressly or directly, into the design of those who are capable of giving such details; and, therefore, while they narrate as historians they hint often as philosophers: they put into our hands, as it were, on every proper occasion, the end of a clue that serves to remind us of searching for, and to guide us to the search of that truth which the *example* before us either establishes or illustrates."

upon the excellence and use of *history* as a STUDY. We come now to the times in which we have lived ourselves.

Mr. *Gibbon* (36), from his early youth, employed the indefatigable energies of his powerful mind almost wholly in the study of HISTORY, and in the attentive perusal (it may be said, perhaps,) of every work of sterling merit, antient or modern, which had been published in his days. As he read, he recorded in writing his sentiments on the merits of the work, and his opinions on the talents of the author. A view of the course and variety of the subjects of his studies was given to the literary world by his friend Lord *Sheffield* after his death; and it may truly be said, that such a picture of learned persevering industry has possibly never been before exhibited to the world. The incessant assiduity with which this system was pursued under every circumstance of life has never, perhaps, been exceeded (if it has ever been equalled) by any individual of the times *past*, or of the *present* day.

At the early age of twenty-four, in the year 1761, in the tumult of a camp at Winchester, Mr. *Gibbon* contemplated the writing of a HISTORY. He says, " My own inclination, as well as the taste of the present age, have made me decide

(36) See Note I i.

in favour of HISTORY. Convinced of its merit, I cannot blush at the choice. But this is not all. Am I worthy of pursuing a walk in literature which *Tacitus* (37) thought worthy of him, and of which *Pliny* (38) doubted if he was himself worthy. The part of an HISTORIAN is as honourable as that of a mere chronicler or compiler of gazettes is contemptible. For which task I am fit it is impossible to know *until I have tried my strength;* and to make the experiment, I ought soon to choose some subject of HISTORY which may do me credit, if well treated, and whose importance, even though my work should be unsuccessful, may console me for employing too much time in a species of composition for which I was not well qualified. I proceed, therefore, to review some subjects for HISTORY; to indicate their advantages and defects; and to point out that subject which I may think fit to prefer."

After exercising his pen upon some historical subjects of minor importance, he *tried his strength* upon a lofty subject, no less than that of the " Decline and Fall of the ROMAN Empire;" and, after a time, he succeeded in sending forth into the world one of the most splendid performances (with all its imperfections) which has ever perhaps appeared in the English language.

Need any man inquire what were Mr. *Gibbon's* senti-

(37) See Note K 1.   (38) Note L 1.

ments upon the subject of HISTORY? Are they not sufficiently attested by the whole course of his studies, and by
the great and noble work which lies before me?

He was of opinion, that " it is the right—it is the *duty*—
of a critical HISTORIAN to collect—to weigh—to select the
opinions of his predecessors."

Sir *William Jones* (39) observes, that " the very soul and
essence of HISTORY is TRUTH, without which it can preserve
neither its name nor its nature, and with which the most
interesting circumstances in a barren chronicle are more
interesting to a sensible reader than the greatest events,
however copiously or elegantly they may be described, in a
romance, or a legend: yet it is strange that in so many
HISTORIES, antient or modern, EUROPEAN or ASIATIC *,
there should be so few, which we can read without asking,
in almost every page, Is THIS TRUE?"

Again,—

"It is in HISTORY as in PHILOSOPHY we can only catch
the general and striking features of TRUTH; it is a folly
to deck her picture with our own imperfect colours, and
to dress up a phantom of our imagination instead of a
REALITY †."

* Sir *William Jones*, vol. v. p. 539.　　　　　† Id. vol. v. p. 548.

Again,—

" In the obscurity of human affairs nothing remains for a wise historian but to confine himself to great and notorious events, in which the true and incontestible part of all history consists; for whenever he descends to particular characters and minute descriptions, or attempts to relate the very words and unfold the sentiments of princes, he will run into wildness and uncertainty, and lead his readers into a kind of fairly land, while they expect to be conducted through the paths of REAL knowledge."

We have thus deduced in detail the sentiments and opinions of some of the most learned and wisest men of antient and of modern times on the use and study of HISTORY, throughout a period of more than 2200 years, namely, from the age of *Thucydides*, who may be said to have flourished about 430 years before the Christian era, until that of Sir *William Jones,* who died, in the prime of life, in the year 1794. These opinions will be admitted to have been uniformly clear and decisive as to the excellence and use of HISTORY as a STUDY of EXAMPLES occurring in *real* life, and which, if duly reflected upon, must necessarily tend to the edification and improvement of mankind.

As peculiarly applicable to this subject, I cannot refrain from recording the opinions of an interesting and philosophic writer of the *present* day, who, be he right or be he wrong, in his estimate of the character of the unfortunate Charles I., (respecting which there is such a redundancy of opposite and discordant opinions, but a statement of which, in these obser- vations, would be irrelevant,) has unquestionably developed and brought to light many of the *secret* springs and causes of action, and has, in a great measure, unveiled the mystery which has hitherto attended many of the motives by which the conduct of the sovereign and the people has equally been governed, during the momentous period to which his commentaries relate. And with his judicious and profound observations on the " philosophy of HISTORY teaching by EXAMPLES," I shall conclude this imperfect dissertation.

" I have sometimes doubted," says Mr. *D'Israeli**, " whe- ther we have derived all that instruction and delight from HISTORY, of which a STUDY involving such extensive specu- lations on human affairs, and such a perpetual development of the moral faculties of man, would appear to be sus- ceptible."

" When philosophers became historians, and we were taught that the commemoration of the past was of secondary importance when compared with the instruction of the pre- sent, the regular narrative of incidents in the natural order of their occurrence exhibiting a vast multiplicity of facts, from their position always incoherent, in their nature often

* Preface to his Commentaries on the Life and Reign of *Charles I.*

trite, trivial, and inconsequential, was superseded by a sys-
tematic arrangement, which conveyed the great results of
human action."

" Instead of the distraction of multifarious events, of which
the reader had neither detected the causes, nor comprehended
the effects, the philosopher discovered the inseparable connection of circumstances, which are often distinctly removed
from each other in order of time. Hence causes were developed like secrets in nature, and principles deduced which,
like laws, govern society."

" A new and greater inconvenience was, however, often
incurred by this modern method of writing HISTORY. *To
establish a pre-conceived theory, either of political feeling* or
curious novelty, the historian sometimes *distorted facts,* or
joined together events which were no otherwise connected
than by his own fallacious imagination."

. "But the page of the popular HISTORIAN, even when un-
alloyed by this depreciating quality, and even when guided
by a searching spirit, still necessarily retained some of the
objectionable characteristics of the mere annalist. In the
rapid succession of events which he records, the imagination
is little affected ;—in the HISTORY of a people, for a tale we
find but a catastrophe, and a great character becomes little
more than a name. We are startled by extraordinary results

M

which violate our conception of nature and truth, and our
sympathies are little excited by the shadowy appearances of
personages who vanish ere we can penetrate into the con-
stituent principles of the minds whose acts are exhibited.
But the harmony of historical proportion would be destroyed
were the HISTORIAN to pursue investigations or agitate inquiries, which would increase our experience of our fellow-
creatures, confirm our self-knowledge, and throw light upon
the obscure, though regulating principles of society."

" It forms a necessary supplement to our knowledge to
combine *secret* with *public* HISTORY,—these *reflect light upon
each other*. The revelations of *private* history give complete-
ness to the imperfect tale of the popular HISTORIAN, and the
great results of human events, which the *private* memoir
cannot afford, are to be found in the record he opens for us.
Vast and innumerable are the sources of *secret* HISTORY
which, during the last half century, have accumulated in
masses; and we are furnished with materials for the HISTORY
of *human nature*, to which the antients could have no access.
One particular department seems peculiar to our own times—
the history of negotiations in the despatches of ambassadors.
Immense archives of contemporary documents are opened to
us in the entire correspondence of eminent men, and the un-
edited history of manuscripts. By these we may best learn
the genius which prevailed when the transactions occurred;—
by these the interest deepens of the great drama of HISTORY.

The narrative opens a living scene, and the *motives* of the personages are sometimes as apparent as their *actions*. It is not fanciful to say, that we often know. Many a *secret* for them is none for us. The letter which was judged to be thrown into the flames when read, we hold in our hands: the cabinet conversation, unheard but by two great statesmen, we can listen to. They viewed the man in his occasional actions; we scrutinize into his entire life. They marked the *beginnings*, but we the *ends*."

" When *Whigs* and *Tories* infused their controversies into their *degraded* HISTORY, trying events and persons by their own conventional tests, they judged of their ancestors as of their contemporaries; narrowing their views by their own notions, their own interests, and their own passions. Such partial estimates of human actions and modes of thinking may become anachronisms in morals and in politics."

" It must, however, be acknowledged that HISTORICAL TRUTH is of a relative nature. There is a difficulty in deciding on events, although the facts be ascertained,—and on historical characters, although the persons are well known; for different men will deduce different results from the same event, and the *motives* of the most open actions may be mixed and ambiguous. One FATAL TRUTH is alone incontestible, that all parties stand in need of mutual compassion, and may certainly triumph in mutual recriminations; and thus the passions, the prejudices, and the parties, which it has ever been the interest of the FEW to excite, to confirm, and to create among the MANY, have prevented mankind from advancing so much as they flatter themselves by the 'fore-passed miseries' of their experience."

"When a great critic declared that an HISTORIAN should be of no religion and of no country, it might have excited inquiry, whether he himself was this 'perfect monster' of passionless integrity? Was there ever man impartial whose business is with the *passions* of mankind. *Rushworth* says of himself, that 'it is possible for an ingenuous man to be of a *party* without being *partial;*'—an airy clench which hardly suited the sobriety of a preface to 'historical collections,' and seems to betray the weak pang of a half-conscience."

"Nevertheless, with all these hopeless imperfections of human HISTORIANS, we must discriminate between the *philosophical,* and the mere *party* spirit. *The* FORMER *addresses* MANKIND; *he opens a volume for their perpetual instruction,* and the noble *end* of THIS HISTORIAN *cannot be obtained, unless he pass beyond the limit of temporary passions and transient interests.* The LATTER is narrowed and devoted to the purposes of a FEW; the writer sets off with the predilections and the prejudices often inherited or taken up in early life; time will not soften this temper, knowledge will not alter these pre-judgments. *His* HISTORY reflecting back all the calumnies, the heats, and the misrepresentations of a former period, gratuitously assuming principles and deducing results accordant with his own system, collecting its materials with sinister industry, and, in a spirit of indiscriminate animosity, must necessarily be unjust, often untrue. *The* PHILOSOPHICAL HISTORIAN *in developing characters looks into* HUMAN NATURE *alone for the principles which are to guide him ;* but the PARTY-SPIRIT raises up the creatures of its own passions, men whom it would elevate above humanity, or disguise into political chimeras. *He who looks round for nature and consults* TRUTH—faithful copyist of the mutable and uncertain purposes of mankind—may perhaps emancipate himself from the bondage of a party ; *careful* of TRUTH, but *careless of its* TENDENCY, *he will show men* AS THEY *are, for never will men be* IMPROVED *by* FLATTERY, *or by* CALUMNY."

Again *,—

" If we are not well acquainted with the AGE, we shall never know the MAN. The philosopher must be an antiquary of human nature. His inquiries, pursued by close studies and patient meditation, can alone prevent those continued false decisions and erroneous conceptions with which *modern* writers of HISTORY sometimes blunder as grossly as modern writers of romance."

* Vol. i. p. 32.

NOTES.

NOTES.

NOTE A.

POLYBIUS was born at MEGALOPOLIS, a city of ARCADIA, 205 years before CHRIST, and was the son of LYCORTAS, chief of the republic of the ACHÆANS. He was trained to arms under the famous *Philopœmen*, and is described by *Plutarch* carrying the urn of that great but unfortunate general in his funeral procession. He arose to considerable honours in his own country; but after the defeat of *Perseus*, near the walls of PYDNA (A.C. 168), he was compelled to visit ROME as a prisoner of war with other principal ACHÆANS, who were detained there as pledges for the submission of their state to the ROMAN dominion. He thus became intimate with the second *Scipio Africanus*, and was present with him at the demolition of CARTHAGE. He saw CORINTH also plundered by *Mummius*, and thence passing through the cities of ACHAIA, reconciled them to ROME.

He extended his travels into EGYPT, FRANCE and SPAIN, that he might avoid such geographical errors as he has censured in others. After the death of his friend and benefactor *Scipio*, he retired from ROME, and passed the remainder of his days at MEGALOPOLIS, where he enjoyed the comforts and honours which every good man ought to receive from the gratitude of his fellow-citizens, and from the self-satisfaction which will ever be an attendant on a benevolent heart. At the mature age of eighty-two years, " he slept in peace the sleep " of death," about 124 years before the CHRISTIAN era.

Diod. Sic. observes, that *Scipio* "was brought up and instructed " from his childhood in the learning of the GREEKS, and when he was " eighteen years of age, applied himself to the study of philosophy,

N

" under the inspection of *Polybius* of MEGALOPOLIS, the historian,
" his tutor, with whom he continued a considerable time*."

NOTE B.

CATULUS, whom *Cicero* introduces in the dialogue with *Antonius*,
is no doubt the same person who is called by *Diodorus Siculus*,
Q. Luctatius Catulus, who committed suicide to avoid assassination in
the bloodthirsty proscriptions of *Marius* and *Cinna*. He had been
consul with *Marius*, A. U. C. 652, A. C. 102. He afterwards took the
part of *Sylla* against *Marius*. At that time *Q. Luctatius Catulus*,
who had had a glorious triumph for his victory over the *Cimbri*,
and had more than an ordinary share in the affections of the
people, was accused by a tribune of a capital offence. Fearing the
imminent hazard of the calumny, *Catulus* made his application to
Marius to entreat him to interpose for his deliverance (for he had
been his friend formerly, but through some suspicion he then entertained of him was become his enemy) ; but he answered him,—" *Die*
" *you must !*" Upon this *Catulus*, perceiving there were no hopes of
his preservation, studied how to die without disgrace; to which end
he destroyed himself by a strange and unusual way : for he shut
himself up in a house, newly plastered, and caused a fire to be
kindled, by the smoke of which, and the moist vapours of the lime, he
was there stifled to death.

NOTE C.

ANTONIUS MARCUS, a famous ROMAN orator, the grandfather of
Marc Antony, the triumvir; he filled the office of *prætor* in SICILY,
and was made *consul* with *A. Posthumius Albinus*, A. U. C. 653,
77 years before the birth of our Saviour. He was afterwards governor of CILICIA in quality of *proconsul*. In order to improve his
talent for eloquence, he became a scholar to the greatest men at
RHODES and ATHENS in his way to CILICIA, and when, on his return
to ROME, he was soon afterwards appointed *censor*, he was one of
the greatest orators known in that city ; and it was owing to him,

* Fragm. lib. xxvi. No. 75.

according to the testimony of *Cicero*, that ROME might boast herself a rival even to GREECE itself in the art of eloquence. He was unfortunately killed in the bloody conscriptions raised at ROME by *Marius* and *Cinna*. He was discovered in the place where he hid himself, and soldiers were sent to despatch him; but his manner of addressing them had such an effect, that none but he who commanded them, and had not heard his discourse, had the cruelty to kill him. His head was exposed before the *rostra*, a place which he had adorned with his triumphal spoils. This happened 90 years before the CHRISTIAN era.

NOTE D.

CATO, the censor, one of the greatest men amongst the antients, was born at TUSCULUM, A. U. C. 519, about 232 years before CHRIST. He began to bear arms at seventeen, and exhibited extraordinary courage. He was a man of great sobriety, and reckoned no bodily exercise unworthy of him. He had but one horse for himself and his baggage, and he looked after it and dressed it himself. At his return from his campaign, he betook himself to plough his ground, not that he was without slaves to do it, but it was his inclination.

He was first *tribune* of the soldiers for the province of SICILY—was *quæstor* in AFRICA under *Scipio*. He was afterwards *prætor*—conquered SARDINIA—governed there with great moderation, and was created *consul*. As a *tribune* in the war of SYRIA, he gave distinguished proofs of his valour against *Antiochus* the Great, and on his return stood candidate for the office of *censor*, and succeeded against seven powerful competitors. He was temperate, brave, and indefatigable; frugal of the public money, and not to be corrupted. There is scarce any talent requisite for public or private life which he had not received from nature, or acquired by industry. He was a great soldier, an able statesman, an eloquent orator, a learned historian, and had great knowledge in rural affairs. Yet with all these accomplishments he had very great faults; his ambition being poisoned with envy, disturbed both his own peace and that of the whole city as long as he lived. Though he would not take bribes, he was unconscionable in amassing wealth by all such means as the law did not punish.

censor after having passed through all the great offices of the commonwealth. There scarce ever was a man who came into the world with greater parts, or cultivated those parts with greater application, —a great general, a great orator, and a great historian, and above all, the most virtuous man of the most virtuous commonwealth. Among his other accomplishments he understood agriculture perfectly, which is a qualification that will always be highly esteemed by a wise people. Dion. Halli. lib. i. cap. 1, note 25.

He died about 150 years before the CHRISTIAN era, aged 85. He wrote several works; 1st, A Roman History; 2d, Concerning the Art of War; 3d, Of Rhetoric; 4th, A Treatise of Husbandry: the last only is extant.

Mr. *Spelman*, in his Dissertation on the Constitution of the ROMAN Senate, observes, that " this power of the *censors* was so great, that " *Cicero* thinks that it ought to have been abrogated. However, great ". as it was, it was not without control,—for the censured persons " had a right of appealing from the *censors* to the PEOPLE ; to whom, " from the suppression of the *decemvirs*, there lay an appeal even " from the *dictators*. This relief, therefore, the *censured* person was " entitled to, when both the *censors* concurred in expelling the indi- " vidual from the *senate ;* but if only one of them thought he deserved " this animadversion, the other might acquit him of it." In a note the translator refers to his authorities for this position: *Cic.* lib. iii. of Laws; *Livy*, lib. iii. c. 55, lib. viii. c. 33, lib. xl. c. 51.

NOTE E.

PICTOR, *Quintus Fabius,* was the grandson of *Fabius* of the *Fabian* family, who was surnamed " *Pictor*," because he painted the temple of *Salus.* This name descended to his posterity, of whom was the consul *C. Fabius Pictor* his son, and *Q. Fabius Pictor* the annalist, the grandson. He was the *first* Roman who wrote an historical account of his country, from the age of *Romulus* to the year of *Rome* 536. He flourished B. C. 225. He is called by *Livy*, " Scriptorum " antiquissimus*," and " apud *Fabium* longe antiquissimum aucto.

* Lib. i. c. 44.

" rem*." This is the historian censured by *Polybius* for his partiality to his countrymen, a partiality occasioned by the hostile feelings
of the GREEKS, for whom he wrote in Greek, that they might think
more worthily of ROMAN story†.

" The only works used by the two ingenious authors, who wrote
" HISTORIES of ROME contemporaneously under *Augustus*, were
" those of *Fabius*, and the later *annalists;* the contents of which they
" moulded into a uniform body, *without any regard to their origin.*"
If *Polybius's* estimate of *Fabius's* adherence to TRUTH in his history
be correct, what can we say to the HISTORIES of *Dionysius* and
Livy ?

NOTE F.

PISO.—The main features of the traditional tale of *Proculus Julius*
were held sacred for centuries by the ROMANS, and commemorated
in sacred songs. But there came a time when simple faith had lost
its strength, and when the esteem for *real* HISTORY had risen in proportion as the period it comprised was longer, and as the nation's
political character had grown in greatness and importance; and then
appeared writers by whom the old body of the old traditions was
perverted, as was this particular one in the grossest manner. These
are the writers whom *Dionysius* and *Plutarch* mention with appro-
bation, calling them rational men, who related what was probable,
and held to what was natural; and among their number the person
whom I believe to have introduced this practice, although it had
earlier models among the GREEKS, or who at least adopted it earlier
than any other ANNALIST, was L. *Piso* the censor, a contemporary
of the *Gracchi;* in other respects a worthy and honourable man, but
who, in what we know of his ANNALS, betrayed great narrowness of
mind and perversity of judgment. The *wish* of these HISTORIANS
was *to gain the whole of the mythical age for* HISTORY: their
assumption, that the poetical stories always contained a *core* of dry
HISTORICAL truth; and their system to bring this *core* to light, by
stripping it of every thing marvellous. The results of this attempt

were extremely various; in the legend of *Romulus* the term was given principally by *Livy**.

The first *Sabine* war grew, from the contests of a few days, into a tedious hard-fought campaign, with pitched battles between great armies. To this war, *Piso* referred the origin of the *Curtian* Lake, for the sake of ridding ROMAN HISTORY of another heroic legend. According to him, *Mettus Curtius*, a *Sabine*, had almost sunk with his horse into the swamp. The same *Piso* exalted *Tarpeia* from a venal traitress into a heroine,—an utterly thoughtless and mad one indeed, whose intention it was to sacrifice herself for her country. " To such lengths could even honest men go," says Mr. *Niebuhr*, " when devoid of understanding, of feeling, and of judgment; but " after these had paved the way, came the *shameless forgers.*" " It is not superfluous to show," says he, " the extreme stupidity of " mind that would fain pass for HISTORY."

" *L. Piso* had a peculiar object in view: he fancied that the antient " legends, however contradictory and incredible, were only history run " wild, and he was the person destined to restore them to their genuine " form†."

NOTE G.

MUTIUS, *Quintus Mutius Scævola*, used his utmost endeavour to reform other men's corrupt manners by his own virtuous example; when proconsul in ASIA, by his moderation and frugality, together with his just and upright dealing, he freed the province from its former miseries and oppressions. By discharging his own expenses, and the expenses of his retinue out of his own private purse, he soon inclined the hearts of all the province towards the people of ROME‡.

In the proscription of *Marius* and *Cinna*, the persons of the greatest quality at ROME, by false accusations were put to death, amongst whom, Q. *Mutius Scævola*, the chief priest, a most honourable and

* Niebuhr's History of Rome, vol. i. p. 231.2. † Id. vol. ii. p. 9.
‡ Diod. Sic. lib. xxxvi. Fragm. 5 and 6.

virtuous person, came to an unworthy end; only the Romans were fortunate in this, that the high priest died not in the most sacred place; for the cruelty of the murderers was such, that they laid him upon the very altar of *Vesta*, and then cut his throat, so that by his own blood he extinguished that fire, which, out of a religious devotion, from antient times, was ever kept burning*.

This was an office of great dignity and power. It was particularly incumbent on him to take care of the sacred rites of *Vesta*†.

NOTE H.

PHERECYDES.—Writings in prose can boast no higher antiquity than the age of *Cyrus* the Great, who flourished between the years 580 and 530 before the CHRISTIAN era. Previous to that time the opinions of the gravest philosophers, the narratives of the historian, and the lighter effusions of genius, were equally delivered in verse. This well established fact affords an answer to any objections to the works of *Homer*, as HISTORICAL compositions. Compositions, in any other form than that in which he wrote, were unknown to the age in which he lived.

PHERECYDES, the philosopher of SYROS, the disciple of *Pittacus* (one of the seven wise men of GREECE), and the master of *Pythagoras*, who died at the age of 85, in the year 515 before the CHRISTIAN era, was the first who delivered to the world the productions of his philosophical meditations in *prose*‡.

Cadmus of MILETUS, who was contemporary with *Pherecydes*, first applied *this form* of writing to HISTORICAL composition§.

* Diod. Sic. lib. xxxvii. Fragm. 16.
† See Adam's Roman Antiquities, and the numerous authorities there cited, p. 278—285.
‡ Paus. lib. i. c. 20; Cicero, Tusc. lib. i. c. 16; Dio. lib. i. c. 50; Servius in Æn. iii. v. 76; Vossius, Il. Gr. lib. iv. c. 4; Pliny, Nat. Hist. lib. vii. c. 56.
§ Pliny, Nat. Hist. lib. v. c. 29; Josephus, cont. Appion; Strabo, lib. vi. c. 259; Suidas in voce; Diod. i.; Dionysius, ii.

When *Pythagoras* heard that *Pherecydes*, once his master, was very sick in the island of DELOS, he sailed out of ITALY thither; where, after he had, for some time, cherished the old man, and used his utmost endeavour to restore him to health, he at length, through old age and the violence of his distemper, died : *Pythagoras* carefully buried him; and so, having performed the office and duty of a son as to a father, returned into ITALY*.

NOTE I.

HELLANICUS of *Mitylene* immediately preceded the great father and prince of *prosaic* HISTORY; being only twelve years older than *Herodotus*. The former was born in the year 496 before the CHRISTIAN era; the latter in the year 484 †.

Sir *Isaac Newton* informs us that he digested his HISTORY by the ages or successions of the priestesses of *Juno Argiva;* while other HISTORIANS digested theirs by those of the *archons* of *Athens,* or the kings of the *Lacedemonians* ‡.

We see from *Cicero*, however, as quoted in the text, that all these HISTORIANS were mere ANNALISTS, in the strictest sense of the term. Their annals were dry registers of dates, persons, places, and events, unembellished by any ornament, or grace of style, or sentiment.

NOTE K.

ACUSELAUS of *Argos* was an historian of about the same age with *Pherecydes*, and is often quoted by *Josephus* §. He is said to have written expressly on genealogies ‖.

NOTE L.

MARIUS, a celebrated ROMAN (originally a peasant of ARPINUM), rose by his military talents to the rank of consul. He first distin-

---

* Diod. Sic., pub. by *Valesius,* lib. vi. No. 35.

† Paus. lib. ii. c. 3; Aul. Gell. lib. xv. c. 23 ; Cic. de Orat. lib. ii. c. 53.

‡ Chronol. ii. 46.   § Cont. Appion.

‖ Suidas in voce; Cic. de Orat. lib. ii. c. 29.

guished himself in AFRICA against *Jugurtha.* By a series of heroic
exploits against the CIMBRI and TEUTONES, and other enemies of his
country, he became the most popular commander of ROME, of which
he was several times consul. His disputes with *Sylla* proved fatal to
the ROMAN people. He died in the midst of this struggle, 86 years
before the CHRISTIAN era, but not until he had deluged ROME with
the blood of his enemies.

NOTE M.

CINNA, with *Marius,* took violent possession of the consulship, and
committed many atrocities. He was opposed by *Sylla,* and at length
was assassinated in a mutiny by a private soldier.

NOTE N.

SYLLA, a ROMAN, of an illustrious family. He signalized himself
by his military successes; and openly attacked *Marius,* upon whose
head he set a price. He put to death the principal persons who
favoured the interests of his rival; and established himself as perpetual Dictator. After being absolute at ROME, he had the courage
to lay down his office, and to retire into private life. He died at
PUTEOLI, Crabbe says, about 75—Lempriere, 78—years before the
CHRISTIAN era, in the 60th year of his age. The last years of his
life were spent disgracefully in low debauchery.

NOTE O.

EPIMENIDES, an antient poet and philosopher, born at GNOSSUS in
CRETE.

The ATHENIANS, being afflicted with the plague, and commanded
by the oracle to make a solemn lustration of the city, sent *Nicias,* the
son of *Niceratus,* with a ship to CRETE, to desire *Epimenides* to come
to them. He accepted their invitation, accompanied the messengers
to ATHENS, performed the lustration of the city, and the plague
ceased. Here he contracted an acquaintance with *Solon.* He rejected all the presents offered him by the ATHENIANS, and would

O

accept of nothing except a little branch of the sacred olive preserved in the citadel; and desired the ATHENIANS to enter into an alliance with the GNOSSIANS. Having obtained this, he returned to CRETE, where he died soon after, aged 157 years.

He was a great poet, and wrote 5000 verses on " the Genealogy of " the Gods," 6500 on " the Building of the Ship *Argos* and *Jason's* " Expedition to COLCHIS," and 4000 concerning *Minos* and *Rhada-manthus*. He wrote also in prose, concerning sacrifices and the commonwealth of CRETE.

NOTE P.

THUCYDIDES was born at Athens, 471 B.C. He was the son of *Olorus;* and was educated in a manner suitable to his quality, that is, in the study of philosophy and eloquence. .He was contemporary with *Herodotus*, who was 29 years of age when he recited his history in public, *Thucydides* being then about 16.

During the PELOPONNESIAN war he was commissioned by the *Athenians* to relieve *Amphipolis*. But his operations were defeated by the quick march of *Brasidas*, the LACEDEMONIAN general; and, being unsuccessful, was banished from ATHENS. He died at ATHENS, where he had been recalled from his exile, in the 80th year of his age, 391 years before CHRIST.

NOTE Q.

HERODOTUS, of HALICARNASSUS, son of *Lycus* and *Dryo*, was born in the first year of the 74th Olympiad, about 484 years before CHRIST. The city of HALICARNASSUS being under the tyranny of *Lygdamis*, *Herodotus* quitted his country, and retired to *Samos;* from whence he travelled over EGYPT, GREECE, ITALY, &c.; and in his travels acquired the knowledge of the history and origin of many nations. He took the opportunity of a general assemblage of the GREEKS, and recited his work at the OLYMPIC games, which rendered him more famous than even those who had obtained the prizes *.

* Encyc. Brit. sub voce.

" It was reserved for him," says Mr. Mitford, " to give grace to " detail in prose narrative*."

NOTE R.

XENOPHON was born at ATHENS, in the third year of the 82nd Olympiad, or before CHRIST, 360 years. After his return into GREECE, on the retreat of the 10,000, he joined *Agesilaus*, king of SPARTA, and fought with him against the THEBANS in the celebrated battle of CHÆRONEA. The ATHENIANS, displeased at this alliance, brought a public accusation against him for his former conduct in engaging in the service of *Cyrus*, and condemned him to exile. The SPARTANS upon this took *Xenophon*, as an injured man, under their protection, and provided him a comfortable retreat at SCILLUNTES in ELEA. Here, with his wife and two children, he remained several years, and passed his time in the society of his friends, and in writing those historical works which have rendered his name immortal. A war at length arose between the SPARTANS and the ELEANS; and *Xenophon* was obliged to retire to LEPREUS, where his eldest son had settled. He afterwards removed with his whole family to CORINTH, where, in the first year of the 105th Olympiad, he finished his days.

NOTE S.

REGULUS (*M. Attilius*), a consul during the first Punic war. He reduced BRUNDUSIUM, and in his second consulship he took sixty-four, and sunk thirty, galleys of the CARTHAGINIAN fleet, on the coasts of SICILY. Afterwards he landed in AFRICA; and so rapid was his success, that in a short time he made himself master of about two hundred places of consequence on the coast. The CARTHAGINIANS sued for peace, but the conqueror refused to grant it; and soon after he was defeated in a battle by *Xantippus*, a SPARTAN general, and 30,000 of his men were left on the field of battle, and 15,000 taken prisoners. *Regulus* was in the number of the captives, and he was carried in triumph to CARTHAGE. He was sent by the enemy to ROME, to propose an accommodation and an exchange of prisoners;

* Hist. of Greece, vol. i. p. 158.

O 2

and if his commission was unsuccessful, he was bound by the most solemn oaths to return to CARTHAGE without delay.

When he came to ROME, *Regulus* dissuaded his countrymen from accepting the terms which the enemy proposed ; and as soon as his opinion had its due influence on the senate, *Regulus* returned to CARTHAGE, agreeable to his engagements.

The CARTHAGINIANS were told that their offers of peace had been rejected at ROME by the means of *Regulus;* and therefore they prepared to punish him with the greatest severity. We are told that he was exposed for some days to the excessive heat of a meridian sun, and afterwards confined in a barrel, whose sides were everywhere filled with large iron spikes, till he died in the greatest agonies.

In the contents or titles (which have been preserved to us) of the lost books of *Livy,* we have the following account of *Regulus :—* "*Attilius Regulus,* consul, having overcome the CARTHAGINIANS in a " sea-fight, passes over into AFRICA ; kills a serpent of prodigious " magnitude with great loss of his own men. The senate, on account " of his successful conduct of the war, not appointing him a successor, "'he writes to them complaining; and amongst other reasons for " desiring to be recalled, alleges that his little farm, being all his sub- "'sistence, was going to ruin, owing to the mismanagement of hired " stewards. A memorable instance of the instability of fortune, exhi- " bited in the person of *Regulus,* who is overcome in battle, and taken " prisoner by *Xantippus,* a LACEDEMONIAN general—the Roman " fleet shipwrecked, which disaster entirely reverses the good fortune " which had hitherto attended their affairs. *Regulus* being sent by " the CARTHAGINIANS to treat for peace and an exchange of prisoners, " binds himself by oath to return if these objects be not attained ; " dissuades the senate from agreeing to the propositions ; and then, in " observance of his oath, returning to CARTHAGE, is put to death by " torture."

" The widow of *Regulus,* and mother of his sons, grievously laid to " heart the death of her husband. She incited her sons," says *Dio-*

dorus Siculus, " to use the captives most cruelly and inhumanly; for
" they were thrust into a little close room, by reason of which they
" were forced to throng upon one another like beasts; and after they
" had been kept without meat for five days, *Bodostor* died through
" vexation of mind and famine. But *Amilcar*, being a man of a great
" spirit, held out still, though he saw no hopes of relief: but told her
" how careful he had been of her husband; and entreated her with
" tears to compassion: but she was so far from being touched with
" the least sense of humanity, that this cruel woman shut up the
" carcass with him for five days together in that close hole, and gave
" him meat only to keep him alive, that he might be the longer sen-
" sible of his miserable condition. *Amilcar*, now despairing by en-
" treating or begging to move her to pity, began to call upon *Jupiter*,
" and cry out to the rest of the gods who took care of mankind, to
" revenge him upon the woman, and repay her with just and due
" punishment."

" However, in the midst of all these torments he was kept alive, till,
" through the mercy of the gods, or some good fortune, he was won-
" derfully and unexpectedly delivered: for even when he was upon
" the point of death, through the stench of the dead body, and other
" miseries he laboured under, some of the meaner servants belonging
" to the house told it to some others abroad, who, in indignation to
" such cruelty and wickedness, forthwith informed the tribunes of the
" people of this horrid fact. Whereupon, when it was discovered, the
" magistrates sent for the *Attilii*, who, for branding the ROMAN name
" with such a dishonourable mark of barbarous cruelty, very narrowly
" escaped being put to death. But the magistrates threatened the
" *Attilii* severely to punish them, if they did not for the future use
" their prisoners civilly, and take due care of them. They imputed
" most that was done to their mother; and, burning the body of
" *Bodostor*, sent the ashes back to his own country; and freed *Amil-
" car* from the calamity and distress he groaned under."

NOTE T.

XANTIPPUS.—He was so ill requited for his splendid services, that
he was ordered to be thrown into the sea on his return home by the

HORACE, Lib. iii. Carmen. 5. The rant, as Lord *Bolinbroke* terms it, which Horace puts into the mouth of *Regulus*, is as follows, viz.:

Hoc caverat mens provida Reguli
Dissentientis conditionibus
   Fœdis, et exemplo trahenti
    Perniciem veniens in ævum,

Si non periret immiserabilis
Captiva pubes.—" Signa ego Punicis
   " Affixa delubris, et arma
    " Militibus sinè cæde," dixit,

" Derepta vidi: vidi ego civium
" Retorta tergo brachia libero,
   " Portasque non clausus, et arva
    " Marte coli populata nostro.

" Auro repensus scilicet acrior
" Miles redibit? flagetio additis
   " Damnum.   Neque amissos colores
    " Lana refert medicata fuco;

" Nec vera Virtus, cùm semel excidit,
" Curat reponi deterioribus.
   " Si pugnat extricata densis
    " Cerva plagis, erit ille fortis,

" Qui perfidis se credidit hostibus;
" Et marte Pœnos proteret altero,
   " Qui lora restrictis lacertis
    " Sensit iners, timuitque mortem.

" Hic, unde vitam sumeret inscius,
" Pacem duello miscuit.   O pudor !
   " O magna Carthago probrosis
    " Altior Italiæ ruinis !"

Fertur pudicæ conjugis osculum,
Parvosque natos, ut capitis minor,
    A se removisse, et virilem
        Torvus humi posuisse vultum;

Donec labantes consilio patres
Firmaret auctor nunquam aliàs dato,
    Interque mœrentes amicos
        Egregius properaret exul.

Atqui sciebat quæ sibi barbarus
Tortor pararet; non aliter tamen
    Dimovit obstantes propinquos,
        Et populus reditus morantem,

Quam si clientum longa negotia
Dijudicatâ lite relinqueret,
    Tendens Venafranos in Agros,
        Aut Lacedæmonium Tarentum.

Which is thus translated by Francis:—

When Regulus refused the terms of peace
Inglorious, he foresaw the deep disgrace
Whose foul example should in ruin end,
And even to latest times our baffled arms attend,

Except the captive youth, in servile chains,
Should fall unpitied.—" In the Punic fanes
" Have I not seen," the patriot-captain cried,
" The Roman Ensigns fix'd in monumental pride?

" I saw our arms resign'd without a wound;
" The freeborn sons of Rome in fetters bound;
" The gates of Carthage open, and the plain,
" Late by our war laid waste, with culture cloth'd again.

" Ransomed, perhaps, with nobler sense of fame,
" The soldier may return. You purchase shame
" With added ruin. To the fleece no more,
" Its rich vermilion lost, the fucus can restore,

" Nor virtue shall its fair complexion gain,
" Or clear by vicious arts th' infected stain.
" If from the toils escaped the hind shall turn
" Fierce on her hunters, he the prostrate foe may spurn

" In second fight, who felt the fetters bind
" His arms enslaved, who tamely hath resign'd
" His captive sword, who bravely might have died,
" Yet on a faithless foe, with abject soul, relied;

" Who, for his safety, mixed poor terms of peace
" Even with the act of war;—oh, foul disgrace!
" Oh Carthage! now with rival glories great,
" And on the ruins raised of Rome's dejected state."

The hero spoke; and from his wedded dame
And infant children turned oppressed with shame
Of his fallen state; their fond embrace repelled,
And sternly on the earth his manly visage held,

Till, by his unexampled counsel sway'd,
Their firm decree the wavering senate made;
Then, while his friends the tears of sorrow shed,
Swift through the weeping throng the glorious exile sped.

Nor did he not the cruel tortures know,
Vengeful prepar'd by a barbarian foe;
Yet with a countenance serenely gay,
He turned aside the crowds who fondly pressed his stay,

As, if his clients reconciled in peace,
The tedious business of the law should cease,
Cheerful he hasted to some calm retreat,
To taste the pure delights which bless the rural seat.

NOTE V.

EPHORUS, a Greek orator and historian of CUMA, or CYME, in
ÆOLIA, who flourished 352 years before the CHRISTIAN era. He
wrote a HISTORY of the GREEKS, from the return of the HERACLIDÆ
into PELOPONNESUS down to the 26th year of *Philip* of MACEDON,

besides other things on moral, geographical, and rhetorical subjects, all of which are lost, except a few fragments published with *Scylax*.

NOTE W.

PLATO—one of the most distinguished philosophers of antiquity; an ATHENIAN by descent, but a native of ÆGINA. He was born about 428 years before the CHRISTIAN era, and, after a life devoted to virtue and philosophy, died at ATHENS at the age of eighty-one. He was the pupil and constant disciple of *Socrates*, after whose death he travelled into various countries, and finally settled at ATHENS; and for forty years presided over a school which derived its name from him; and delivered his lectures, which were attended by numerous and respectable auditors. His philosophy is of the sublimest description.

NOTE X.

CICERO, the celebrated ROMAN orator, was born in the year of ROME 647, about 107 years before CHRIST. His father, *Marcus Tullius*, who was of the equestrian order, took great care of his education, which was directed particularly with a view to the bar.

Cicero was at his TUSCULAN villa, when he first received the news of the proscription, decided on by *Octavius*, *Antony*, and *Lepidus*, and of his being included in it. It was the design of the triumvirate to keep it a secret, if possible, to the moment of execution, in order to surprise those whom they had destined to destruction before they were aware of their danger, or had time to make their escape; but some of *Cicero's* friends found means to give him early notice of it; upon which he set forward to the seaside, with a design to transport himself out of the reach of his enemies. There finding a vessel ready, he presently embarked; but the winds being adverse, and the sea uneasy to him, after he had sailed about two leagues along the coast, he was obliged to land, and spend the night on shore. From thence he was forced, by the importunity of his servants, on board again; but was soon afterwards obliged to land at a country-seat of his, a mile from the shore, weary of life, and declaring he was resolved to die in that country which he had so often saved. Here he slept soundly for some time, till his servants once more forced him away in a litter towards the ship,

P

having heard that he was pursued by *Antony's* assassins. They had scarcely departed when the assassins arrived at his house, and, perceiving that he had fled, pursued him immediately towards the sea, and overtook him in a wood that was near the shore. Their leader was one *Papilius Lenas*, a tribune of the army, whose life *Cicero* had formerly defended and saved. As soon as the soldiers appeared, the servants prepared to defend their master's life at the hazard of their own; but *Cicero* commanded them to set him down and make no resistance. The assassins soon cut off his head and his hands, returning with them to ROME, as the most agreeable present to their cruel employer. *Antony*, who was then at ROME, received them with extreme joy, rewarding the murderer with a large sum of money, and ordering the head to be fixed upon the rostra between the two hands—a sad spectacle to the city. It drew tears from every eye, to see those mangled members, which had been used to exert themselves so gloriously from that place in defence of the lives, the fortunes, and the liberties of the ROMAN people, so lamentably exposed to the scorn of sycophants and traitors.

" The deaths of the rest," says an historian of that age, " caused " only a private and particular sorrow; but *Cicero's* a universal one. " It was a triumph over the republic itself; and seemed to confirm " and establish the perpetual slavery of ROME."

NOTE Y.

DIODORUS SICULUS lived about threescore years before our SAVIOUR's birth, in the time of *Julius Cæsar*, and in the reign of *Augustus*. He wrote a general history, from the beginning of the world to his own time, in forty books, called the " *Historical Library*," of which only fifteen are extant. The rest have been swallowed up by the voracious and never-to-be satiated appetite of time.

Here may be found EXAMPLES which may justly put CHRISTIANS to the blush, who come not up to the moral virtues of poor heathens, heretofore famous (upon that account) in the ages wherein they lived;— as *Themistocles* for his faithfulness to his country,—*Aristides* for his justice,—*Scipio* for his chastity,—*Cato* for his sobriety,—and several others for eminent and virtuous qualifications.

The works of the present author are well known among the learned to be a treasury of antient history. Amongst others, *Henry Stephen,* in his tract of *Diodorus,* gives him this honourable encomium: " *Quantum solis lumen inter stellas, tantum inter omnes, quotquot* " *ad nostra Tempora pervenerunt, historicos (si utilitas potius, quam* " *voluptatis aurium habenda est ratio) noster hic Diodorus eminere* " *dici potest.*" And *Justin Martyr,* and some others, call him the most famous author of all the GREEK historians. Among other excellences of this author, he is peculiarly observable to have a regard and respect to the providence of GOD in the affairs of the world; and is the only antient author that takes notice, in the course of his HIS-TORY, of the times wherein the most famous historians, philosophers, and poets flourished *.

NOTE Z.

The epitaph on the monument of the poet *Drayton,* ascribed to *Johnson,* is in complete accordance with this sentiment.

" Do, pious Marble, let thy readers know,
" What they and what their children owe
" To Drayton's name, whose sacred dust
" We recommend unto thy trust.
" Protect his mem'ry, and preserve his story;
" Remain a lasting mon'ment of his glory;
" And when thy ruins shall disclaim
" To be the treasurer of his name,—
" His name, which cannot fade, shall be
" An everlasting mon'ment to thee."

Again,—

" The Pilgrim oft,
" At dead of night, 'mid his oraison, hears
" Aghast the voice of Time,—disparting towers,
" Tumbling, all precipitate down dashed
" Rattling around—loud thund'ring to the moon."

Dyer's Ruins of Rome.

* Booth's Preface.

DIONYSIUS of HALICARNASSUS (an appellation which indicates the place of his birth) follows *Diodorus Siculus*.

What he says of himself in the Preface to his HISTORY is all that is known of him. "*Dionysius* lived at ROME," says his translator, " in " the AUGUSTAN age,—an age celebrated above all others in the " ROMAN HISTORY, both for the great writers it produced, and for the " distinguishing encouragement given by *Augustus* to those writers. " He was cotemporary, and probably acquainted with *Livy*, *Virgil*, " and *Horace*, and many other learned and polite authors, with whom " that age was adorned, and was himself a conspicuous star in that " bright constellation."

Mr. *Spelman* observes, that " it is impossible to read his HISTORY " without discovering in the author a mind fraught with all the ele- " ments of humanity—a sincere, a mild, and an honest heart—an " unaffected love of virtue—and, what is more amiable than a detes- " tation of vice, a compassion for it. He congratulates indeed the ' happy, and condoles with the miserable, but without insulting even ' those who deserve their misery. He is never satisfied with cele- ' brating the bravery, the patriotism, the frugality, and contempt of " riches of the old ROMANS, nor with lamenting the degeneracy of " those in his own time."

This learned translator has the following appropriate observation :— " *Dionysius*," he says, " teaches by PRECEPT what his and every " other HISTORY will teach by EXAMPLES, that the prosperity of every " nation is owing to their public and private virtue, and their adversity " to the want of both."

" HISTORY is the tribunal before which all princes must one day " appear, and derive their lasting glory or dishonour from her deci- " sions. When they themselves are no more—when the mercenary " scribblers of their time are as much forgotten as their works—then ' HISTORY takes her seat, and, like *Justice* with her balance, but " with eagle eyes, weighs every action, and explores the actor's heart—

" strips Ambition of her vain disguise, and treats a conqueror like a
" successful robber;—then will just praise be given to the prince, who
" made the happiness of his people his only care, and their law his
" only guide; whose only errors, if they were errors, proceeded from
" an excess of goodness misapplied, and are almost transformed to
" virtues by the dignity of the principle from whence they flowed.
" Such a prince will HISTORY paint in her fairest colours, and deco-
" rate him for nations yet unborn to love, and for princes yet unborn
" to imitate."

The best edition of the works of this author is that of Oxford, in
1704, in *Greek* and *Latin*, by Dr. *Hudson*.

NOTE B 1.

LARTIUS.—It does not appear to be quite clear who was first created
dictator, or in what year. *Livy* says that in the most antient writers
he finds it asserted, that the first dictator created was *Titus Lartius*,
A. U. C. 253, nine years after the expulsion of the kings.

The first cause of creating a dictator was the fear of domestic sedi-
tion. The authority of the consuls not being sufficiently respected, it
was judged proper, in dangerous conjunctures, to create a single magistrate with absolute power.

The power of the dictator was supreme both in peace and war.

NOTE C 1.

LIVY was descended from a noble family in ROME, and was born
at PATAVIUM, now called PADUA, in ITALY, in the 694th year of
ROME, 58 years before the commencement of the CHRISTIAN era.

Like many other literary men, his life was contemplative rather
than active: very few particulars, therefore, concerning him, have
come down to us. He resided at ROME for a considerable time, where
he was much noticed and highly honoured by *Augustus*.

He appears to have conceived the project of writing his HISTORY
immediately upon his settling at ROME.

wards emperor.

After a time, he sought tranquillity and retirement in the beautiful country and delightful climate of NAPLES. Here, enjoying uninterrupted literary ease and quiet, he continued his labour, and finished his work; comprising, in 142 books, the History of ROME from the foundation of that city to the death of *Drusus*, containing a period of 743 years, ending nine years before the birth of our SAVIOUR. Having completed this great work, he returned to spend the remainder of his days in his native country, where he died, A. D. 17, at the age of 75 years.

NOTE D 1.

NIEBUHR, the historian of ROME, is a son of the celebrated traveller of that name, whose merits are so well known in this country.

NOTE E 1.

The learned translator of *Dionysius's* Antiquities, in his Dissertation on the Constitution of the ROMAN Senate, observes that, " con-" cerning the *original* institution, *Dionysius* is much more particular " than *Livy* in every thing relating to this subject." From which of the *approved* ROMAN authors named by him could he have procured the FABLE ?

NOTE F 1.

Dionysius gravely relates, as matter of HISTORY, the following idle and most improbable tale respecting the *Horatii* and the *Curiatii.* .
" *Sicinius*, an ALBAN, having, about the same time, married his
" twin-daughters to *Horatius*, a ROMAN, and to *Curiatius*, an ALBAN,
" and their wives being with child at the same time, each of them was
" brought to bed, at her first lying-in, of three male children. All
" these children, their parents (looking upon the event as a happy
" omen both to their cities and families) brought up till they arrived
" to manhood. To these youths the gods had given beauty and

" strength, and a greatness of mind not inferior to THAT which men
" of the happiest disposition could boast of *."

He has the following observation on the murder of the sister by her
brother *Horatius* :—" Among the spoils of the slain, the friends of
" *Horatius* carried an embroidered robe, which she herself, with the
" assistance of her mother, had wrought, and sent as a present to her
" lover, to be worn by him on their nuptial-day. As soon as she saw
" this robe stained with blood, she burst out into violent lamentations,
" and reproached her brother for the loss of her cousin and lover.
" *Horatius*, inflamed with passion at her reproaches, ran his sword
" through her sides, and having killed his sister, he went to his
" father: but so averse to vice, and so *exalted were the manners and*
" *minds of the* ROMANS at that time, (to compare them with the
" actions and lives of THOSE of our age, so cruel and severe, and so
" little differing from a savage fierceness,) that the father, when
" informed of this heinous fact, was so far from resenting it, that he
" looked upon it as a *glorious and .becoming* action ; neither would
" he suffer his daughter's body to be brought into the house, nor
" allow her to be buried in the monument of her ancestors, or to be
" honoured with a funeral pomp, with personal ornaments, or other
" customary solemnity ; but she lay exposed in the place where she
" was slain ; and the passengers, covering her with stones and earth,
" buried her as a corpse destitute of all regard †."

NOTE G 1.

Sir WALTER RALEIGH.—This illustrious person was born at
HAYES, in the parish of BUDLEY, in the county of DEVON, in the
year 1552. He lived in great credit and in prosperity during the
reign of *Elizabeth*, and enjoyed the favour of that great princess,
except in the instance of his attachment to the daughter of Sir
Nicholas Throckmorton, formed without her previous sanction. He
afterwards married her, however, and regained the Queen's favour.

He was beheaded on the 19th of October, 1618.

* Lib. iii. v. 13.   † Lib. iii. c. 20.

Lord BOLINBROKE was born 1672, at BATTERSEA, of an illustrious family; and died there, 15th of November, 1751.

NOTE I 1.

Mr. GIBBON was born on the 8th of May, 1737, and died on the 18th of January, 1794.

NOTE K 1.

TACITUS—a celebrated ROMAN historian, who flourished in the reigns of *Domitian* and *Nerva.*

NOTE L 1.

PLINY the Elder—a celebrated philosopher, was born at VERONA, and lost his life in an eruption of Mount VESUVIUS, A. D. 79.

NOTE M 1.

Sir WILLIAM JONES, Chief Justice of INDIA, was born in 1748. He died at CALCUTTA, in the prime of life, 17th of April, 1794.

London : Printed by WILLIAM CLOWES, 14, Charing Cross.

CHRONOLOGY.

SIR ISAAC NEWTON'S CHRONOLOGY

GREEKS AND LATINS.

WRITINGS in prose can boast of no higher antiquity than the age of *Cyrus* the Great, who flourished between the years 580 and 630 before the CHRISTIAN era. Previously to that time, the opinions of the gravest philosophers, the narrations of the historians, and the lighter effusions of genius were equally delivered in VERSE.

This well-established fact affords a complete answer to any objections to the works of *Homer*, as HISTORICAL compositions, on the ground of their being in *verse*. Compositions in any other form than that in which he wrote were unknown to the age in which he lived.

Pherecydes, the philosopher of SYROS, the disciple of *Pittacus* (one of the seven wise men of GREECE), and the master of *Pythagoras*, who died at the age of eighty-five, in the year

B 2

515 before the CHRISTIAN era, was the first who delivered to the world the productions of his philosophical meditations in *prose**.

Cadmus, of MILETUS, who was contemporary with *Phere-cydes, first* applied this form of writing to HISTORICAL composition†.

Acuselaus, of ARGOS, an historian of about the same age, who is often quoted by *Josephus,* is said to have written expressly on Genealogies‡.

Nearly about the same period (B.C. 572), the sanguinary laws of *Draco* were promulgated in writing at ATHENS§.

Following these, in the next generation, was *Hecatæus,* an historian of MILETUS, who was born A.U.C. 549||, and another *Phcrecydes,* who was surnamed *Atheniensis.* They both of them flourished in the reign of *Dorius Hystaspes.* The latter wrote, in ten books, a History of the Antiquities and Genealogies of ATHENS, which was held in great estimation among the antients¶.

---

* Pausan. i. 20; Cic. Tusc. i. 16; Dion. i. 50; Servius in Æn. iii. 76; Plin. Nat. Hist. vii. 56.

† Plin. Nat. Hist. v. 19; Josephus cont. Apion; Strabo, vi. 259; Suidas in voce; Diod. i.; Dionys. of Hal. ii.

‡ Cont. Apion, init.; Suidas in voce; Cicero de Orat. ii. 29.

§ Plutarch, Vit. "Solon." || Herod. ii. 143.

¶ Dion. Hal. i. initio.

Hellanicus, of MITYLENE, immediately preceded the great father and prince of prosaic history, being only twelve years older than *Herodotus* *.

Sir *Isaac Newton* informs us, that he digested his history by the ages or successions of the priestesses of *Juno Argiva*; while other historians digested theirs by those of the *archons* of ATHENS, or the kings of the LACEDÆMONIANS †.

We learn, however, from *Cicero*, that all these histories were mere annals, in the strictest sense of the term. They were dry registers of dates, persons, places, and events, unembellished by any ornament or grace of style, or sentiment‡. It was reserved for *Herodotus* " to give grace to detail in *prose* narration §."

So long as the testimony of an antient author is in coincidence with the favourite system, which, *conte que conte*, is to be supported, whether it be ushered forth by the parent of the system, in that garb of *confidence* which should alone belong to *historic authenticity*, or in that garb of a cautious *hesitation*, which should ever attend the propagation of *traditionary rumours*, the authority, if we are to credit chrono-

---

* *Hellanicus* was born in the year 496 before the CHRISTIAN era; *Herodotus* in the year 484. Paus. ii. 3; Aul. Gell. xv. 23; Cicero de Orat. ii. 53.

† Chron. ii. 46.   ‡ Cic. de Orat. ii. 12.

§ Mitford's Hist. of Greece, vol. i. p. 158.

logers, is nevertheless, in either case, equally decisive and unquestionable. But whenever the tenor of such testimony is unfavourable, or calculated to excite a doubt as to the truth or the consistency of the system, our ready and confident chronologer does not hesitate at once to pronounce that *Herodotus,* or *Thucydides, in this* is mistaken,—*in that Pausanias* is in error,—*Strabo* has misconceived the sense of some passage of a still more antient author whom he has quoted, or *Plutarch* has identified and confounded events, which are wholly distinct and independent, both in age and character, of each other, and thus involved himself in a puzzle from which our more enlightened chronologers alone can extricate him.

These antient authors, we are told, did not possess the lights, which a further lapse of more than fifteen centuries has thrown upon our *modern* chronologers. The judicious *Mitford* has an observation which very forcibly applies to this subject, and to those *new lights* which have burst forth upon our modern chronologers. " It seems," says he, " as if doubts had decreased in modern times in proportion, not to the acquisition of means for discovering truth, but to the loss of means for detecting falsehood." Let us examine, however, a little into the nature and character of those lights which have given to modern chronologers such advantages over all the venerable, but, as they would contend, less enlightened, authorities of antiquity, and thus fortunately afforded them the opportunity (of which they have not hesitated to avail themselves) of correcting the errors into which the authorities of antiquity may have fallen.

These new lights will be found, upon investigation, to be (for the most part) little more than the gratuitous and fanciful theories—the dreams, or the inventions of a host of deep-read, learned, and ingenious, but *speculative* men,—historians, antiquaries, chronologers, and critics,—who have flourished in the intermediate ages between *remote* antiquity and modern times; some of them, indeed, at periods so distant from modern times, as almost to have acquired the title of " antient," and, under that imposing name and character, to steal from us, in favour of their assertions and opinions, a degree of respect, regard, and confidence, which otherwise we should not have bestowed on them, and to which they will be found in reality to have little claim. Few of these intermediate, learned and ingenious personages, even the most distant from our own times, were still so many centuries removed from the occurrence of well-authenticated or apocryphal events, whose chronology they take upon themselves decisively to fix and determine, as to exclude them from any title to our credence or confidence, except in so far as it may be justified by the weight and respectability of the authorities which they have quoted—by the accuracy or probability of the data upon which they have relied—and by our own acquiescence in the fairness or propriety of the they have drawn from them.

" Learned men, in learned and inquisitive ages," says my Lord *Bolinbroke,* " who possessed many advantages that we have not, and, among others, that of being placed so many centuries nearer the *original* proofs that are the objects of so much laborious research, despaired of finding them, and gave fair warning to posterity, *if posterity would have taken it.*"

An instance will serve to show with what facility these *learned* chronologers deceive themselves and delude the world; and upon what loose and unsatisfactory data (for evidence it cannot be called) they found the most arbitrary and positive conclusions, which they usher forth into the world, and impose as a tax upon the credulity of mankind, with the same unblushing confidence as if they were *really* necessary deductions from universally received and well-established HISTORIC FACTS.

Herodotus informs us, upon the authority of the ministers of the THEBAN *Jupiter,* that " the PHŒNICIANS had violently carried off from THEBES two priestesses; one of whom had been sold into LIBYA, the other into GREECE. And they added, that the commencement of those oracles must be assigned to these two women." Not quite satisfied with the mere assertion of the priests, *Herodotus* desires to know the authority on which this assertion rests. He is answered, " that, after a long and ineffectual search after these priestesses, they had finally learned what they had told him."

Herodotus then proceeds to state the information which he received from the priestesses of the oracle of DODONA, as to the origin of that institution, and which was confirmed in every particular by the other ministers employed in the service of the temple :—" Two black pigeons flew from THEBES in EGYPT; one of them settled in LIBYA, the other at DODONA; which latter, resting on the branch of a beech tree, declared, with a human voice, that this, by divine appointment, was to be an oracle of *Jove*. The inhabitants, fully impressed that this was a divine communication, instantly complied with the injunction. The dove which flew to LIBYA in like manner commanded the people to fix there an oracle of *Ammon*, which is also an oracle of *Jupiter*."

It is remarkable, and worthy of observation, that in communicating his opinion upon this information, *Herodotus qualified it with a doubt* of its authenticity. " IF," says he, " the PHŒNICIANS *did*, in *reality*, carry away these two priestesses, and sell one to LIBYA, the other to GREECE, this latter must have been carried to the THESPROTI, which

C

country, though part of what is now termed GREECE, was formerly called PELASGIA. That, although in a state of servitude, she erected, under the shade of a beech tree, a sacred edifice to *Jupiter*, which she might very naturally be prompted to do from the remembrance of the temple of *Jupiter* at THEBES, whence she was taken. There she instituted the oracle, and having learned the GREEK language, might probably relate, that, by the same PHŒNICIANS, her sister was sold for a slave to LIBYA." He then proceeds to explain the allegory of the two black doves, and to state, that " the two oracles of EGYPTIAN THEBES and of DODONA have an entire resemblance to each other;" and very justly infers from thence, " that the art of divination, as practised in the GRECIAN temples, was derived from EGYPT; and that the EGYPTIANS were the first who introduced the sacred festivals, processions, and supplications, and from them the GREEKS were instructed." And he considers this as " a sufficient testimony that these religious ceremonies were, in GREECE, of modern date, whereas in EGYPT they had been in force from the remotest antiquity."

Let us see what the *learned* chronologers *build* upon this *traditionary* information, which is delivered, even by the sufficiently credulous *Herodotus* himself, in a manner expressive of his doubt, if not of his disbelief, of its authenticity. The unprejudiced and judicious inquirer after historic truth (whose judgment and common sense have not been perverted by any early acquired or preconceived prejudices in favour of any particular theories or systems of ebronology, or absorbed and buried in a bewildering mass of useless learning,) will be astonished to learn, that upon this *traditionary, loose,* and *vague* authority, has not only been founded the most arbitrary and positive conclusions, as to HISTORICAL facts, but even uncertain dates and periods of events are pretended to have been thereby FIXED with the utmost exactness and precision.

This *dubious* event of the forcible abduction, by the PHŒNICIANS, of two priestesses of the oracle at THEBES, the learned *Jackson* does not hesitate to identify (as if it were really a *well-authenticated historic fact*) with the great event of the invasion and subjugation of EGYPT by the PHŒNICIAN shepherds*. The antient invasion of THEBES by the PHŒNICIANS, mentioned by *Herodotus,* "when the two priestesses were taken captives, *could be no other,*" says *Jackson,* "than that of the PHŒNICIAN shepherds, who conquered EGYPT, and ruled for many years there."

Mr. *Jackson* chooses to *imply* "invasion and conquest," but without the slightest authority for such an implication: for "invasion and conquest" are *not* "*mentioned* by Hero-

* Jackson's Chronological Antiquities, vol. iii. p. 241.

dotus," as Mr. *Jackson* asserts, or even *hinted at* by that credulous author. *Herodotus* merely speaks of the forcible abduction of two females by the PHŒNICIANS; but in *what manner* they were taken away, his *traditionary* information and the HISTORIAN himself are wholly silent.

" By this account," says he, in the same unwarrantable tone of confidence, " which the EGYPTIAN priests of THEBES gave to *Herodotus,* we are able *to fix, with great exactness,* the time of the founding of the two antient and famous oracles of JUPITER; one in LIBYA, and the other by the *P*ELASGI at DODONA. The PHŒNICIANS invaded and conquered EGYPT, as we are assured from *Manetho's* Dynasties, in the year before CHRIST 1982, and *hereabout,* or a year or two after, *we may place* the foundation of the two before-mentioned antient oracles of LIBYA and GREECE."

Is it to be endured that the *vague* and *traditionary rumours* of events in remote antiquity, handed down to us with all the errors, inaccuracies, and aberrations from the truth, which are inevitably incident to an *oral* transmission through many generations, or possibly even centuries, are to be assumed as *well authenticated historic facts;* for the purpose merely of drawing from them deductions favourable to some theory or fanciful system of chronology, and that these rumours and deductions, with all their fallacies and absurdities, are to be foisted upon us, under the sanction of high *learned* authority, as HISTORIC TRUTHS ? The attempt is an insult to the sober reason and the dispassionate judgment of mankind.

I confess I entirely concur with the learned and judicious *Mitford**, in the preference which he gives to Sir *Isaac Newton's* System of Chronology over that to which the favour of learned men has been more generally extended. That the chronology of our great philosopher may be liable to objection in some of its *details* is not at all surprising— *humanum est erra*re, and *even* the great *Newton* was not *infallible.* Of this I am satisfied, however, that the *leading principles* upon which he has founded his system of correction and amendment of the early chronology of the GREEKS and of the ALBAN and ROMAN kings ;—the grounds upon which he has expunged from it some centuries of primeval darkness and of historical vacuity, in which, as *Mitford* justly observes †, " neither man acquired fame, nor event had any consequence," appear to me so forcible and convincing—because they are entirely consistent with reason and common sense,—because they are bottomed on the *experience* derived from periods of *authentic history* and *certain chronology*,—that I confess I am lost in wonder and astonishment at the rejection of this rational system by so many learned men, who seem to me to shut their eyes, and

* Vol. i. p. 174. † Vol. i. p. 163.

to blind their judgments against the most obvious and palpable absurdities which are so forcibly pointed out by our
great philosopher, as existing in the system of GRECIAN and
LATIN chronology which they patronize, and to which they
cling with a sort of affectionate pertinacity, which is only to
be accounted for by the force of early prejudices, or by the
acquisition of too much learning, without the solidity of head
or understanding which can enable them to digest the useless
mass of learning which they have swallowed;—" too much
learning hath made them mad."   Would it not, on the contrary, be wholly repugnant to *unprejudiced* reason, and
utterly inconsistent with common sense, to acquiesce in those
miserable expedients which have been, and still are, resorted
to by chronologers, antient or modern, for the purpose of
supporting and maintaining their *lengthened* system of
GRECIAN chronology, which it was the object of Sir *Isaac
Newton's* system, by judicious curtailment, to rectify?

Whenever it is convenient or necessary to fill up a chasm,
or to stop a gap in *their* chronology, respecting which *authentic* HISTORY is wholly silent, these early-prejudiced or
over-learned system weavers do not hesitate, in order to suit
their purpose, to alter the course of nature, or to manufacture, *ad libitum*, and without any authority whatever, duplicate kings, duplicate heroes, duplicate philosophers, and
duplicate poets, living at different ages, but bearing the *same*

name,—possessing the *same* or similar qualities of mind and body—doing the *same* or similar acts—and acquiring the same reputation. Such a spurious manufacture, if soberly and dispassionately considered, will appear to be the illegitimate offspring only of learned absurdity. It is a manufacture utterly inconsistent with probability, and in reality rests upon no foundation whatever of HISTORIC TRUTH. Why are we called upon to surrender up at discretion our reason and common sense? Why are we called upon to give credence, so authoritatively demanded of us, to such absurd—such unsanctioned—duplicate creations? Why are we called upon, in opposition to our common sense, to believe that the ALBAN kings, the ROMAN kings, and the LACEDÆMONIAN and other GRECIAN kings (as long as kingly government existed in GREECE), reigned each for a *longer* average period in succession than all the other kings of the world who have appeared in the annals of *authentic* HISTORY besides? Upon no other maintainable ground in truth, than that it is necessary for the support of their system that we should do so. Can any man, who is in a state of freedom to exercise a cool, dispassionate, and sober judgment, yield his acquiescence to a system which requires to be so supported? It was to expose and to correct such gross—such palpable— absurdities that the great *Newton* framed successfully, for the most part, as I think, his System of GRECIAN and LATIN Chronology.

The more the generally received system of chronology, which is so pertinaciously favoured by the learned, is considered—the more it is tried by well *authenticated* HISTORIC facts—the more shall we find it liable to objection.

According to this system the return of the HERACLIDÆ is fixed in the year before CHRIST 1104; the capture of AMPHEIA in the year 743, which leaves a period of 361 years between the dates of these events.

According to the system of Sir *Isaac Newton*, the return of the HERACLIDÆ is placed in the year before CHRIST 825; the capture of AMPHEIA in the year 652; leaving an interval of 173 years between these two events.

Pausanias has given us the pedigrees of the respective kings of LACEDÆMON, of MESSENIA, and of ARCADIA, in uninterrupted succession, from the date of the return of the HERACLIDÆ to the commencement of the first MESSENIAN war *.

If these pedigrees are to be relied on, they confirm, in a very satisfactory manner, each other, and the system of Sir *Isaac Newton*.

* Lib. iii. c. 2 and 7; lib. iv. c. 3 and 4; lib. viii. c. 5.

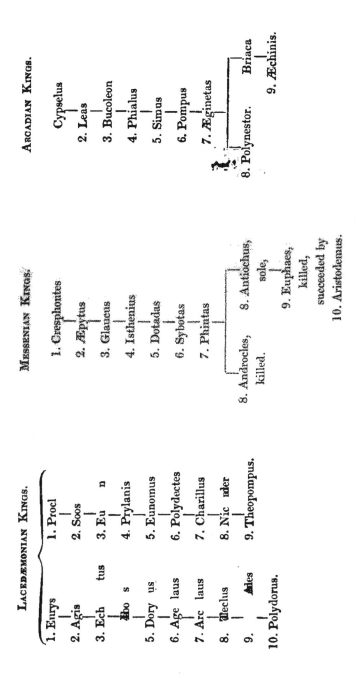

ARCADIAN KINGS.

Cypselus
2. Leas
3. Bucoleon
4. Phialus
5. Simus
6. Pompus
7. Æginetas
8. Polynestor.
Briaca
9. Æchinis.

MESSENIAN KINGS.

1. Cresphontes
2. Æpytus
3. Glaucus
4. Isthenius
5. Dotadas
6. Sybotas
7. Phintas
8. Androcles, killed.
8. Antiochus, sole,
9. Euphaes, killed, succeeded by
10. Aristodemus.

LACEDÆMONIAN KINGS.

1. Procl
2. Soos
3. Eu   n
4. Prylanis
5. Eunomus
6. Polydectes
7. Charillus
8. Nic   nder
9. Theopompus.

1. Eurys
2. Agis
3. Ech   tus
4. Bo   s
5. Dory us
6. Age laus
7. Arc laus
8.
9.   Ates
10. Polydorus.

D

The MESSENIAN king *Euphaes* commenced his reign only about the time of the capture of AMPHEIA : so the *first* MESSENIAN war began in the reign of the LACEDÆMONIAN king *Alcamenes*, but arrived at its greatest height in the reign of his son *Polydorus* *.

We cannot reckon, therefore, more than a succession of eight MESSENIAN kings between the return of the HERA-CLIDÆ and the commencement of the first MESSENIAN war. Of the LACEDÆMONIAN and ARCADIAN kings we may reckon a succession of nine kings between these two events.

Let us apply these successions of kings to the interval, according to each system of chronology, and mark the result in each case.

Eight kings in succession, filling up a space of 361 years, would produce an average of 45 years for the duration of the reign of each.

Nine kings in succession, filling up the same space, would produce an average of more than 40 years for the reign of each.

Each of these results would be absurd, as being contrary to all experience derived from *authentic* HISTORY and *certain*

* Pausan. iii. 3.

chronology. Even allowing these reigns to be equipollent with generations, that is, $33\frac{1}{3}$ years for each reign (for which, however, there is no pretence whatever), still these pertinacious chronologers would have a vacuity to supply of 95 years in the one case, and of 61 years in the other. So much for the fashionable chronology.

Eight kings in succession, filling up a space of 173 years, would produce an average of $21\frac{1}{2}$ years for the reign of each.

Nine kings in succession, filling up the same space, would produce an average of $19\frac{1}{4}$ years for the reign of each.

Either of these results would agree with Sir *Isaac Newton's* principle*,—would be consistent with the course of nature, as ascertained and defined by the experience of *authentic* HISTORY and *certain* chronology,—and would therefore be consistent with sound reason and common sense. Sir *Isaac Newton* has calculated his reigns and periods to the end of the first MESSENIAN war, which lasted 21 years, and was terminated therefore in the year before CHRIST 632.

Sir *William Jones* †, upon this subject, has the following remark : "Human nature is nearly the same in all ages; and it has been proved by the strongest induction, that kings seldom reign, one with another, longer than 18 or 20 years each."

* See Chronology, p. 51.   † Vol. v. p. 554.

D 2

" It is with the utmost diffidence that I venture to add an observation of my own upon any work of *Newton*, whose admirable tracts on the abstract sciences, and on the application of those sciences to natural philosophy, exhibit the noblest specimen of perfection to which the human intellect can be exalted; and whose treatises on lighter subjects, though incapable, from their very nature of strict demonstration, are not without many strokes of that piercing genius which raised him above all men who have ever lived."

> Superior beings, when of late they saw
> A mortal man unfold all Nature's law,
> Admired such wisdom in an earthly shape,
> And show an *Newton* as we show an ape.
> Could he whose rules the rapid comet bind,
> Describe or fix one movement of his mind?
> Who saw its fires here rise, or here descend,
> Explain his own beginning or his end *?
>
> Nature and Nature's laws lay hid in night,
> God said, " Let Newton be, and all was light."
>
> *Pope's Epitaphs.*

* Pope's Essay on Man, 2nd epistle. It is an interesting subject to trace the progress of a thought in the mind of a man of genius. The above lines were originally thus written, with the alterations as shown underneath:—

> " Angels themselves, I grant it, when they saw
> One mighty man unfold all Nature's law,
> Admired an angel in a human shape,
> And showed a *Newton* as we show an ape.
> Thou, then, who tell'st each planet where to roll,
> Describe or fix one movement of thy soul;
> Who mark'st their points to rise or to descend,
> Explain thy own beginning or thy end."

Sir *William* proceeds to observe, " that it appears to him that Sir *Isaac Newton's* medium of 20 years is too general, and that, in some ages and nations, it must be considerably less, in others far greater, according to the necessary difference of government or manners in the different empires of the world. Thus, by comparing the duration of the modern ASIATIC dynasties, since the decline of the Califate, with the reigns of the several princes, I have observed that those monarchs have seldom sitten on the throne longer than *ten* or *twelve* years at a medium; for, if one or two of them have contrived to hold their seats *forty* years, the greater part of them have reigned but *six* or *seven,* and many have been dethroned in a few months, some even in a few days, after their accession. This can be owing to nothing but the imperfection of those unhappy governments, where a sultan no sooner has the diadem on his head than his ministers, sons, or brothers, form a confederacy against him; so that he either perishes in the field, or closes his days in prison, to make room for one of his relations, who frequently meets with the same fate: this is apparent from almost every history of *modern* ASIA. The case was very different in the infancy of the PERSIAN empire: the sovereigns were almost deified by the people whom they had civilized; the temperance of those early ages might tend to lengthen their natural lives; and few of them were disturbed by civil wars or rebellion: so that we may safely allow the space of 560 years to the two first families of PERSIAN kings, or *twenty-*

from the death of *Darius,* in the 330th year before Christ, will place the foundation of the Persian monarchy in the 890th year before the same epoch, about 14 years, according to *Newton,* after the burning of Troy, and just a *century* before some general or feudatory of *Tahmuras* founded the dynasty of the Assyrians."

The objection of Sir *William Jones,* however, to the *generality* only of the medium, and the circumstances assigned as the reasons for his objection, appear to me to amount to a decisive confirmation of the *Newtonian* System of Chronology.

CŒTERA DESUNT.

London : Printed by William Clowes, 14, Charing Cross.

LOOSE AND UNCONNECTED THOUGHTS

RESPECTING

ROMAN AND GRECIAN HISTORY.

LOOSE AND UNCONNECTED THOUGHTS,

&c.

IF we were to divide the whole duration of the national existence of ROME into ages, with reference to the different ages of the existence of man, we should probably allot the whole period which elapsed from its foundation to its capture by the GAULS to its *infant* age and condition: and when we reflect that the most powerful of all the petty nations of ITALY (not excepting even ROME itself) could scarcely have vied in extent of territory, and probably in effective population, even with any of our modern English counties of a moderate size,—and that if we were to describe a figure nearly in the shape of a parallelogram, having the south-western coast of ITALY for one of its longest sides, and if we were to include within this figure the territory of infant ROME and of all these petty nations combined, it would not embrace an extent of country of more than two hundred miles in length and fifty miles in breadth, containing a superficies of not more than ten thousand square miles,—we shall be forced to admit, that it is from other causes, rather than their own *intrinsic* importance, that we must seek to explain the lively interest with which we are animated by the recital of the events of these early periods of ROMAN HISTORY.

If the GALLIC irruption had terminated the independent national existence, and with it all the splendid portion of the history of ROME, or even if (surviving that catastrophe) the growth and acme of its national power and greatness had never extended itself beyond the boundaries which Nature would seem to have prescribed as the limits of an empire or kingdom of ITALY, (by which it would have acquired no extraordinary preeminence in the scale of relative national importance,) the history of all its petty wars, and military achievements,—its boasted civil and municipal institutions, —its violent and incessant party dissensions,—and its internal political struggles between eminent men for influence and power,—would probably have been perused, not studied, with no greater degree of interest than the history of CARTHAGE itself (if that history had been handed down to us by any *Carthaginian* author with equally circumstantial details), or than the early history of any other of the petty nations of antiquity, or of more modern times. As far as we are possessed, however, of these details, respecting CARTHAGE, conveyed to us, as they have been, in all that hostile spirit, and with all that poisonous venom which the most violent national and political prejudices could engender, we are compelled to feel that CARTHAGE (at the periods to which these details relate, and which were written by an arrogant enemy) is very little, if at all, inferior to ROME itself in the scale of national grandeur and importance, and in every other quality which could render a nation great and powerful. Impartial judgment will not fail to elevate its splendid hero, *Hannibal*, to a level at least, if not to a superior grade in talent and ability, with any hero whom ROME could produce, not even excepting that greatest of all its heroes, *Julius Cæsar* himself. But the immortal *Hannibal* was crossed, and ultimately ruined, by the rancorous jealousies of his countrymen, and by the internal political dissensions of his country. The expression " *delenda est Carthago*" affords in itself decisive evidence no less of the *fearful apprehensions* than of the high national and political estimation in which CARTHAGE was held at ROME.

It may possibly be said, that the interest of a still more lively and animated description, which is avowedly excited in us by the early history of the little communities of GREECE (which, in geographical importance, were scarcely superior to those of ITALY, of which we have been speaking), affords a practical refutation of this observation. To this it may be answered, that there is no similitude or resemblance whatever in the character or circumstances (as calculated to excite our interest) of the early events of ROMAN, as compared with the early events of GRECIAN HISTORY.

A concise summary of the latter will illustrate, and, it is conceived, will fully establish the justice of this position.

The histories, or, to speak more correctly, the speculative theories of learned and fanciful men, which profess to inform us of the aboriginal settlement and peopling of the nations of EUROPE, must, from the very nature and absolute uncertainty of the evidence upon which they are founded, be incapable of producing either a well-founded conviction, or any rationally explainable interest in the mind of any student of history. In the study of history the degree of legitimate interest which it excites must be in proportion to the strength or weakness of our conviction of its TRUTH.

We shall, for these reasons, pass over as objects more properly belonging to antiquarian research, and therefore as foreign to our present inquiry, all the theories as to the aboriginal settlement of GREECE and ITALY, with this one observation merely,—viz., that as EUROPE must have been gradually peopled by successive migrations in a direction from east to west, or by the swelling and gradual over-flowing in the same direction of the stream of population of the more eastern and earliest settled countries in EUROPE, the probability is in favour of the greater antiquity of the aboriginal settlement of GREECE than of ITALY.

The commencement of GRECIAN HISTORY cannot with

safety be carried farther back than three or four generations before the siege of TROY, or, according to the *Newtonian* chronology (to which, with some modifications, I entirely subscribe), about one thousand years before the *Christian* era. The ages more remote have properly acquired not only the character, but the name of " FABULOUS : " and even the earlier part of those which have been denominated the "HEROIC" ages, is involved in so much obscurity, or is so much disguised by allegory, or mingled and tainted with fiction, that it is a task of no inconsiderable difficulty to separate and distinguish with confidence or satisfaction the TRUTH from the FABLE.

Of that which is denominated, and has been generally received as ROMAN HISTORY, no reliance whatever can be placed upon the period of it which preceded the foundation of ROME, and very little indeed (in my humble judgment) upon that which succeeded it, until we arrive at about half a century before its capture by the *Gauls;* this would fix the date of the commencement of *Roman* STORY, according to the same chronology, at about six hundred and fifty years before the *Christian* era, and *Roman* HISTORY at about three hundred years after that period.

The *first* great epoch of GRECIAN HISTORY is distinguished by one of the most celebrated and interesting events recorded in antient history. These events seize with an irresistible hold upon our feelings, from their transmission down to us by the inimitable hand of the great master poet and HISTORIAN * of antiquity.

The independent sovereigns of GREECE, the descendants or the successors of *Perseus* and of *Pelops*, of *Hercules*, of *Cadmus*, of *Minos*, of *Cecrops*, of *Theseus*, and of the heroes of the ARGONAUTIC expedition, unite in a grand and mighty league' for the purpose of avenging upon a distant and a powerful ASIATIC kingdom a flagrant injury (aecompanied by breach of hospitality and insult) which had been offered by one of the sons of its sovereign to one of the princes of GREECE. A gallant host of one hundred thousand heroes from the southernmost coast of PELOPONNESUS to the northern boundary of THESSALY, and from CRETE, and the smaller islands of the GRECIAN community, assemble at AULIS in BŒOTIA (the appointed port of general rendezvous), and are transported from thence in a fleet of one thousand two hundred vessels to the shores of ASIA. The supreme command of this majestic armament, by the common consent of the sovereigns engaged in it, is vested in *Agamemnon,* who swayed the sceptre of MYCENÆ, of many islands, and of ALL ARGOS.

---

* Mr. Mitford, in his valuable History of GREECE, has satisfactorily vindicated and established the claim of *Homer* to the character and authority of an HISTORIAN, as well as a poet. The character of a faithful delineator of the manners and customs, domestic and political, of the age in which he lived, has never been denied him.—Vol. i. pp. 61, 63, 127, 160. See also Gillies' History of GREECE, vol. i. p 36.

Πολλῆσιν νήσοισι καὶ Αργει παντι ανασσειν,

who was the grandson of *Pelops,* and the brother of the prince whose injuries had excited this powerful confederation associated for the purpose of avenging them ; and each component nation of this grand confederacy was led on to vengeance and to glory by its own immediate sovereign in person. Their voyage was prosperous; their landing, after a sharp and sanguinary contest, was effected on the TROJAN coast, and their superior numbers compelled the TROJANS to abandon their territory to the ravages of the invading army, and to seek their protection within the lofty walls of their capital.

The combatants about to be engaged on either side in this awful and momentous contest were not unworthy of each other. The PHRYGIAN kingdom, of which TROY was the capital, could boast of an antiquity equal at least to that of any of the GRECIAN states. Its sovereigns could exhibit a genealogy as remote at least in its recorded or traditionary commencement as those of any of the princes of GREECE, and equally with them could conceal or dignify the meanness or uncertainty of its origin in all the fabulous and poetic splendour of a divine transmission. *Priam,* the reigning monarch, was the fifth in lineal descent from *Dardanus,* its founder, who, in the language of poetry and fable, was the son of *Jove.*

Erichthonius, the son and successor of *Dardanus,* is famed

C

in poetry and history for his enormous wealth, and still more for the remarkable sources from whence it was derived.

It was the good fortune of *Tros*, the son of *Erichthonius*, to give his name to that celebrated city of which his son was the real founder. *Ilus*, the son of *Tros*, removed the seat of empire from one of the mountains of IDA on which *Dardanus* had placed it, to the fertile plain which was watered by the rivers SIMOIS and SCAMANDER, and founded there the future capital of the PHRYGIAN empire. During the reign of *Ilus* and his successors this city had experienced those vicissitudes of good and evil fortune which are the lot of nations as well as of individuals. In his reign, as well as in that of his son *Laomedon*, TROY is said to have been subjected to capture and pillage. To provide against the recurrence of similar misfortunes, *Laomedon* is said to have inclosed it within walls and battlements of such an immense height and strength, and of such superior and matchless construction, as to have been deemed, in the easy credulity of those times, the work of more than mortal hands.

CÆTERA DESUNT.

Before we proceed in descending chronological order, it is incumbent upon us to notice two remarkable institutions of early GREECE, which claim chronological precedence over the TROJAN war itself. The far-famed oracle of DELPHI, and the celebrated council of the AMPHYCTYONS, were both of them of such remote antiquity (though of undoubted REAL existence), that their *origin* is involved and altogether lost in the darkness and obscurity of the "FABULOUS" ages. When we consider these two singular institutions with reference to the periods of their establishment, they cannot fail to excite our curiosity—our interest—and our wonder. The first—if not the offspring, the adopted child and creature at least of wily priestcraft, working for its own interested purposes upon the weakness of human nature—had for its object to acquire and to preserve an influence over the conduct and actions of nations and of private individuals through the powerful agency of credulity and religious superstition;—the other—the offspring of a political wisdom and prudence, quite extraordinary for the age which gave it birth—had for its object the creation and maintenance of a bond of political and social union, and of national good fellowship between the different states composing the general community of GREECE. This object was supposed to be attained by the establishment of a tribunal of mutual resort for the settlement of their international differences, and the prevention thereby of the horrors and miseries of war and bloodshed amongst themselves;—for concocting the means of mutual support in case of *foreign* molestation ;—and for the encouragement and protection of their common religion. The whole tenor, however, of GRECIAN history shows the scheme to have been in some measure UTOPIAN, and that the laudable political objects of this celebrated institution were rendered nugatory, and its authority unavailing, by the violences, the mutual jealousies, and the eagerness for superiority or independence which prevailed amongst the various GRECIAN states which were represented in it ; and it would probably, at a much earlier period, have sunk into insignificance and obscurity, had not its consequence been from time to time kept alive by its association and intimate connection with its more thriving sister institution at DELPHI. In later periods of GRECIAN HISTORY we find it employed as an instrument in the hands of a politic, designing, and powerful prince to further his deep-laid schemes for his own aggrandizement, and for the subversion of the liberties and independence of GREECE.

CÆTERA DESUNT.

OBSERVATIONS

RESPECTING

THE AUTHENTICITY

OF

THE ARUNDELIAN MARBLES,

OR, IN MORE ACCURATE LANGUAGE,

THE PARIAN CHRONICLE.

OBSERVATIONS

AUTHENTICITY OF

THE PARIAN CHRONICLE.

I HAVE read with great attention the " weak and inconsistent arguments," (as they are termed by Dr. *Hales,*) of the "ingenious classical sceptic, Mr. *Robertson,*" who has ventured to call in question the authenticity and antiquity of the PARIAN Chronicle. I have read with equal attention, and with the most anxious disposition to be convinced, the arguments of the learned Mr. *Hewlett,* in his "Vindication of the authenticity of the PARIAN Chronicle," by which he has, in the opinion of Dr. *Hales,* so " ably exposed " the weakness and inconsistency of those of the classical sceptic. But I am bound in truth and candour to confess that they wholly failed to convince me; nay, more, that they have not in any degree tended to remove or weaken the doubts and difficulties which the arguments of his opponent had raised

A 2

in my mind as to the authenticity of this Chronicle. I am conscious that there may be more of boldness than prudence in hazarding this assertion. In any event I subject myself to the angry anathema, which the learned Mr. *Hewlett*, at the commencement and at the close of his unfair, uncandid, and intemperate vindication, hurls forth against all who shall presume, by doubts, to disturb what he is pleased to term " the rational convictions of the mind." I humbly confess, in spite of Mr. *Hewlett's* anathema, that I have no such " rational convictions." The confident and arrogant tone of the vindicator forms a striking contrast with the modest and diffident tone with which the dissertator concludes his work. " Whether it is an authentic monument of antiquity or a modern compilation; whether its authority is indisputable, or, as I am inclined to think, APOCRYPHAL, I shall now leave to the determination of the judicious and impartial reader. Though its authenticity, I believe, has hitherto been unquestioned; nay, though it has been held in the highest estimation by men of distinguished learning, I flatter myself there can be no impropriety in this disquisition."

But this diffidence, however, has the effect only of making the intemperate and uncandid Mr. Hewlett still more angry. He even converts it into a ground of charge against the dissertator. After literally quoting the passage, he applies to it this sneering and sarcastic observation:—

" From these and other passages, and indeed from the motto prefixed to the book—*Ea quæ disputavi, disserere malim quam judica*re, Cic.—it appears that the author has not embraced any decided opinion upon the subject." Could any thing be more unfair, more uncandid, or more illiberal than this observation ?

Of the nine different considerations which gave birth to the doubts entertained by Mr. *Robertson*, as to the authenticity of the PARIAN Chronicle, the fourth, the sixth, and the eighth appear to me to have great weight.

1st. As to the fourth consideration, viz.

" The GREEK and ROMAN writers, for a long time after the date of this work, complain that they had no chronological account of the affairs of GREECE."

1st. *Julius Africanus,* who died about the year of CHRIST 233, asserts that the GREEKS had no accurate history before the OLYMPIADS, and that all their accounts of preceding ages are confused and inconsistent." Apud *Euseb.* Evang. lib. x. c. 10.

2d. *Justin Martyr,* who wrote about the year 140, makes the same observation.

3d. *Plutarch* ventures no further into Grecian antiquity than the time of *Theseus*. His *ne plus ultra* is not much more than one-half of a century before the siege of Troy. All beyond "is full of prodigy and fiction—the region of poets and fabulists—wrapped in clouds, and unworthy of belief." In Vit. Thes. The same writer takes notice of the inconsistencies of the Greek historians in many points of chronology, concerning some of the most illustrious characters, and the most important transactions of later times, in which a general agreement might have been expected. "There is nothing but uncertainty," says he, "and contradiction in the accounts which historians have given us of *Lycurgus*, the celebrated Spartan lawgiver." In Vit. Lycurg. *Plutarch* wrote about A. D. 120.

On another occasion (in Vit. Solonis) *Plutarch* observes, "that some authors think they can prove by chronological arguments that the story concerning the interview between *Solon* and *Crœsus* is a fiction; but a story so famous, attested by such a number of witnesses, and, what still more deserves to be considered, so agreeable to *Solon's* character, and so worthy of his magnanimity and wisdom, should not, in my opinion, be rejected upon a pretence of its not agreeing with some chronological canons, as they are called, which themselves continue to this day *endeavouring to correct, without being able to bring them to any consistency.*"

To the above passage in *Plutarch,* Mr. *Robertson* applies the following apposite and forcible observation :—" In this instance we find the date of a most important transaction in the most polished state of GREECE, the legislation of *Solon* at ATHENS, a subject of dispute and uncertainty."

The defect of historical records in those early times, and the ignorance of the best informed writers as to the most remarkable transactions of neighbouring kingdoms, is strikingly illustrated in the utterly irreconcileable variances between the accounts given by *Herodotus* and *Xenophon,* of the most important circumstances in the history of *Cyrus* the Great. According to *Herodotus, Cambyses,* the father of *Cyrus,* was a PERSIAN of inferior rank; according to *Xenophon* he was king of PERSIA. According to the former he *dethroned* his grandfather, *Astyages,* and transferred the empire of the MEDES to the PERSIANS; according to the latter *Astyages* died in peace, and left his kingdom to his son *Cyaxares.* According to the former, *Cyrus,* after a reign of twenty-five years, was slain in a battle with *Tomyris,* queen of the MASSAGETES, who cut off his head and threw it into a vessel of human blood, with a sarcastic reflection on his cruelty and ambition; according to the latter, *Cyrus,* after a reign of conquests and glory, died like a philosopher, in his own palace, surrounded by his family and friends. Now *Herodotus* was born only forty-five, and *Xenophon* only seventy-nine years after the death

Her*odotus* was born in the year 484; *Xenophon* in the year 450 B. C. These authors lived within a century of the events which they so differently describe. Of the events and their eras, which our *Pa*rian chronicler promulgates in a tone of so much confidence, many of them happened (if they happened at all) upwards of ten centuries *before* the death of *Cyrus*, and more than thirteen centuries before the chronicler's own time. To return from this digression,—

4th. *Josephus*, who was born A. D. 37, asserts, that " the antient Greek writers destroyed one another's credit" by their charges of inaccuracy and falsehood against each other.

5th. *Varro*, the profound antiquary of Rome, who died in the year before Christ 26, divided the time anterior to his own age into three parts; the first (extending from the creation of the world to the Ogygean deluge) he termed αδηλον, "the obscure," or unknown period; the second (extending from the deluge to the first Olympiad) he termed μυθικον, "fabulous," *quia in eo multa fabulosa referuntur;* the third (extending from the first Olympiad to his own time) he termed ἱσορικον, "the historic era," *quia res in eo gestæ, veris historiis continentur. Varr.* Frag. p. 219.

6th. *Thucydides*, who was born 471 years before Christ,

remarks, that " the transactions of an earlier date than the PELOPONNESIAN war, and those which were still more antient, could not, through length of time, be adequately known."

7th. *Diodorus Siculus*, who flourished about sixty years before CHRIST, informs us that he was thirty years in composing his historical library, and that he travelled through many parts of EUROPE and ASIA, in order that he might see those places which he had occasion to mention; but with regard to the times and chronological periods which preceded the TROJAN war, he admits that all his inquiries were of little avail. As to them, he says, " he cannot with any confidence determine, *because he had no certain foundation to rely upon.*"

This assertion of *Diodorus Siculus*, as Mr. *Robertson* justly observes, is extremely unfavourable to the credit of the PARIAN Chronicle. His reasoning and conclusions are, in my humble judgment, so clear and satisfactory, that I shall give them in his own language.

" We must either suppose," says he, " that the PARIAN Chronicle was not *existing* in the time of *Diodorus*, which at once decides the question; or, that *Diodorus* had not heard of it, which is scarcely credible, considering his abilities, and the pains he took to collect information from

B

worthy of credit, which will hardly be admitted by the advocates for the ARUNDELIAN Marbles."

"The same inference may be drawn from the foregoing remarks of *Africanus, Justin Martyr, Plutarch, Josephus, Varro,* and *Thucydides;* for they all agree that the earlier periods of the GRECIAN history were involved in darkness and confusion."

"But if the PARIAN chronologer could ascertain the dates of the most important events which happened in GREECE, five, six, seven, eight hundred years before the OLYMPIADS; such as, the first establishment of the kingdom of ATTICA by *Cecrops*—the deluge in the time of *Deucalion*—the coming of *Danaus* into PELOPONNESUS—the arrival of *Cadmus* in BŒOTIA—the siege of TROY, &c., with a particularity which we scarcely find in a modern history, there could be no want of light or information, &c., consequently the complaints of all the writers above mentioned are groundless and absurd."

"If *Thucydides,* as well as other writers, complained that there was nothing but uncertainty in the earlier periods of the GRECIAN history, from whence can we suppose the author of this inscription collected such a clear, determinate, and comprehensive system of chronology?"

We shall now proceed to the sixth consideration, as Mr. *Hewlett* combines the two in his answer to the reasonings and conclusions of Mr. *Robertson.*

2d. As to the sixth consideration, viz.—

" The PARIAN Chronicle is not once mentioned by any author of antiquity, and this silence is by no means a circumstance in its favour."

" The PARIAN Chronicle," Mr. *Robertson* observes, " is not a small inscription, of no importance in the republic of letters. It is"—or rather, he should have said, it professes to be—" a curious, learned, and comprehensive system of chronology, inscribed at a considerable expense on a tablet of marble, comprehending a detail of the principal epochas of GREECE during a period of one thousand three hundred years."

" In this inscription," says *Prideaux,* " we have more events in the early ages of GREECE specified and recorded, than are to be found in almost all the writers of antiquity." Marm. Oxon. Præf. p. 5.

" The epochas of *Cecrops, Ducalion, Hellen, Cadmus, Danaus, Minos, Triptolemus, Hesiod, Homer,* and others ascertained."

" Here the question which has been a thousand times debated, whether *Homer* or *Hesiod* is the more antient author, is *precisely determined.* Here likewise the year, the month, and the day of the month in which TROY was taken, is particularly specified."

" These are such wonderful discoveries in antient history, that if this chronicle had existed for two hundred and sixty-four years before the birth of CHRIST, and more especially if it had been compiled by PUBLIC AUTHORITY, or even KNOWN at PAROS, it must have excited a general attention, and would certainly have been copied or cited, or praised or censured, or mentioned by some writers of succeeding times."

" But neither *Strabo, Pliny, Pausanias,* nor *Athenæus,* who mention the most considerable chronicles of different countries; neither *Apollodorus, Diodorus, Tatian, Cleomenes, Alexandrinus,* nor *Eusebius,* who professedly treat of the fabulous ages of GREECE, take the least notice of this wonderful monument of antient learning. In short, we do not find in any writer of antiquity, either poet or historian, geographer or chronologer, mythologist or

scholiast, the most distant allusion to the PARIAN Chronicle."

" At last, after it had existed above one thousand eight
hundred years, without being either named or cited, it is
dug out of the ground, and brought to EUROPE in triumph;
it is explained, quoted, applauded by critics and commen-
tators; in a word, it is deposited in the bosom of our
Alma Mater, and esteemed κτημα ες αει, ' a glorious and
everlasting acquisition.' "

" Under these circumstances," concludes Mr. *Robertson,*
" it will be impossible to account for the profound silence
of the antients, and their gross inattention to a writer, who
now excites the curiosity and admiration of the literary
world, and professes to unravel all the chronological perplexities of the fabulous and heroic ages of GREECE."

We shall now proceed to consider the answers of the
learned Mr. Hewlett to the arguments of the classical
sceptic, whom he appears to hold in such sneering contempt.

With respect to the conclusion drawn by Mr. *Robertson,*
from the facts above stated, that " no regular scientific
chronology existed from the time of *Herodotus* to *Polybius*,"
Mr. Hewlett observes (p. 63) that " it is utterly impossible
for a writer of the eighteenth century to determine what

could know what the History of *Ephorus* contained; unless he could examine the Chronica of *Apollodorus;* and, above all others, the *Acta Chronica*, and other writings of *Timæus Siculus.* This last writer, however captious, or however credulous he might have been as an historian, is said by *Diodorus Siculus* to have been extremely accurate as a chronologer. These, and a great number of authors whose names, perhaps, have never reached us, are necessary to inform us of the state of chronology in GREECE."

I cannot attach any weight whatever to this observation of Mr. *Hewlett,* because we must suppose that *Diodorus Siculus* (who for thirty years was anxiously engaged in inquiring after information upon the subject) perfectly well knew what the History of *Ephorus*—what the Chronica of *Apollodorus*—what the *Acta Chronica*, and other writings of *Timæus Siculus*—and, to sum up the whole, what the writings of every other author, of his own, or of preceding times, whose works were accessible to him, contained. But this same *Diodorus* positively assures us, that all his anxious and *"perilous"* inquiries had been of no avail, as to the early periods of GRECIAN history; they had afforded him no *"parapegmata,"* upon which he could rely for deciding upon the chronology of any events which preceded the TROJAN war. If he is entitled to our credit for this assurance, we have a right, nay, we are bound to assume, that neither *Ephorus,* nor *Apollodorus,* nor *Timæus Siculus,* nor any other known authors in the time of *Diodorus Siculus,* contained any information in regard to the early history or chronology of GREECE, which we could ourselves have relied on, if the works of all these various authors had been extant at this day. I am at a loss therefore to discover to what legitimate object this observation of Mr. H*ewlett* can tend.

· From this preliminary observation (without either sense or meaning) of Mr. H*ewlett,* we shall proceed to his remarks on the arguments which Mr. *Robertson* " means to found on the silence of *Diodorus Siculus* with respect to the PARIAN Chronicle, and his neglect of chronology before the TROJAN war."

He quarrels in the first instance with that gentleman's translation of the important passage in question, and gives us one of his own, which is certainly a more *literal* one, but which avails nothing in his argument, inasmuch as the *spirit* of the passage, and the *rational inferences* from it, as bearing upon the point in dispute, remain the same.

He contends that although *Diodorus* could not "fully determine those early periods, as he has succeeding ones, yet he has observed a sort of relative chronology, and settled the time of one epocha by that of another." He adduces three instances of this, but they are so vague and unsatisfactory as to add little weight to the argument. He denies that "*Diodorus* made no attempt to circumscribe these times which precede the TROJAN war," but he " admits that he could not do it so accurately as in subsequent periods."

" It was not the want of materials, such as they were," says Mr. H*ewlett*, "which perplexed the historian, but it was the irreconcileable diversity of opinions. In the prosecution of his extensive plans he could not dwell with the patient labour of *Timæus* to settle a period of chronology in those remote ages, and was happy, perhaps, to hasten on to more interesting and important subjects."

Now this reasoning is really so absurd as scarcely to deserve the trouble of a serious refutation. Can any man believe that if the " patient labour of *Timæus*" had successfully struck out, or settled a period of chronology in those remote ages, that *Diodorus Siculus*, who so highly extols his diligence and accuracy, would have omitted to adopt it, and introduce it into his history, "however extensive his plan," or however " happy he might have been to hasten on to more interesting and important subjects." Our learned Mr. H*ewlett* is far from being happy in his references to this same *Timæus*. " *Diodorus*," says Mr. H*ewlett*, " has remarked of *Timæus* that he was extremely accurate in his chronology, and laboured to render his work as copious as possible." From such a writer therefore, alone, the epochas of "the PARIAN Chronicle might have been transcribed, without having recourse to other authorities." Now if the writer of the PARIAN Chronicle could have transcribed his epochas from the work of *Timæus, Diodorus* could have done the same thing. But he has not done it; and that negative circumstance amounts, in my humble judgment, to that sort of moral proof which ought to satisfy every rational and unprejudiced mind, either that there was no such thing in *Timæus,* or, if there were, that *Diodorus* did not deem it sufficiently worthy of credit for him to rely upon it.

Mr. *Hewlett* then attempts to prove by several loose and vague quotations from *Diodorus* that there were several antient " writers," as well as the author of the PARIAN Chronicle, " who professed to unravel the perplexities of the fabulous ages, though not to the entire satisfaction of *Diodorus.*" " The following," says he, " is an important passage: 'I can neither determine,' says *Diodorus,* ' who were the first kings, nor can I agree with those historians who profess to know.' Among those historians, doubtless," says our learned vindicator, " he would have classed the author of the PARIAN Chronicle, if he had seen his performance, and passed it over in silence."

It is very singular that Mr. *Hewlett* does not appear at

all conscious that his arguments (feeble as they are), in *support* of the *authenticity* of the PARIAN Chronicle, strike forcibly at the very root of its *authority* as a *table* of certain *chronology*. As to the *value* of this Chronicle as an *authoritative* system or epitome of chronology, even if its *authenticity* were undoubted, we shall have some observations to make at the close of these remarks.

Mr. *Hewlett* then enters into a course of reasoning in the endeavour to prove that the circumstance of the PARIAN Chronicle not appearing to have been quoted by *Diodorus*, or any other antient author, ought not to be admitted as an argument against its authenticity. "It is not the custom of *Diodorus*," says he, "nor is it the custom of the antients in general, to quote authorities of any kind with tolerable precision." This may be true, but it seems to bear very little upon the question; for I cannot divest myself of the conviction, (whether it be a "*rational*" conviction, or not, must be left to others to decide,) that if the PARIAN Chronicle existed in the time of *Diodorus*, and was known to him, the style and tone of pretension,—the decided and authoritative manner which characterize that table of chronology would necessarily have induced so curious, so anxious, and so indefatigable an inquirer as he evidently was, to investigate the subject for the purpose of ascertaining whether there were really any good or sufficient grounds for placing a reliance upon the *truth*, and the *authenticity* of the events, and upon the chronology which it so *authoritatively* promulgates. Were any individual to take up this table, for the first time, and without any previous information or knowledge of the subject, he could not but suppose that its author had merely transcribed, or had digested a series of events and dates, universally known to all the world, and historically authenticated and established. "I have described," says our chronologer in this tone of pretension and authority, "preceding times—beginning from *Cecrops*, &c." "Since *Cecrops* reigned at ATHENS was 1318 years, &c." But all the authors of antiquity whose works have happily come down to our times,—the predecessors—the contemporaries —the successors of the chronologer of PAROS,—either candidly confess their ignorance or their doubts, or differ so positively, or materially, as to the early events and chronology of antient GREECE, as to destroy each other's credit. (*Joseph.* Cont. Ap. l. i. s. 3.) Our confident *PARIAN* chronologer, *alone*, has no doubt or hesitation whatever. He *alone* is indued with clear and accurate perceptions— with certain and determinate information—upon points respecting which all *other* learned men of antiquity doubted or disagreed. After lying buried for nearly nineteen centuries, our PARIAN chronologer comes forth; but by whom—or when—or where—he has been found, not one of his panegyrists or vindicators is able to inform us, and he is ushered forth into the world with the authority almost of an inspired writer, for the purpose of converting darkness and obscurity, into light and certainty.

From all these premises, I must confess it does appear to me that one or other of these two alternative conclusions is inevitable; 1st, either that the PARIAN Chronicle did not exist, or was unknown in the days of *Diodorus Siculus*, and those other respectable writers of antiquity, who have transmitted down to us their candid confessions of ignorance, or their doubts as to the early history and chronology of antient GREECE; or, 2dly, if it then existed, and was known to those writers, that it was not held by them in any estimation, or as entitled to any credit, as an authoritative document in history or chronology. If the first of these alternative conclusions be preferred and adopted, there is an end at once of its authenticity, unless indeed it may be supposed to have existed unknown to all the world, except the learned (if any such there were) in the island of PAROS. This appears to be our author Dr. *Hales's* solution of the difficulty, which we shall presently consider. If the second of these alternative conclusions be preferred and adopted, it will be very immaterial, as far as the interests of history and chronology are concerned, whether it be authentic or not. It would still, if authentic, be curious, as a relic of antiquity, but beyond that, it would have *no value* whatever. Because then it would have been known, but known as a document which was held in no estimation by any of these writers.

Dr. Hales thinks that " the most rational solution of the silence of subsequent classical writers respecting this curious chronicle" (which is the principal argument used to impeach its genuineness) " may be derived from the insular and secluded situation of the island of Paros." (vol. i. p. 236.)

Now in offering this solution of the difficulty, the learned Dr. Hales seems wholly inconsistent with himself, for he has just before stated that " Paros was one of the most flourishing and opulent of the Cyclades." From whence did its opulence and prosperity arise? No doubt from its great *intercourse*, and extensive communications, commercial and political, with the rest of Greece, both European and Asiatic, and with Egypt. Politically it was intimately connected with Athens. Its famous marbles alone would necessarily be the means of a constant commercial intercourse with the rest of the civilized world, which it supplied with the abundant product of the bowels of its soil, for the erection of the most splendid temples and edifices of antiquity. The doctor is sadly mistaken in his geography with regard to Paros when he terms it *secluded*, if by seclusion he meant, that it had not ready and easy opportunities of access, and communication with the surthe CYCLADES, and is nearly midway between CARIA in ASIA MINOR, the PELOPONNESUS, the island of CRETE, and ATHENS.

We proceed on to the eighth consideration.

8th. The discovery of the Chronicle is related in a very obscure and unsatisfactory manner, with some suspicious circumstances, and without any of those clear and unequivocal evidences, which always discriminate truth from falsehood.

. " It is remarkable," says Mr. *Robertson*, " that the place (a very important circumstance) where it was found is not ascertained."

The generality of writers who have had occasion to mention it, have supposed it was found in the island of PAROS.

Du Pin, Du Fresnoy, Dr. *Rawlinson*, and Abbé *Banier* were of this opinion.

" Others," as *Palmerius* and *Batavius*, " tell us that it was not found at PAROS, but in ASIA MINOR, at SMYRNA."

" If we consult the editors of the *Marmora Arundeliana* we shall find no satisfaction in this particular."

Selden says, " we may reasonably conjecture that the author was a PARIAN." *Prideaux* is wholly silent upon the subject. *Maittain* speaks of this fragment, as if he had not known where it was discovered. Dr. *Chandler* believes it was found at *Paros*, and afterwards removed to SMYRNA. This is the last account we have of the PARIAN Chronicle.

" In the inscription itself we have no data by which we can any ways discover the place where the marble was erected."

" If this monument was erected at SMYRNA, for what purpose does the writer mention *Astyanax*, the archon of PAROS, and not one circumstance relative to SMYRNA ?"

" If it was erected at *Paros*, why does he not mention more archons of that city than one? Or how shall we account for his profound silence, with respect to all the events and revolutions which must have happened in that island, and have been infinitely more interesting to the natives than the transactions of any foreign country ?"

It would appear from *Gassendies's* life of *M. de Peirese*, that the ARUNDELIAN Marbles "had been exposed to sale before they fell into the hands of Mr. *Petty*."

" These Marbles," says *Gassendies*, " were first discovered and dug out of the ground, in consequence · of the application and order of *Peirese*, who paid fifty pieces of gold for that purpose by the hands of one *Samson*, his agent ·at SMYRNA. But when they were ready to be sent on board, by some artifice of the vendors, *Samson* was thrown into prison, and the Marbles, in the mean time, left in a state of confusion."

" Such," observes Mr. *Robertson*, " were the first ostensible possessors of these Marbles ! and so dark and unsatisfactory is the account which is transmitted to us of their discovery ! They had been totally unknown or unnoticed for almost 1900 years, and at last they are dug out of the ground—nobody can tell us when or where."

In answer to these objections on the part of Mr. *Robertson*, Mr. *Hewlett* answers,—1st. " *Du Pin, Du Fresnoy,* Dr. *Rawlinson,* and Abbé *Banier* expressly affirm that the *Marmor Chronicon* was found in the island of PAROS, and the expression of *Palmerius* that they were found at SMYRNA, alludes to the collection of Marbles mentioned by *Gassendies,* and might only mean that they were first seen, or discovered then by Mr. *Petty;* it does not deny that the

Parian Chronicle was first dug up in the island of Paros and afterwards removed to Smyrna." And as to *Petavius*, says Mr. He*wlett*, " he seems not to have had any clear idea of what the Arundel Marbles were." But before we can make the concession to Mr. He*wlett*, that any weight whatever is due to the positive affirmation of *Du Pin*, *Du Fresnoy*, Dr. *Rawlinson*, and the Abbé *Banier*, upon which he relies, it is incumbent upon him to shew—what I apprehend he is unable to shew—that these writers had *oth*er genuine sources of authentic information upon the subject than those which we possess, namely, those derived from the editors of the *Marmora Arundeliana,* which we have seen offered no satisfaction whatever on the subject. Their positive affirmation therefore amounts to nothing at all. Mr. He*wlett* admits that " *Selden* is inexcusable for not having prefixed to his commentary an accurate and circumstantial narration of its discovery from Mr. *Petty's* own words, or the Earl of *Arundel's* relation.' There is no doubt that *Selden* himself believed that the author was a Parian. But I cannot by any means agree with Mr. He*wlett* that " *Selden* fully admitted that the Parian Chronicle was found in Paros." "It is reasonable," says *Selden,* " to suppose that the author was a Parian from this consideration. He has distinguished his chronological performance by the name of an archon who was his countryman, that he might thus compliment his country." Now, surely, if *Selden* knew that the marble was found in Paros,

D

undoubtedly he would. And here I must be permit
express my surprise with the classical sceptic, that,
author of the Chronicle intended to compliment his co
men, he should have omitted to record many inter
events which must have happened in PAROS.

CÆTERA DESUNT.

London:—Printed by WILLIAM CLOWES, 14, Charing Cross.

ANNOTATIONS

MITFORD'S

HISTORY OF GREECE.

4to.

SECOND EDITION, FIRST VOLUME.

LONDON:

WILLIAM CLOWES, 14, CHARING CROSS.

1834.

ANNOTATIONS, &c.

[" *Was inspired generally with a spirit of emigration.*"

▮▮▮▮▮▮▮▮▮▮▮▮▮▮▮▮▮▮▮▮▮▮▮▮▮▮▮▮▮▮▮▮▮▮
▮▮▮▮▮▮▮▮▮▮▮▮▮▮▮▮▮▮▮▮▮▮▮▮▮, or at least
had been improved, even before the general DELUGE, is evident from the scripture HISTORY of the antediluvian ages.
Lamech, of the line of Cain, was the sixth in descent from
Adam.

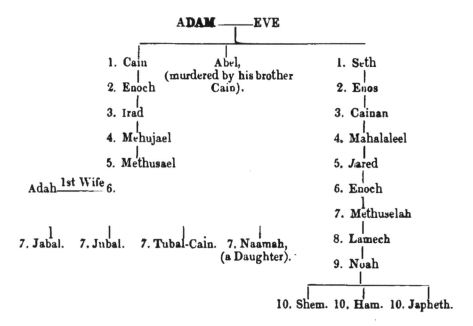

	ADAM———EVE	
1. Cain	Abel,	1. Seth
2. Enoch	(murdered by his brother	2. Enos
3. Irad	Cain).	3. Cainan
4. Mehujael		4. Mahalaleel
5. Methusael		5. Jared
Adah —1st Wife— 6.		6. Enoch
		7. Methuselah
7. Jabal. 7. Jubal. 7. Tubal-Cain. 7. Naamah, (a Daughter).		8. Lamech
		9. Noah
	10. Shem. 10. Ham. 10. Japheth.	

We are not informed how long our first pareuts continued
in the enjoyment of innocence and the garden of EDEN,

interval between their expulsion from PARADISE, and the birth of their first-born son *Cain*. *Adam*, we are told, was about one hundred and thirty years old when his third son *Seth* was born. But this information does not enable us to ascertain the difference between the ages of *Cain* and *Seth*. Their respective lineal descendants, *Lamech* and *Enoch*, were both however in the sixth degree from *Adam*, their common progenitor. *Lamech* had by two wives, *Adah* and *Zillah*, three sons and a daughter:

1st. "*Jabal*, the eldest son, is said to have been the father of such as dwell in tents, and of such as have cattle." Gen. iv. 20. Agriculture therefore must have been his pursuit.

2d. "*Jubal*, the second, was the father of all such as handle the harp and the organ." ver. 21. The manufacture of musical instruments and the science of music were his pursuits, which argues a considerable degree of civilization.

3d. *Tubal-Cain*, the youngest, was "an instructor of every artificer in brass and iron."ver. 22. The manufacture of metals and the cultivation of the arts useful to mankind were therefore his pursuits.

If the duration of the lives of the descendants of *Cain*

were equal to that of the lives of the descendants of *Seth* (of which we are wholly without information) the sons of *Lamech,* and the invention of the science of music, and of the arts of manufacturing brass and iron, would have been contemporaneous with *Methuselah,* the grandfather of *Noah.* If, on the other hand, the curse of GOD upon their ancestor, for the murder of his brother *Abel*,* carried with it (as a consequence) the shortening of the duration of life to any thing like the period assigned to the days of man, as stated by the royal *Psalmist,* then the age in which the sons of *Lamech* lived, and the invention of these arts, would necessarily be referrible to a much e*arli*er *date* in antediluvian HISTORY.

It is a curious circumstance that the only inventions of arts which are noticed in SCRIPTURE as existing before the general DELUGE, are ascribed to the descendants of *Cain.*

———————

[" *A soil of exuberant fertility, &c.*" p. 4.]—Of all the countries which came within the observation of Her*odotus,* this was by far the most fruitful in corn. Fruit trees, such as the vine, the olive, and the fig,. they did not even attempt to cultivate. But the soil was so well adapted for

———

* " Now art thou cursed from the Earth which hath opened her mouth to receive thy brother's blood from thy hand. When thou tillest the ground, it shall not henceforth yield unto thee her strength: a fugitive and vagabond shalt thou be in the earth."—Gen. iv. 11, 12.

hundred, and the ear of their wheat as well as barley was four digits in size. The immense height to which *millet* and *seasamum* (a plant cultivated as a pulse in the Levant and eastern countries) would grow, Herodotus himself witnessed; but he is fearful of specifying, lest he should be deemed to violate probability. lib. i. c. 193.

[" *Astronomy and Dialling, &c.*" p. 5.]—As to the *pole*, the *gnomon* (Quære, a dial with index? See *Beloes's* note on Herod. lib. ii. c. 109), and the *division* of the *day* into twelve parts, the GREEKS received them, says Herodotus, from the BABYLONIANS. Herod. ib.

[" *The Euphrates or Tigris,*" p. 5.]—The ASSYRIANS have but little rain; but their lands are fertilized, and the fruits of the earth nourished by means of the river, which does not however, like the EGYPTIAN NILE, enrich the country by overflowing its banks, but is dispersed by manual labour, or by hydraulic engines. Herod. lib. i. c. 193. The EUPHRATES occasionally overflows its banks; but its inundations do not, like those of the NILE, communicate fertility. *Pliny*, lib. xviii. c. 17, observes that the streams of the

EUPHRATES and the TIGRIS do not leave behind them the mud which the NILE does in EGYPT.

[" *By no means necessary for the origin of navigation*," p. 6.]—The SCRIPTURE HISTORY of the antediluvian ages is wholly silent upon this interesting subject. We know not, therefore, whether in the times before the general deluge mankind had made any or what progress in the art of navigation; or whether, if at all existing, it had been made subservient merely to the purposes of migration from one spot to another, whenever any increase of population might require an extended occupation of country; or fancy and the desire of roving might have induced a search after new habitations; or whether it had ever been applied to the civilizing objects of commerce and traffic between the people of the antediluvian world, who, in process of time, from one or other of these causes, might have become more or less distantly situated from each other. The extent of population to which mankind had arrived, and the extent of country which it occupied at the era of the flood, are equally matters of vague conjecture; but it may reasonably be inferred from the tenor of SACRED HISTORY, and particularly from the manner in which the grand *postdiluvian* separation of mankind and the division of the earth is mentioned, that there had not, up to that period, been any *general* dispersion of the human race over the habitable globe. The only

in SCRIPTURE, is that which was the consequence of the curse of *Cain*. " A fugitive and vagabond shalt thou be in the earth," Gen. iii. 12 ; " and *Cain* went out from the presence of the LORD, and dwelt in the land of NOD, on the east of EDEN." ver. 17. Still we must suppose that convenient means had been devised, at very early periods, for crossing at least the great rivers TIGRIS and EUPHRATES, which completely intersected the countries respectively considered to have been the original seats of the habitation of man*.

The natural property of wood, as the lighter body, to float upon the surface of water, must necessarily have been exhibited to the inhabitants of the banks of the TIGRIS and EUPHRATES, and must very soon have forced itself upon their observation, in the periodical inundations of those rivers. Rapid torrents must, on these occasions, have hurried along with them the trunks and branches of trees which they had torn up and swept away in their progress. Similar observations must have shewn them that wood so floating could be more or less easily moved, and be propelled, on the surface of the water, with different degrees of velocity, according to the degrees of force applied to it.

* We shall hereafter see an allusion, in PAGAN story, to the commencement of rude and simple navigation several generations before the flood.

Although unable, in either case, to assign to the *effects* produced their proper and legitimate *causes*, they must also, from observation, have been familiarly acquainted with the *natural* property which water possesses, from its superior density over atmospheric air, to penetrate through any apertures in a hollow vessel, and to occupy, according to its quantity, a given space in that part of the interior cavity which is below the level of the aperture by which it had been admitted. But they did not know, because it was imperceptible to their senses, that this given space which to them appeared a *vacuity* had in reality been occupied and filled by another, though an invisible fluid, no less essential to the support of animal life than that by which it had been displaced, and as to its external properties differing from it only in the assumption of a more expanded and rarified form of existence.

The RAFT, consisting merely of rough pieces of timber tied or rudely connected together, as the *simplest* and *most obvious*, would probably be the FIRST effort of the application of these natural properties of wood to any practical objects of experiment or use; the CANOE the NEXT; and LAST of all, in this first stage of nautical science, the BOAT or BARGE would in all probability, for a considerable period, have proudly vaunted itself as the *ne plus ultra*—the perfection of the art of navigation.

magnitude, and liable to such extraordinary periodical fluctuations in the mass or body of water which they would discharge, and the extent of its surface, as those of the TIGRIS or EUPHRATES) must long have preceded that by *bridges* constructed of *brick* or *stone*. The *first* bridge, in all probability, consisted merely of the trunks of trees tied together, and connected by some means with the bank on either side.

This is all that we can venture even to conjecture as to the art of navigation, during the antediluvian ages, which were brought to a conclusion by the most awful and stupendous event in the history of mankind, by which the whole race of man, with all his arts and inventions, had nearly been annihilated, and the whole habitable globe had nearly become a dreary and desolate wilderness.

The wickedness of man " had become great in the earth; every imagination of the thoughts of his heart was only evil continually." (Gen. vi. 5.) It had not only grown up to a height so enormous as to exclude the possibility of any longer continuance of the DIVINE forbearance, and so as to forfeit all claim to any extension of the DIVINE goodness and mercy—so *universally* had it pervaded the *whole mass* of mankind,—that one individual alone, with his family, could be found worthy of being made a solitary exception out of the universally-impending destruction. This one individual had "found grace in the eyes of the LORD, because he was a just man, and perfect in his generations, and walked with GOD." (Gen. v. 8, 9.) From our conviction of the unbounded and impartial goodness and loving-kindness of the ALMIGHTY we must be assured, that, if there had been on the face of the earth *another* human being just and perfect as *Noah* was, HE also would have been saved.

The beneficent purpose of preserving this just man and his family, and through him the human race, and the whole animal creation from the impending ruin, gave occasion to an effort in the art of ship-building which has never been equalled in succeeding ages.

Whatever may have been the progress made in this art prior to the GENERAL DELUGE, it is certain that, either from former experience, or through DIVINE instruction communicated for the *especial occasion*, both the venerable postdiluvian patriarch and his three sons must have been sufficiently acquainted with its *general principles* to enable them to construct a vessel, the largest in size and capacity of any which has ever been built in ancient or modern times*.

---

* The dimensions of the ark were 300 cubits in length, 50 in breadth, and 30 in height; and it consisted of three floors or decks, Gen. vi. 15, 16. Reckoning the cubit at 18 inches, it will be found that it must have been of the burthen of 42,413 tons, and must therefore have been equal in capacity

for the accomplishment of the object, that *Noah* and his sons should be made acquainted with the *principles* of the art, which it was the DIVINE WILL that they should be the instruments of thus reducing into practice.

To this, however, it may be answered, that, although the DELUGE itself, with all its incidents and consequences, was unquestionably (next to the CREATION itself) the most stupendous miracle that DIVINE OMNIPOTENCE has ever displayed to mankind, yet we know that the ALMIGHTY condescended to effect the preservation of the human and animal creation through the instrumentality of human agency, and by a work the execution of human hands. " And GOD said to *Noah make thee* an ark of gopher-wood, &c. &c. *Thus* did *Noah*, according to all that GOD commanded him *so did he.*" Gen. vi. 14—22.

We must therefore presume that this work of *human hands* was so constructed as to be competent, according to

or stowage to eighteen of our first rate men-of-war, which are between 2,200 and 2,300 tons burthen. *Hales's* Chron. vol. i. p. 328. From the following passages in Scripture, it is inferred, that the time employed in constructing the ark was 120 years. "And the LORD said, my spirit shall not always strive with man, for that he also is flesh; *yet his days shall be* 120 *years.*" Gen. vi. 3. "When once the long-suffering of GOD waited, in the days of *Noah*, while the ark was preparing." 1 Pet. iii. 20.

the *ordinary course* of the operations of *Providence*, and without any necessity for the further continuance of a special miraculous interposition, to effect the great and benevolent purposes for which it was designed. But even granting that the workmen might not, *at the time* of their formation of the ark, have been acquainted with the PRINCIPLES of the art, which (by the DIVINE command and with DIVINE aid) they were reducing into practice, yet their experience of the safety and security with which, though tossed to and fro by every wind, it had floated for 150 days* on the surface of the troubled waters of the flood, and had withstood " the

---

* " In the 600th year of *Noah's* life, in the 2d month, the 17th day of the month, the same day were all the fountains of the great deep broken up, and the windows of heaven were opened (Gen. vii. 11); and the waters prevailed upon the earth 150 days (ver. 24). And after the end of 150 days the waters were abated. And the ark rested, in the 7th month, on the 17th day of the month, upon the mountains of *Ararat*" (viii. 3, 4). But although the waters began to abate after 150 days, and the waters decreased continually (ver. 5), yet it was not until the 1st day of the 10th month, or 74 days after the waters began to abate, that the tops of the mountains were seen (ver. 5), nor until the 1st month, the 1st day of the month of the succeeding year, or 314 days after the commencement of the flood, that "the waters were dried up from off the earth," and " *Noah* removed the covering off the ark, and looked and behold the face of the ground was dry " (ver. 13). But, in all probability, it was not sufficiently so for the comfortable habitation of man, for *Noah* did not quit the ark until he had received the divine command to do so, and which was not delivered until a period of 56 days more had elapsed. " In the 2d month, on the 27th day of the month, was the earth dried, and GOD spake unto NOAH, saying, Go forth out of the ark, thou, and thy wife, and thy sons, and thy sons' wives with thee." "Bring forth every living thing," &c. And *Noah* went forth, and his sons, and his wife, and his sons' wives with him, every beast, &c. went forth out of the ark (viii. 14—19); so that *Noah* and his family continued in the ark for 370 days, or a year and 10 days, according to the primitive sacred year.

most awful and grateful sense of the DIVINE omnipotence and goodness towards them and their families, could not fail, at the same time, forcibly to have excited their deep and profound reflection, and to have called forth all their reasoning faculties, in the consideration of the *immediate human means* (the work of their own hands) by which their lives, and the race of man, and that of the whole animal creation had been in so singular and wonderful a manner preserved. These reflections would naturally lead them to an investigation of *cause* and *effect*, with particular reference to this interesting object of their contemplation; and it would require no very difficult or tedious course of reasoning to trace the *effects* which they had so recently and so impressively experienced up to their natural *causes*.

The *natural properties* of *wood* to float, or to be moved more or less easily on the surface of water (the first step in this investigation), and the natural property of *water* to penetrate through any apertures into the cavities of hollow vessels, have already been noticed as problems in natural philosophy, which must, at a very early period, have attracted the particular attention of mankind, whose repeated observation of facts could not fail, sooner or later, to have led them to the application of these properties to the convenient pur-

* *Hales's* Chron. vol. iii. p. 337.

poses of crossing or navigating rivers, either for objects of extended settlement, or of migration, or of commercial or other intercourse, between people of the same or of different nations, more or less distant totally from each other.

We must therefore conclude that *Noah* and his sons were familiarly acquainted with these properties, and with the possibility of their useful or convenient application to any of the before-mentioned purposes of life, to such an extent as that, up to the era of the FLOOD, they may have been generally so applied, without ascribing the acquisition of this knowledge to any special DIVINE interposition.

From their own observation of the form and mode of construction of the ARK, during the long period in which, under DIVINE instruction, they were engaged in the work, and from their own experience of the admirable manner in which it had answered all the purposes for which it was designed, they must have satisfied themselves that, by a similar adaptation together of pieces of wood of the same form and description as those which they had used in the construction of the ark, a vessel or machine could be constructed, varying in its size and capacity with reference to the size and dimensions of the materials used, and which, " if pitched within and without with pitch," as the ARK had been, would not only *retain* the *natural property* inherent in each of its component parts of floating upon the water, but would *acquire* the *artificial*

C

the surface of the water, without danger of sinking, or of injury or inconvenience from any access of that element, a quantity or burthen of commodities suited to its capacity, and also of affording a safe and commodious floating habitation for man.

During a period of more than twelve months of complete abstraction from all earthly objects, *Noah* and his sons, cooped up in the ARK, had no other subject of contemplation than that of their own wonderful preservation, and of the means by which, under Divine *Providence*, it was in course of being effected. When they quitted the ARK, therefore, they must have been sufficiently skilled in the practical art, if not in the theoretical principles, of ship-building, to have enabled them to apply the information which they had acquired in the improvement of navigation to any extent of which, in the infant condition of this SECOND race of mankind, it might, during the continuance of their lives, have been susceptible. Whether the gradually but continually swelling and multiplying population, or the migrations, of man, had led him to the shores of the OCEAN in the lives of *Noah* and his sons seems very uncertain. I think we should infer from SACRED HISTORY that they had not. If they had not been led to the shores of the OCEAN there could have been no occasion for the application of the knowledge which they possessed, in the art of ship-building, to any other objects of human convenience than those of the crossing or navigation of RIVERS; and the application of their knowledge would therefore have been confined to the construction of such small vessels as were best suited to those latter purposes. They could not have been aware of the possibility of its useful adaptation to such more enlarged and extended objects as the OCEAN at a future period presented to the restless and enterprising spirit of their posterity.

And as the ALMIGHTY had " established his covenant with them, that all flesh should not any more be cut off by the waters of a flood, neither should there any more be a flood to destroy the earth," (Gen. ix. 11,) they knew that there never would be occasion for another ARK. They might therefore have deemed it a useless and unnecessary labour to instruct their children in all the knowledge which they possessed themselves of an art which, under these circumstances, could no longer be made subservient to the necessities or the convenience of mankind. And thus the knowledge may have died with the survivors of *Shem, Ham,* and *Japhet,* and of their children living, and of an age capable of observation, at the time of the FLOOD; and the ARK, in succeeding generations, might have been known and contemplated in no other manner than as an object of historical tradition, and as the wonderful and miraculous means by which their parents had been preserved from the general destruction.

in the early ages of the world, of the knowledge of so important an art. It was in the chosen line of *Shem* alone that
any accurate account of the creation, the primitive history
of mankind, the universal DELUGE, and the means by which
the human race had been preserved, through the DIVINE
goodness, from extinction, had probably been handed down
by tradition through each succeeding generation of his posterity. (*Jackson's* Chron. Antiq. vol. iii. p. 84.) The ARK
itself, and everything connected with it (excepting some loose
traditions of a DELUGE), were, in all probability, forgotten
after four or five generations of the posterities of *Ham* and
Japhet had elapsed. Their descendants very soon fell into
idolatry, and ceased "to walk in the ways of the living GOD*."

" In the days of *Peleg* was the earth divided." (Gen. x.
25.) According to the genealogies of the *Masorete* and
Samaritan Hebrew texts, and of *Josephus*, *Peleg* was the

---

* The race of *Shem*, who were in the direct ascending line from *Abraham*,
was also tainted with idolatry. It seems to be pretty generally agreed, that
the idolatry of deifying and worshipping dead men first began in PHŒNICIA
and EGYPT, and was propagated from thence to other nations, viz. to ARABIA
and CHALDEA from EGYPT, and to GREECE from PHŒNICIA. Several of the
learned have supposed that *Serug*, the great grandfather of *Abraham*, was the
first of the race of *Shem*, who laid the foundation of it in CHALDEA. But for
this supposition there does not appear to be any authority in Scripture. *Jackson's* Chron. Antiq. vol. iii. p. 42, 43 ; *Hales's* Chron. vol. i. *Terah*, the father
of *Abraham*, was certainly an idolater. "Your fathers," said *Joshua* to the
children of ISRAEL, "dwelt on the other side of the flood" (i. e. the EU-
PHRATES) "in old time, even *Terah* the father of *Abraham*, and the father of
Nahor, and they served other gods." Joshua xxiv. 2.

fourth, but, according to the *Septuagint* version and *St. Luke's* genealogy of CHRIST, ch. iii. ver. 36, he was the fifth in descent from *Shem* *. The date of his birth, with reference to that of the DELUGE, is variously represented, according to the various ways in which the patriarchal generations after the flood have been reckoned. According to the *Masorete* Hebrew text (which is followed in one translation of the Bible in common use) his birth is placed only 101 years after the flood, whereas in the *Samaritan* Hebrew it is placed 401, in the *Septuagint* 531, in *Josephus* 411, and, according to *Dr. Hales's* correction of *Josephus*, 401 years after that event (Chron. vol. i. p. 72, 104); which agrees with the *Samaritan* Hebrew, and also with the *Septuagint*, if the interpolation of the second *Cainan* be rejected.

According to this corrected chronology of *Josephus*, and to that of the *Samaritan* Hebrew text (to which, for several reasons, I give the preference over that of the *Masorete Hebrew*), the migration of the *primitive* postdiluvian families to their respective settlements, under the DIVINE dispensation,

* In the *Septuagint* Version, and in *St. Luke's* genealogy of CHRIST, a second or postdiluvian *Cainan* is interpolated between *Arphaxed* and *Saleh*; and a generation of 130 years is assigned to him. He is altogether omitted in the *Hebrew* texts. The conflicting authorities for the rejection or the admission of this second *Cainan* are fully discussed by *Mr. Jackson* in his Chron Antiq. vol. i. p. 79, and *Dr. Hales* in his elaborate chronological work (vol. i. p. 90), who take opposite sides of the question, which, however, is one of very minor importance. It appears to me that our *Bible* genealogies of the postdiluvian patriarchs make the period between the flood and the birth of *Abraham* so short as to be quite inconsistent with all the leading and prominent events and facts which the same history of that period embraces.

It is not at all necessary, however, to suppose that the art of navigation was resorted to in any of these *original* migrations. The *first* settlement of ASIA and of AFRICA would unquestionably have been effected by means of emigrations over LAND. Even the *Japhetic* wanderers, " by whom the ISLES of the Gentiles were divided" (Gen. x. 5), would, most probably in the *first* instance, have peopled the *continent* of EUROPE, either wholly by successive *land* emigrations, or, if in part, by the passage of the DARDA-NELLES—that latter operation would have been as easily achieved, and by the same simple means, as the passage of their own TIGRIS or EUPHRATES, or of any of the larger rivers of Northern ASIA or of EUROPE, which might have intercepted the course of their emigrations.

We have thus arrived at the period of the first grand division of the earth, and the dispersion of mankind, without being able to ascertain from SACRED HISTORY whether any or what material progress or improvement had been made in the science or art of NAVIGATION beyond those first practical rudiments of it displayed in the construction and limited use of the CANOE, the BOAT, or the BARGE, and which have already been noticed as the probable acquisitions of a very early period of the antediluvian world.

The first mention in PAGAN story of any thing like an attempt at navigation is that recorded in the PHŒNICIAN History of *Sanconiatho*, which was translated into Greek, in the reign of the Emperor *Adrian*, by *Philo* of *Byblus*, some fragments of which are preserved by *Eusebius*.

Usorus, the brother of *Hypsaranius* (who is supposed to be the same with *Mehujael*, the great grandson of *Cain*, (Gen. iv. 17, 18,) "having taken a tree and broken off its boughs, was the first who ventured (in a CANOE made of it) into the sea." *Jackson's* Chron. Antiq. vol. iii. p. 15.

Now *Mehujael* was the fourth in descent from *Cain;* and, if there was no distinction in the duration of the antediluvian life of man amongst the descendants of *Adam*, he would have been contemporaneous with *Mahalaleel*, of the line of *Seth*, who, according to the chronology of the *Septuagint* and of *Josephus*, was born 795 years after the creation, and 1,461 years before the flood.

According to the PHŒNICIAN HISTORY, therefore, the date of the invention of the CANOE would be assignable to the 14th century before the flood.

Two or three generations after *Usorus*, *Chryson* (the *Tubal Cain* of SACRED HISTORY) invented " the hook, bait, and fishing line, and small fishing BOAT, and was the first

sons of the *Dioscuri* made SHIPS of BURTHEN, in which they sailed, and being cast upon the coast near MOUNT CASSIUS (about 40 miles from PELUSIUM—*Strabo*, lib. xvi. p. 1,103), they consecrated a temple in the place, p. 23. This is the first attempt at SAILING in SHIPS of which any mention is made in PAGAN HISTORY.

Saturn, the son of *Uranus* (who, according to the history of *Sanconiatho*, was born about 400, and died about 800, years after the flood—*Jackson's* Chron. Antiq. vol. iii. p. 40, 42), after *traversing various countries*, is said to have given the kingdom of ATTICA to his daughter *Athenæ* or *Minerva*, p. 30. Such a voyage would imply a considerable progress in the art of navigation.

The *P*ELASGI, who formed so large a portion of the population of primitive GREECE, are considered by the learned *Jackson* as the descendants of the PHŒNICIAN *Dioscuri* or *Cabiri*. They inherited and improved upon the naval spirit and enterprise of their progenitors, and are said to have acquired their name from their *wandering* propensity, and their frequent passing *by sea* from one country to another— (the sea being called *Pelagus*, from the Hebrew word *Peleg*, as dividing one country from another). Chron.

Antiq. vol. iii. p. 61, 103, et seq.) We learn from *Strabo* that on this account they were called by the Attic historians πελαϱγοὶ, from storks, which are birds of passage, lib. iii. p. 339. This wandering spirit led the PHŒNICIAN *P*ELASGI in very early times to quit their ASIATIC homes, and to carry by sea the *P*ELASGIC name, and with it the art of navigation and the *Cabini* mysteries, into other countries, and amongst the rest into the islands and continent of GREECE.

Jackson places the *first* or the *Japhetic* settlement of GREECE in the seventh century, and the *second* or the PHŒNICIAN PELASGIC about the ninth century after the flood. We have seen that the *first* was, in all probability, effected by emigrations over *land*. The *second*, if it ever took place (of which I entertain great doubts), would most probably have been effected through maritime enterprise.

This theory of the PHŒNICIAN origin of the GRECIAN *P*ELASGI supposes an intermediate peopling of GREECE from *P*HŒNICIA through the medium of navigation, after the original JAPHETIC migration and the settlements consequent thereon in GREECE, but some centuries before the first colonizations from EGYPT of which we have any certain accounts in HISTORY. It will be again adverted to in the course of these remarks on GRECIAN HISTORY. I shall therefore content myself here with observing, that it is a theory, for which there is no direct authority in antient authors, but which rests altogether on inferences, the force or propriety of which may be variously estimated, according to the bias of the reader's mind upon the subject, and is consequently built upon far too *conjectural* a basis to justify its HISTORICAL recognition.

If Mr. *Jackson's* theories be well founded, the art of navigation must have made a very considerable progress a century or more before the days of *Abraham* ; the PHŒ-NICIAN *P*ELASGIC maritime emigrations into, and settlement of, GREECE having taken place in the ninth century after the DELUGE, whereas, according to the patriarchal genea-logies of the *Septuagint* and *Josephus, Abraham* was not born till about one thousand years after that event.

———————

[" *The occupants of Phœnicia coming from the coast, &c.*" p. 6.]—We are informed by *Herodotus,* that the PHŒ-NICIANS migrated from the borders of the RED SEA to the coasts of the MEDITERRANEAN SEA, and soon distinguished themselves by their long and enterprising voyages. They exported the produce of EGYPT and ASSYRIA. lib. i. c. 1. This migration of the PHŒNICIANS is thus explained by our great philosopher Sir *Isaac Newton.*

DAVID, king of ISRAEL, in the twelfth year of his reign,

B. C. 1048, conquered the EDOMITES. "And he put garrisons in EDOM; throughout all EDOM put he garrisons, and all they of EDOM became *David's* servants." 2 Sam. viii. 14; 1 Chron. xviii. 13. "Moreover *Abishai*, the son of *Zeruiah*, slew of the EDOMITES in the valley of SALT eighteen thousand." 1 Chron. xviii. 12. Many of the EDOMITES, who were merchants and seamen, says our philosopher, fled from the RED SEA to the PHILISTINES on the coasts of the MEDITERRANEAN SEA, where they fortified *Azoth*. These EDOMITES carried with them to all places their arts and sciences, amongst which were navigation, astronomy, and letters; for in IDUMŒA they had constellations and letters before the days of *Job*, who mentions them. These EDOMITES, translating the word ERYTHREA into that of PHŒNICIA, gave the name of PHŒNICIANS to themselves, and that of PHŒNICIA to the sea-coasts of *Palestine*, from AZOTH to ZIDON.

The PHILISTINES, thus strengthened by the accession of the fugitive EDOMITES, invaded and took ZIDON, as a town very convenient for the merchants who had fled from the RED SEA. A considerable body of the ZIDONIANS under *Abibalus*, the father of H*iram*, fled by sea, and built or much enlarged TYRE, about the sixteenth year of the reign of *David*. Hence Isaiah calls TYRE "the daughter of ZIDON," and its people " the inhabitants of the isle, whom the merchants of ZIDON replenished," ch. xxiii. 2, 12.

according to all that thou desirest; for thou knowest that there is not among us any that can skill to hew timber like the ZIDONIANS." 1 Kings v. 6. The *new* inhabitants of TYRE had not then lost the name of the ZIDONIANS, nor had the old inhabitants, if there were any considerable number of them gained the reputation of the *new* ones for skill in hewing of timber, as they would have done, had navigation been long in use at TYRE. The artificers who came from ZIDON were not dead; the flight of the ZIDONIANS being in the reign of *David,* and, by consequence, in the beginning of the reign of *Abibalus,* the father of H*iram,* and the first king of TYRE mentioned in history, the ZIDONIANS continued in the possession of the trade of the MEDITERRANEAN as far westward as GREECE and LIBYA, and the TYRIANS, in conjunction with *Solomon* and the kings of JUDAH, established and carried on, until after the TROJAN war, the richer trade of the RED SEA : so also did the merchants of ARADUS, for in the PERSIAN GULPH are two islands called TYRE and ARADUS, which had temples like the PHŒNICIANS. The TYRIANS and ARADIANS sailed thither and beyond to the coasts of INDIA, while the ZIDONIANS frequented the MEDITERRANEAN. (*Strabo,* lib. xvi.) At length, in the reign of JEHORAM, the EDOMITES revolted

from the dominion of the kings of JUDAH, "and made themselves a king." 2 Kings viii. 20, 22; 2 Chron. xxi. 8, 10.
And the trade of JUDAH and TYRE on the RED SEA being
thereby interrupted, the TYRIANS retired from the RED SEA
and built ships for traffic in the MEDITERRANEAN, and began
to make long voyages to places which had not been frequented by the ZIDONIANS.   Hence we perceive the reason,
says *Newton*, why *Homer*, who celebrates ZIDON, makes no
mention of TYRE.   EDEN, ERYTHRA, and PHŒNICIA are
names of the same signification, the words denoting a
" RED COLOUR," which makes it probable that the ERY-
THREANS, who fled from *David*, settled in great numbers in
PHŒNICIA, that is, in all the sea-coast of SYRIA from EGYPT
to ZIDON; and by calling themselves PHŒNICIANS, in the
language of SYRIA, instead of ERYTHREANS, gave the name
of PHŒNICIA to all that sea-coast.   In support of this
hypothesis, Sir *Isaac Newton* quotes *Strabo*, lib. i. p. 42 ;
Chronol. p. 12, 97, 104—110, 125, 167.

[" *Thus arose commerce.*" p. 6.]—That the MIDIANITES
and ISHMAELITES, who bordered upon the RED SEA, near
MOUNT HOREB, on the south side of EDOM, were merchants
so early as the days of *Jacob*, is evident from SACRED
HISTORY.   "And they" (the sons of *Jacob*) " lifted up
their eyes and looked, and behold a company of ISH-

MAELITES came from GILEAD with their camels bearing spicery, and balm, and myrrh, going to carry it down to EGYPT." Gen. xxxvii. 26. "Then there passed by MIDIANITES, merchantmen, and they (the sons of *Jacob*) sold *Joseph* to the ISHMAELITES for twenty pieces of silver." ver. 28. " And the MIDIANITES sold *Joseph* into EGYPT, unto *Potiphar*, an officer of *Pharaoh's*, and captain of the guard." ver. 36. From the same unquestionable authority, we learn that, in the days of *Moses* and the judges of ISRAEL, the MIDIANITES and ISHMAELITES abounded in gold and other precious metals, the fruits of merchandize. When the children of ISRAEL were avenged of the MIDIANITES, it was commanded, that of the spoil taken from them, "the gold, and the silver, the brass, the iron, the tin, and the lead, and everything that might abide the fire," should be made to " go through the fire that it might be clean." And the captains of thousands, and the captains of hundreds of the host of ISRAEL, " brought unto *Moses* an oblation for the Lord, what every man had gotten, of jewels of gold, chains, and bracelets, rings, earrings, and tablets." Numbers xxxi. 22, 23, 48, 50. Again, when the army of the MIDIANITES were defeated by *Gideon*, the men of ISRAEL, at his request, gave to him, " every man the earrings of his prey (for they had golden earrings, because they were ISHMAELITES), besides ornaments and collars, and purple raiment, that was on the kings of MIDIAN, and beside the chains which were about their camels' necks."

Judges viii. 24, 25, 26. These passages in SCRIPTURE afford abundant proofs, not only that the MIDIANITES and ISHMAELITES were merchants in very early times, but they had grown wealthy from their merchandize, and that they carried on a lucrative commercial intercourse with EGYPT.

["*The rich vales, &c.*" p. 11.]—*Thucydides* enumerates as amongst the richest tracts of country in GREECE, THESSALY and BŒTIA, and *P*ELOPONNESUS, with the exception of ARCADIA. Of ATTICA, he says, that the barrenness of its soil preserved it, through the longest space of time, quiet and undisturbed in one uninterrupted series of possession. *Thucyd.* lib. i. c. 2.

["*Piratical warfare, &c.*" p. 12.]—These piratical expeditions of the GRECIAN and other inhabitants of the seacoasts and islands were conducted, says *Thucydides*, by persons of the greatest ability amongst them, for the purpose of enriching the adventurers, and subsisting their poor. They landed and plundered by surprise unfortified places and scattered villages, and from thence they principally gained a subsistence.

Not only in those early times was it that piracy was esteemed an honourable employment, for even in his time, *Thucydides* observes, there were many people of the con-

that in those early times, the people of the CONTINENT exercised robberies upon one another; and that, even in his time, many people in GREECE were supported by the same practices. He instances the OZOLIAN LOCRIANS, the ÆTOLIANS, and ACARNANIANS, and their neighbours on the CONTINENT, and notices the custom, introduced by a life of rapine during their early periods of barbarism, of wearing their weapons, which in his time they still retained, and which, he observes, once prevailed all over GREECE, as their habitations had no manner of defence; travelling was full of hazard; and their whole lives were passed in armour, like barbarians. In short, the customs and manners of antient GREECE were the same as those of all barbarians, of all ages and all countries, and even "quite similar," says *Thucydides*, " to those of the present barbarian world."

The cities of GREECE, which were of later foundation, and built since the improvement of naval skill, had been placed for the better increase of wealth on the sea-shore, and walled about, and principally upon necks of land jutting out into the sea for the sake of traffic, and greater security from the insults of neighbouring people; whereas those of an earlier date, being more subject to piratical depredations, were situated at a greater distance from the sea, on the continent as well as in the islands; for those who lived upon the coast, although inexpert at sea, were in the habit, says *Thucydides,* of making excursions into the interior of the country for the sake of plunder.

The people of the islands, that is, the CARIANS and the PHŒNICIANS, were by far the most expert of these early piratical adventurers. *Thucyd.* lib. v. 6.

———

["*And Thasus, &c.*" p. 12.]—THASUS was a small island in the ÆGEAN sea, not far distant from the coast of THRACE. Fable or tradition has ascribed its first settlement to *Thasus,* whom some of the fables have dignified with a divine origin, as the son of *Neptune;* according to others he was the son, (*Pausan.* lib. v. c. 25,) and to others the grandson, (*Apollod.* lib. iii. c. 1, s. 1, 2,) of AGENOR, the father of *Cadmus, Phœnix, Cilix,* and *Europa.* After the failure of his mission, together with the other sons of AGENOR, in search of the lost *Europa,* he is said to have settled in this island, to which he gave his name.

———

["*Of the different kingdoms or provinces of Greece, from the earliest accounts to the Trojan war,*" p. 13, 28.]—The accounts which have been handed down to us by *Pausanias* and others, of the *first* foundation of the different kingdoms

E

Times"—if not altogether fabulous, are built upon such vague and uncertain authority, and partake so much of the character of fable, that they could not, with safety or any degree of propriety, be admitted into the pages of HISTORY, which ought never to be tainted with the most distant appearance or semblance of *fiction*. But although very properly excluded from the *text*, they may probably be permitted to take their humble and unassuming station in a *note*, for the *amusement* merely, and gratification of a pardonable *curiosity*, even in the student in HISTORY—as food for the consideration and ill-bestowed useless labours of some inquisitive and poring but injudicious antiquary *— and as an appropriate basis or foundation whereon self-sufficient, credulous, and self-deceiving chronologers, may raise their airy and fanciful superstructures of wild, extravagant, absurd, and visionary theories and systems of chronology, which, generally speaking, are calculated only to mislead the sober judgments of mankind—to perplex the student in HISTORY—to render more difficult the task of the HISTORIAN—to increase unnecessarily the uncertainty which unfortunately must ever, in a greater or a less degree, be

---

* It is by no means intended in this remark to disparage the valuable, and (in the elucidation of HISTORY) highly important labours of the antiquary, when directed to *useful* and *legitimate* objects. The remark is confined to those who bring discredit on a rational pursuit by its application to *trifling* and *frivolous* objects.

incident to the HISTORY of very remote ages—and finally, to sum up the whole in a word, to render that which is already (alas) too much " confused worse confounded."

I shall avail myself of the permission thus assumed, during the course of my study of the interesting HISTORY which this highly valuable and ingenious work of our learned and judicious author embraces.

These fables or traditions of antient GREECE are, however, extremely contradictory in the genealogies of their kings and heroes ; but it would be a waste of time to dwell a moment upon these contradictions for the purpose of establishing any preference of one genealogy over another. The endeavour to reconcile the discordancies between *fabulous* genealogies would be an idle attempt; yet, idle as these useless and uninteresting pursuits are, they have wasted hours, days, weeks, months, and years of learned labour, which, if devoted to other studies, might have produced results evidently useful and beneficial, or at least interesting, to mankind.

The only thing therefore that can be done is to set forth these contradictory genealogies as we find them in the pages of antiquity, leaving it to those who have a *taste* for such pursuits to decide between them.

invented many useful arts conducing to the comfort of
▓▓▓▓▓, ▓▓▓ ▓▓ pretends not to inform us whence or
when they came thither.

2dly. Many ages after the ETIOCRETANS had been settled
in this island the PELASGI planted amongst them a ▓▓▓▓▓.
This people, says he, were continually inured to arms, and
wandering up and down their antient habitations, (id. ib.)

3dly. A colony of DORIANS, from LACONIA and the
territory of OLYMPIA, in PELOPONNESUS, under the conduct
of *Teutamus*, the son of *Dorus*, and grandson of *Hellen*,
the son of *Deucalion*, and grandfather of the celebrated
Minos, established themselves in CRETE.

And, lastly. A promiscuous herd of barbarians from the
neighbouring countries poured into CRETE, (id. ib.)

According to this account, therefore, it would seem that
CRETE was peopled at various times by colonies from
different countries, speaking different languages, until in
process of time they dropt their own, and adopted that
of the antient CRETANS. *Diod. Sic.* (id. ib.)

Sir *Isaac Newton* supposes that these colonies could not have arrived in CRETE more than two or three generations before the days of *Asterius* and his son *Minos*: and he founds this rational supposition and want of experience in navigation in (Chron. p. 183.) [illegible]

2dly, *Were there supposed two princes of the name of Minos in different periods, &c.?* p. 14.]—This supposition seems to have occasioned no little confusion in the early, we may say, fabulous account of GREECE. *Diodorus Siculus* speaks of *Minos*, the adopted son of *Asterius*, and of another *Minos*, the grandson of the former, who he says was the first of the GRECIANS who formed a navy, and acquired the dominion of the sea, (lib. iv. c. 4.) He describes him, as afterwards, with a mighty fleet, invading SICILY, and there dying of the steam and heat of a bath, (lib. iv. c. 5.) He says, the islands called CYCLADES were formerly desolate; but *Minos*, having a strong army, and, with a powerful navy, being master of the sea, sent colonies out of CRETE, and peopled many of these islands, (lib. v. c. 4.)

HERODOTUS, speaking of *Polycrates*, says that, except *Minos*, the CNOSSIAN, or whoever before him accomplished it, he was the first GREEK who formed the design of making him master of the sea, (lib. iii. c. 122*.)

* See also as to *Minos*, lib. vii. c. 169, and note of Mr. *Beloe*, vol. iv. p. 99.

THUCYDIDES says, that *Minos* is the earliest person known from tradition to have been master of a navy, and to have been chiefly lord of the sea which is called the GRECIAN. To him were the islands of the CYCLADES subject; nay, most of them he planted himself with colonies, having expelled the CARIANS, and substituted his own sons in the different commands. And there, of course, he exerted his utmost power to clear that sea of pirates for the more secure conveyance of his own tributes.

PAUSANIAS describes *Minos* as ruling over all the GRECIAN sea, (lib. i. c. 27.) According to this author, the use of sails was first discovered by *Dædalus,* who, with his son *Icarus,* was thus enabled to escape the vessels of *Minos* which were in pursuit of him; but from the sequel of the story we may infer, that this new invention, by which they effected this deliverance from one danger, was the cause of another, which proved fatal to *Icarus.* For our author says, that *Icarus,* being unskilled in the art of piloting the ship, overset it and was drowned. In what manner *Dædalus* was preserved is not stated, (lib. ix. c. 11.)

––––––––

[" *In earlier times, however, some settlements had been made, &c.*" p. 16.]—But, according to *Thucydides,* these earlier settlements, which were discernible even in his time, were all INLAND, and at some distance from the sea, both in the islands and on the continent.

[" *The Pelasgian name is eminent, &c.*" p. 19.]—The fable or tradition of the earliest history of ARCADIA may be found in *Pausanias*, (lib. viii. c. 1, 2, 3, 4, 5.) At the period when *Pausanias* first introduces us to the people who inhabited the country, which afterwards acquired the name of ARCADIA, they were as wild and barbarous as the savage beasts of prey which roamed at large over their common mountains, and equally with them shared the common bounties of nature. They had then neither habitations or clothing to shelter and protect them from the inclemency of the weather; and their food consisted only of herbs and roots of the coarsest, and some of them of a pernicious, kind. At this period there appeared amongst them a person, (whether a native or a foreigner *Pausanias* does not inform us, but most probably the latter, and an EGYPTIAN,) who not only excelled in stature, strength, and comeliness of person, but "surpassed all others in the endowments of his mind." He taught them arts by which they might improve their condition in life—to build cottages, and to make garments from the skins of swine. He persuaded them also to relinquish their coarse and pernicious food for one more palatable and wholesome, namely, the acorn of the beech tree*, or chesnuts, which, *Pausanias* informs us, long continued to be the diet of the ARCADIANS. Having thus acquired an influence over the people they elected *Pelasgus* to be their king, and their country thenceforth assumed the name of PELASGIA.

According to Sir *Isaac Newton's* Chronology, *Pelasgus* came into ARCADIA from EGYPT about the year B. C. 1100. (p. 11, 168.)

Pelasgus was succeeded by his son *Lycaon*, who is represented to have been in nowise inferior to his father in mental endowments, or in attention to the civilization of his subjects. He first brought them to congregate in towns and villages, and built the city of LYCOSURA†. He also instituted games in honour of *Jupiter Lycæus*‡, and practised the horrid rites of human sacrifice on the altar of the

---

* See note, p. 7, of this vol.

† LYCOSURA was visited by *Pausanias* in his travels through GREECE: it did not in his time contain many inhabitants. "Certainly," says he, "LYCOSURA is the most antient of all the cities existing on the continent, or in the islands, and was the first that the sun ever beheld. Hence from this men then learnt to build other cities." (lib. viii. c. 38.)

‡ The temple of *Jupiter* LYCÆUS. After relating some idle tales of wonderful particulars with which the mountain LYCÆUS abounds, *Pausanias* proceeds to inform us, that, "upon the highest summit of the mountain there was," in his time, "a heap of earth which formed an altar of LYCÆAN *Jupiter*, from which the greatest part of PELOPONNESUS might be seen," and that the sacrifices on this altar to the LYCÆAN *Jupiter* were conducted in a secret and mysterious manner, and that he was not permitted accurately to investigate them. (Id. ib.)

deity. From this circumstance, our great philosopher supposes, that *Pelasgus*, his father, " might have come with this people from the SHEPHERDS in EGYPT—from the region of HELIOPOLIS, where they sacrificed men, till *Amosis* abolished that custom." p. 168.

Lycaon is supposed to have been contemporary with CECROPS, king of ATHENS. *Chron.* p. 10, 11. B. C. 1085.

In the third age after *Pelasgus*, in the reign of *Nyctimus*, the eldest of *Lycaon's* sons, PELASGIA is said greatly to have increased in the number of its cities and in the extent of its population. In the beginning of his reign the GREEKS have placed the flood of *Deucalion*, B. C. 1045. *Lycaon* had twelve or thirteen other sons, of whom no other actions are recorded than that of building cities, which were generally honoured with their own names, the recital of which could not interest any class or description of readers. The youngest, however, of his sons was of a more enterprising character, and merits particular notice and attention, as being the first individual who led a colony from GREECE. Having obtained men and money from his brother *Nyctimus*, he sailed to ITALY, and having found in the western parts of that country a large region fit for pasturage and tillage, but yet for the most part uninhabited, or but thinly peopled, he cleared some of it from the bar-

F

barians, and built small cities contiguous to one another, *Dion. of Halicar.* lib. i. c. 12. The country from him was called ŒNOTRIA; and he became the JANUS of the LATINS. He carried with him, and established there, the horrid rites of human sacrifices; " from whence you may know," says Sir *Isaac Newton,* " that *Janus* was of the race of *Lycaon,* which character agrees to *Œnotrus,*" p. 154, 155. This emigration of *Œnotrus* was in the year B. C. 1028.

Some years after the emigration of *Œnotrus* (according to Sir *Isaac Newton* B. C. 943, according to others, sixty years before the destruction of TROY, which would answer to 964, B. C.), *Evander* (who is said by *Pausanias,* lib. viii. c. 43, to have been "the best warrior of all the ARCADIANS," and who is fabled to have been the son of *Mercury* and *Themis,* called by the ROMANS *Carmenta*), accompanied by his mother, led an army of ARCADIANS from the ARCADIAN PALLANTIUM into ITALY, and built a city or village on one of the seven hills on which ROME was afterwards situated, which was called after the name of the parent city, but was afterwards corrupted by the ROMANS into *P*ALATIUM.

*Evande*r and his mother are reported to have first brought into ITALY the use of GREEK letters, which they had themselves been recently taught in ARCADIA. *Dion. Halicar.* lib. i. c. 31, et seq.

A few years after *Evander,* *Hercules* is said to have

carried a GRECIAN colony into ITALY, and to have abolished the rites of human sacrifice. Id. c. 34, et seq.

It is singular, that with so many sons of *Lycaon*, not one of them, excepting his eldest son *Nyctimus*, who died without issue, should have succeeded to the father's throne.

Lycaon had an only daughter, *Callisto*, who is fabled to have been with child by *Jupiter*—to have been transformed by the jealousy of *Juno* into a bear—and to have been killed by *Diana* out of regard to her sister deity. The male child she carried in her womb was saved by *Mercury*, and the unfortunate mother, in her state of animal transformation, formed the constellation called the GREAT BEAR.

Her son *Arcas* succeeded his uncle *Nyctimus*, and gave his name to the country, which thenceforth dropped the appellation of PELASGIA, and assumed that of ARCADIA.

The succession of *Arcas*, according to Sir *Isaac Newton*, happened about the year B. C. 1020. He received bread-corn from *Triptolemus*, and taught his subjects to convert it into bread. He instructed them also in the useful art of weaving garments.

Arcas had three sons, *Agan*, *Aphidas*, and *Elatus*, and we are told by *Pausanias*, that when they came of age he divided his kingdom between them. Sir *Isaac Newton* has omitted them altogether in his succession of ARCADIAN kings. Surely the *th*ree should be reckoned as *one* in that succession.

Agan had one son *Clitor*, who it is said became the most powerful of all the kings of his time, and built a city, which after him was called CLITORA; but he died without issue.

Aphidas had also a son, named *Aleus*.

Elatus had five sons, of whom it is unnecessary to name any other than *Æpytus*, who himself succeeded to the sovereignty, and *Stymphalus*, who was the stem of all the ARCADIAN kings from H*ippothous*, the grandfather of *Cypselus*, down to *Aristocrates II.*, the twenty-fifth king and last of the dynasty.

Elatus is reported, in after times, to have migrated to PHORIS, and to have built the city of ELATIA. Upon the death of *Clitor*, without issue, the sceptre came into the hands of *Æpytus*, who, dying of the bite of a serpent, was succeeded by *Aleus*, the son of *Aphidas*, whom Sir *Isaac Newton* supposes to have been born about seventy-five years before the ARGONAUTIC expedition, which would answer to the year before CHRIST 1012. His grandfather, *Arcas*, Sir *Isaac* supposes to have been born about the end of the reign of *Sante*, which would answer to the year B. C. 1060.

Lycurgus, the eldest of the three sons of *Aleus*, succeeded his father; lived to an extreme old age; and survived both his sons, *Ancæus* and *Epochus*. The former was an ARGONAUT, and was slain by the CALYDONIAN boar in the year B. C. 934. He left one son, *Agapenor*, who led the ARCADIANS to the Siege of TROY. He was probably too young to be intrusted with affairs of government on the death of his grandfather; for we find the sovereignty collaterally devolving upon *Echĕmus*, the son of *Areopus*, and the grandson of *Cepheus*, the youngest of the three brothers of *Lycurgus* : *Agapenor* succeeded to *Echĕmus*.

Having now arrived on the confines of HISTORIC ground, and having in another part of the volume treated of *Echĕmus*, and the ARCADIAN kings who followed him in succession, we shall dismiss the subject, furnishing merely a pedigree of the ARCADIAN kings from *Pelasgus* to *Cypselus*, who reigned in ARCADIA at the time of the DORIAN conquests in *P*ELOPONNESUS.

Pedigree of the Arcadian Kings, from PELASGUS (B.C. 1100) *to* CYPSELUS (B.C. 825), *embracing a period of 725 years.*

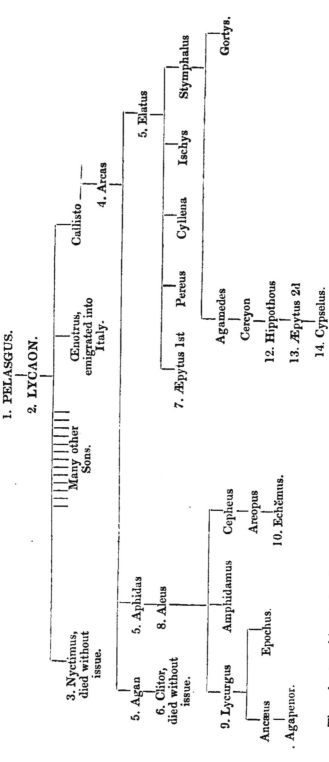

These fourteen kings, after the rate of between nineteen and twenty years to a reign, one with another, took up about 275 years; and these years, counted back from the return of the *Heraclidæ*, place the age of *Pelasgus* about the year B.C. 1100.

[" *The establishment of Egyptian colonies in Greece, &c.*"
p. 20.]—The hypothesis of our great philosopher Sir
Isaac Newton, as to the colonization of GREECE by the
EGYPTIANS and PHŒNICIANS, seems to be as rational, and
therefore as much entitled to our respect, if not to our
absolute credence, as any others which have been proposed
upon this darkly-illumined subject.

1st. THE EGYPTIANS.

The CANAANITES, who fled from *Joshua*, retired in great
numbers into LOWER EGYPT, which they conquered and
retained under their dominion until the days of *Eli* and
Samuel. They fed on flesh, and sacrificed men after the
manner of the PHŒNICIANS; and were called SHEPHERDS
by the EGYPTIANS, who lived only on the fruits of the
earth, and abominated FLESH-EATERS. UPPER EGYPT,
from SYENE to HELIOPOLIS, which before had been under
many kings, had become consolidated, in the days of *Eli*,
into one kingdom under *Mephres*, who reigned in the year
B. C. 1125, and his successor *Misphragmuthosis*, the latter
of whom some time afterwards made lasting war upon the
SHEPHERDS. In the course of this war, which was most
probably of considerable duration, many of the SHEPHERDS
were compelled to fly into PALESTINE, SYRIA, and LIBYA,
and others, under *Lelex, Inachus, Pelasgus, Cecrops,* and
other captains, into GREECE. The rest of the SHEPHERDS

were shut up by *Misphragmuthosis* in a part of LOWER
EGYPT called ABARIS, or PELUSIUM. *Chron.* p. 10.

The war against the SHEPHERDS, which had been commenced by *Misphragmuthosis,* was continued during the
reign of his son and successor, AMOSIS, or ISTHMOSIS, who,
about the year B. C. 1070, or in the beginning of the reign
of *Saul,* expelled the remaining SHEPHERDS from ABARIS
or PELUSIUM, and thus acquired the dominion over all
EGYPT. *Chron.* p. 11. The SHEPHERDS retired in very
great numbers to the PHILISTINES. In the third year
of the reign of *Saul* "the PHILISTINES gathered themselves together to fight with ISRAEL, 30,000 chariots, and
6,000 horsemen, and people as the sand which is on the
sea-shore in multitude," 1 Sam. xiii. 5. To the expulsion
of the SHEPHERDS by the kings of EGYPT Sir *Isaac Newton*
ascribes the numerous host of the PHILISTINES in the days
of *Saul,* and the several colonies which came in those times
out of EGYPT and PHŒNICIA into GREECE, in the days of
Eli, Samuel, Saul, and *David.* Some of them fled in the
days of *Eli* from *Misphragmuthosis,* who conquered part
of the LOWER EGYPT; others retired from his successor
Amosis into PHŒNICIA and ARABIA PETRÆA, and there
mixed with the old inhabitants, who not long after being
conquered by *David,* fled from him, and the PHILISTINES
by sea, under the conduct of *Cadmus* and other captains,
into ASIA MINOR, GREECE, and LIBYA, to seek new seats,

and there built towns and erected kingdoms, and set on foot the worship of the dead. Chron. p. 167, 168, 174, 205, 206. Before these days, says our philosopher, GREECE and all EUROPE seems to have been thinly peopled, from the northern coasts of the EUXINE SEA, by wandering CIMMERIANS and SCYTHIANS, descendants of *Japhet*, who led a rambling sort of life, like the modern TARTARS in the northern parts of ASIA—were without houses, and sheltered themselves from rain and wild beasts in thickets and caves of the earth, p. 184.

2d. THE PHŒNICIANS.

We have before traced the fugitive EDOMITES, before the conquering arms of *David*, from the shores of the RED SEA to the coasts of the MEDITERRANEAN. We have seen them, in conjunction with the PHILISTINES, invading and taking possession of ZIDON.

———————

[" *The character of a Poet was a character of dignity.*" p. 97.]—*Pausanias* remarks, that poets have often lived with kings;—for prior to *Euripides, Anacreon* was familiar with *Polycrates* the SAMIAN tyrant ; *Æschylus* and *Simonides* betook themselves to *Hiero* of SYRACUSE ; *Philoxenus* associated with *Dionysius*, who afterwards tyrannized in SICILY ; and *Antagoras* the RHODIAN and *Aratus Solensis* were the familiars of *Antigonus*, king of MACEDONIA. As to

Hesiod and Homer, says he, they either were not fortunate
enough to be the companions of kings, or else they volun-
tarily despised an association with them ; the former,
perhaps, through the rural life which he embraced, and his
unwillingness to travel, lib. i. c. 2.

————

["Achaia remained during some generations, &c." p. 190.]
—The district in PELOPONNESUS, generally known in GRE-
CIAN HISTORY by the name of ACHAIA, was not originally
so called.   Before the return of the Heraclidæ the
ACHAIAN name embraced another and a far more extensive
portion of the PENINSULA. We have seen that Homer
denominates the ARGIANS, with all the people of the north-
eastern coast, ACHAIANS; and that he even distinguishes
the whole of PELOPONNESUS from the rest of GREECE by
the name of ACHAIAN ARGOS, p. 24 of this volume.

Pausanias however asserts, that the LACEDÆMONIANS
and ARGIVES alone of all the PELOPONNESUS, prior to the
return of the Heraclidæ, were called ACHAIANS.   The
ACHAIA of later GRECIAN HISTORY, the district of which we
are now speaking, was then denominated ÆGIALEIA, lib. vii.
c. 1. When Tisamenus was expelled by the Heraclidæ
from ARGOLIS and LACONIA, the inheritance of his ancestors,
he, with his ACHAIAN followers, took forcible and hostile
possession of ÆGIALEIA. He was slain in the contest;
but his ACHAIAN followers defeated the IONES (who then

occupied the country, and who retreated to ATTICA), and maintained themselves in the possession of it; and from thenceforth ÆGIALEIA assumed the name of ACHAIA. Id. ib.

Polybius speaks in terms of unqualified praise of the form of government of the ACHAIANS, which he describes to be of "very antient date." In his judgment, that democratical species of government, under which liberty and equality are secured, "was more just and perfect among the ACHAIANS than in any other state." "They were distinguished," says he, "for integrity and love of virtue above all other people," lib. ii. It may not be inapposite to introduce here the definition which the same respectable author elsewhere gives us of what he esteems to be a *just* democracy. Speaking of the various forms of government, he observes: "nor is that to be esteemed a *democracy,* in which the whole multitude usurp the liberty of pursuing their own counsels and designs without control. But when we see a people, who, from the antient manners of their country, are accustomed to pay due worship to the gods, to revere their parents, to shew respect to the aged, and to obey the laws—*when,* in the assemblies of citizens like these, the resolutions of the greater are made the rule of government—*then* we behold the form of a *just* democracy," lib. vi. Upon this definition, however, we must be permitted to observe, that an habitual observance by a people of their religious and moral duties—of the

various obligations of social and private life—and an obe-
dience to those laws which form an essential feature of our
author's "*just democracy*"—are no less essential to the due
and efficient administration of *every other* form of government, and to the well-being and happiness of the people
under it. Wherever these essentials are found equally to
exist in *those* whose *province* it is to *rule,* and in those whose
duty it is to *obey* (which our author assumes in his definition), we may safely venture to pronounce, that, in *such a*
case, and *so long as such* a state of things should continue,
the *form* of government would not be material. Applying
his own sentiment to *other forms* of government, we may say,
that *when* we see *such* a people as he describes—and *when*
their ruler or rulers (whether one, a few, or many) are, like
those whom they *govern*—observant of all their religious,
moral, and social duties—*then* we behold a *just* government—
be it a *monarchy,* be it an *aristocracy,* or be it a *democracy.*
I fear, therefore, we must consider our author's "*just demo-*
cracy" rather as an UTOPIAN government than as one that
ever did or ever can exist. The ACHAIAN government, if
it really justified the warm panegyric which *Polybius* has
bestowed upon it, may probably be considered as approxi-
mating, the nearest of any other, to his UTOPIAN democracy,
and may therefore, with due allowances, be not unfairly
adduced as the nearest practical illustration of it.

Speaking of that dark and treacherous policy which is

too common in the world, but which, although utterly
unworthy of a king or a nation, too frequently actuates their
conduct, and of the supposition of some men, that, because
these arts are common in the world, the practice of them is
become necessary in the administration of public affairs, he
observes, that " the ACHAIANS were *at all times* distinguished by different sentiments: so far were they from
forming any secret designs against their friends, in order to
enlarge their power, that they disdained even to subdue
their enemies with the assistance of deceit. In their opinion,
victory was neither honourable nor secure, unless it was
obtained in *open* contest and by force of superior courage.
Upon this account they established it as a law amongst
themselves, never to use any concealed weapons, nor to
throw darts at a distance, being persuaded that an open
and close engagement was the only fair method of combat.
For the same reason it was that they not only made a
public declaration of war, but sent notice also to the other
party of their resolution to try the fortune of a battle, and
of the place likewise in which they had determined to
engage." " In the present times," says *Polybius,* " a general
is supposed to be ignorant of his profession if he discovers
his intentions." He gives credit to the ROMANS, however,
and to them *alone,* for retaining some slight traces of the
antient virtue. " For they make beforehand a denunciation
of war; they seldom form ambuscades; and they fight always
man to man in close engagements." And he concludes with

an expression of great regret, that, "in general, artifice so much prevails, that it is now become the chief study of men to deceive each other, both in the administration of civil affairs and in the conduct of war," lib. xii.

It was not until the *latter* ages of GREECE, at no very distant period before its final subjugation to the ROMAN power, that the ACHAIANS made any conspicuous figure in GRECIAN affairs. But see vol. iii. of this History, p. 430.

———

[" *Great grandsons of Hyllus associating with themselves Oxylus, &c.*" p. 128.]—The ancestors and descendants of *Hyllus*, of whom the latter are usually denominated the *Heraclidæ*, and the ancestors of *Oxylus*, are said to be as follow, viz. :—

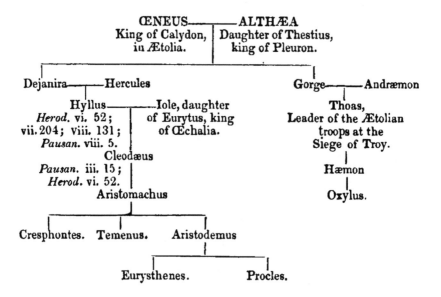

OENEUS———————ALTHÆA
King of Calydon,　Daughter of Thestius,
　in Ætolia.　　　king of Pleuron.

Dejanira————Hercules　　　　　Gorge————Andræmon

　Hyllus————Iole, daughter　　　Thoas,
Herod. vi. 52;　of Eurytus, king　Leader of the Ætolian
vii. 204; viii. 131;　of Œchalia.　　troops at the
Pausan. viii. 5.　　　　　　　Siege of Troy.

　　Cleodæus
Pausan. iii. 15;　　　　　　　　Hæmon
Herod. vi. 52.

　　Aristomachus　　　　　　　　Oxylus.

Cresphontes.　Temenus.　Aristodemus

　　Eurysthenes.　　　Procles.

The first attempt of the descendants of *Hercules* to recover the dominion of Peloponnesus was made by his son *Hyllus*. The hatred which *Eurystheus*, king of Argos, bore to *Hercules* and his descendants was not satisfied with the expulsion of the Heraclidæ from Peloponnesus. They had been kindly received by the Athenians. His hatred and his jealous fears of their growing influence made him anxious to pursue them to destruction. He invaded Attica; but the Heraclidæ, assisted by the Athenians, completely defeated his army. He was killed by the hand of *Hyllus*, whom he had so bitterly persecuted; and all his sons fell in this battle.

This brilliant success induced *Hyllus* to undertake the invasion of Peloponnesus; but he in his turn was killed in single combat by *Echĕmus*, king of the Tegeans, and the design was abandoned. Her*od*. lib. ix. c. 26; *Pausan.* lib. viii. c. 5; *Diod. Sicul.* lib. iv.

A second attempt was made by his son *Cleodæus*, but without success.

———

["*Cresphontes took possession of Messenia, &c.*" p. 128.] —Messenia being one of the most fruitful provinces in the whole Peloponnesus was naturally an object of desire, and

Theras, the natural uncle of the infant sons of *Aristodemus*, contended, in their behalf, with *Cresphontes* for the possession of that country. It was ultimately agreed that they should draw lots for it. Through stratagem and fraud in the drawing of the lots, *Cresphontes* obtained the possession of MESSENIA, *Pausan*. lib. iv. c. 3. It should seem that this circumstance was not forgotten in after times, and it may probably have had some effect in keeping alive the feelings of animosity between the two people, lib. iv. c. 4.

The fable or tradition of its earliest history, according to *Pausanias* and others, is as follows :—

Three different dynasties reigned over MESSENIA before the return of the HERACLIDÆ and the establishment of the dynasty of which *Cresphontes* was the founder and stem, and which was the consequence of that invasion.

MESSENIA was a desert when *Polycaon*, the younger of the two sons of *Lelex*, king of LACONIA, married *Messene* of ARGOS, the daughter of *Triopas*, and the grand-daughter of *Phorbas*, kings of that country. Whether *Lelex* was a native of GREECE or an EGYPTIAN seems doubtful. *Pausan.* lib. i. c. 39; lib. iv. c. 1.

The pedigree of *Messene*, according to *Pausanias*, (lib. ii. c. 16; lib. iv. c. 1,) was as follows :—

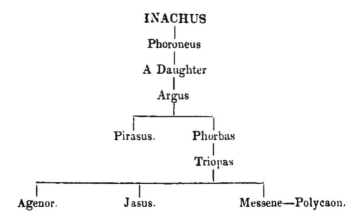

INACHUS
|
Phoroneus
|
A Daughter
|
Argus

Pirasus.   Phorbas
|
Triopas

Agenor.   Jasus.   Messene—Polycaon.

Messene, proud of her descent through a line of kings, could not endure to be the wife of a *private* individual. Collecting a body of ARGIVES and LACEDÆMONIANS, *Polycaon* and *Messene* took possession of the country, which after her was called MESSENIA, and they became its first sovereigns.

All the antiquarian zeal, and diligent inquiries of *Pausanias* could not enable him to ascertain who were the children of *Polycaon* and *Messene*. It should seem, however, that after five generations the race became extinct; and thus ended the first dynasty of MESSENIAN kings.

SECOND DYNASTY.

Upon the failure of the descendants of *Polycaon* and *Messene*, *Perieres*, the son of *Æolus*, was called to the government of MESSENIA.

H

There are two different accounts of the fabulous or traditionary descent of *Perieres*. *Apollod.* Fab. Gen. 1, 2, 8, a. b.

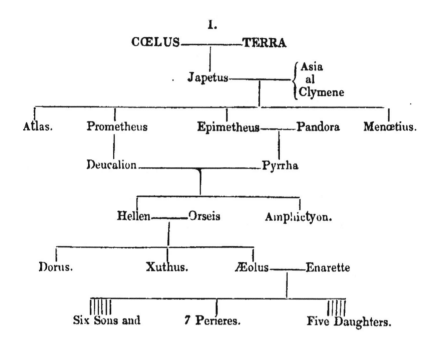

According to other accounts he was thus descended.
Apollod. Fab.

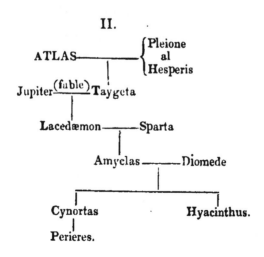

The first is the MESSENIAN, the second the LACEDÆMO-
NIAN account. *Apollod.* Heyne Observ.

Perieres married *Gorgophone,* the daughter of *Perseus,*
who, after his death, according to *Pausanias,* married
Œbalus, the son of *Cynortas,* by whom she had *Hippocoon,*
Tyndarus, and *Arene,* lib. iii. c. 1 ; lib. iv. c. 2.   Of this
lady, *Pausanias* observes, that she was the *first* woman who
set the example to her sex of marrying a second husband;
it having been usual, before her time, for women on the
death of their husbands to abstain from marrying again,
lib. ii. c. 21.

The children of *Perieres* by *Gorgophone* were, according
to *Pausanias, Aphareus* and *Leucippus.   Apollodorus* adds
another, whom he calls *Borus.*

The two brothers, *Aphareus* and *Leucippus,* reigned
jointly over MESSENIA ; but the former exercised the chief
sway.

Aphareus married his uterine sister, *Arene,* the daughter
of *Gorgophone* by *Œbalus,* and built a city in MESSENIA,
which, after her, he named ARENE.

Aphareus had by *Arene* three sons: *Idas,* who was an

ARGONAUT; *Pisus,* the reputed founder of PISA in ELIS; and *Lynceus.*

Leucippus had only daughters, two of whom were betrothed to *Idas* and *Lynceus,* but were ravished by *Castor* and *Pollux.* The fate of these two brothers, *Idas* and *Lynceus,* is differently related, but with this agreement, that they both came to an untimely end, and both of them, as well as *Pisus,* died without male issue,

Thus terminated the short dynasty of the house of *Perieres;* and the sceptre of MESSENIA devolved on the race of *Neleus,* in the person of *Nestor,* his son, the venerable hero of the TROJAN War.

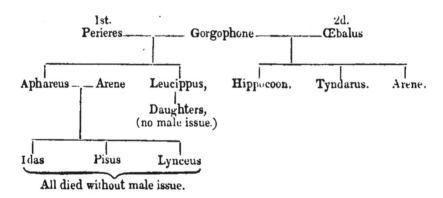

THIRD DYNASTY.

Nestor, the son of *Neleus,* upon whom the government of MESSENIA (with the exception of that part of the country which was subject to the sons of *Æsculapius*) devolved, on the failure of the line of *Perieres*, was collaterally related in blood to that house, if we adopt the first of his aforegoing pedigrees.

Cretheus, *Salmoneus*, and *Perieres*, were three of the sons of *Æolus*, the son of *Hellen*. *Salmoneus* had a daughter named *Tyro*, who, according to the fable, had twin sons by *Neptune*, *Pelias* and *Neleus*. *Tyro* afterwards married her uncle, *Cretheus*, the founder and king of IOLCHOS, in THESSALY, by whom she had three sons, *Æson*, *Amythaon*, and *Pheres*. On the death of *Cretheus*, *Pelias* and *Neleus* usurped the sovereignty of IOLCHOS, in exclusion of *Æson*, the rightful heir. But *Pelias* and *Neleus*, afterwards quarrelling, the latter fled from IOLCHOS, and went to his cousin, *Aphareus*, at MESSENIA, who not only received him kindly, but assigned to him a portion of his maritime territory, in which he built PYLOS. He married *Chloris*, the daughter of *Amphion*, by whom he had twelve sons, whose names are all mentioned by *Apollodorus*, and one daughter.

Neleus and all his sons, with the exception of *Nestor*, were killed by *Hercules*.

Thus it appears that *Neleus* was the great nephew of *Perieres*, being the grandson of his brother, *Salmoneus*.

Nestor married, according to some, *Eurydice*, the daughter of *Clymenus;* according to others, *Anaxibia*, the sister of *Agamemnon,* and had seven sons and two daughters. Of the sons, *Antilochus* and *Thrasymedes* distinguished themselves with their father at the Trojan War; and from *Pisistratus,* another son, was probably descended, his namesake, who, between four and five centuries afterwards, made so distinguished a figure in Athenian story. See Herod. lib. v. c. 65. It seems probable also that the rival family of *Alcmæon* was descended from *Thrasymedes,* another of the sons of the venerable *Nestor.*

Nestor survived the Trojan War, and had the good fortune (of which many of the Grecian chiefs were deprived) to revisit his country, where he ended his days in peace. The time and manner of his death is unknown, and we possess no information as to the affairs of Messenia from the period of his death to that of the return of the Heraclidæ.

We have, in *Pausanias,* lib. ii. c. 18, the following account of the royal family of Messenia at the time of their expulsion by the Heraclidæ.

" They expelled from Messenia the posterity of *Nestor :* *Alcmæon,* the son of *Syllus,* and the grandson of *Thrasy-*

medes; and *Pisistratus,* the grandson of *Pisistratus;* and besides these, the children of *Pæon,* the son of *Antilochus; Melanthus,* the son of *Andropompus,* the grandson of *Borus,* and the great-grandson of *Penthilus,* who was the son of *Periclymenus."* *Periclymenus* was the eldest of the twelve sons of *Neleus,* and brothers of *Nestor,* who was the youngest. *Pausanias* goes on to state, that " *Tisamenes* came with an army and his sons into that part of GREECE which was called ACHAIA; and likewise the posterity of *Neleus,* except *Pisistratus* (for he did not know to what people he betook himself); but all the rest came to ATHENS; and from these the progeny of the PÆONIDÆ and the ALCMÆONIDÆ were denominated."

Having now arrived upon HISTORIC ground, we shall content ourselves with furnishing the pedigree of *Nestor.*

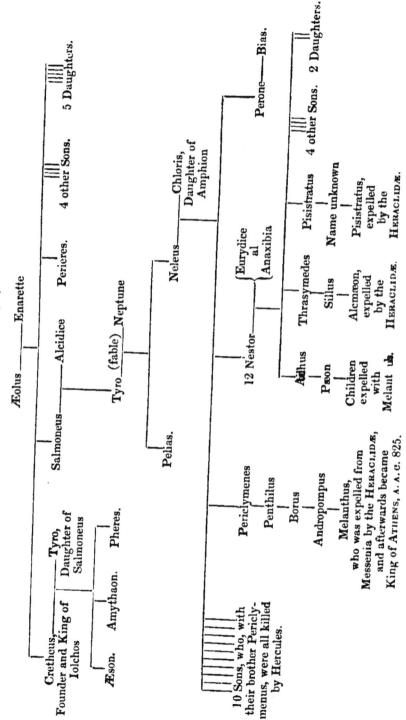

Pedigree of NESTOR, *King of Messenia.*

["*An entire revolution took place in the population of the whole Peninsula, excepting Arcadia, &c.*" p. 129.]—
Pausanias says, however, that the antient MESSENIANS were not "expelled from their kingdom by the DORIANS; for they willingly submitted to their new king *Cresphontes*, and gave the DORIANS a part of their lands," lib. iv. c. 3. It is probable, therefore, that the antient royal family of MESSENIA, and those immediately connected with them, only were expatriated, and that the mass of the people remained and amalgated with their DORIAN conquerors. The posterity of the venerable *Nestor*, with the exception of *Pisistratus* (of whose destiny *Pausanias* declares himself to be ignorant), settled themselves with *Tisamenes*, the son of *Orestes*, and his followers, in the new ACHAIA. *Pausan.* lib. ii. c. 18. *Melanthus*, the king of PYLOS, and others retired to ATHENS, where a brilliant destiny, the reward of his bravery and prowess, awaited him. He exchanged the sovereignty of PYLOS for that of ATHENS, and transmitted it to his son *Codrus*. *Pausan.* ib.; *Strabo*, lib. ix. p. 393; p. 245 of this volume.

ACHAIA must also be considered as an exception to the general consequences of the DORIAN revolution, inasmuch as, although its population was changed, in consequence of that event, it did not receive a DORIAN population in the place of it, but an ACHAIAN population from ARGOLIS and LACONIA; and with its population it also exchanged its name from ÆGIALEA to ACHAIA, which it ever after retained. See pp. 128, 131, 190 of this volume.

[" *But the oracle which held its reputation and extended, we may say, over the world, was Delphi,*" p. 136.]—The respect and religious veneration with which this far-famed institution was clothed—the influence which it acquired, and by which it held enchained and retained in superstitious bondage for so many centuries, not all GREECE alone, but every country and people of the then known world which adored or acknowledged the gods of GREECE— and by which, with a despotic sway, it governed and regulated the conduct not of nations only, but also of private individuals, in all the important transactions and concerns of human life—in all events political, military and civil— foreign and domestic—public and private—were altogether, and nothing more than, the creatures of OPINION. It would seem, therefore, to have been not merely an essential, but an indispensable requisite, towards the inception, the birth, the growth, and the maintenance and preservation of that respect, veneration, and influence, that the votaries of this superstition should not only possess an entire faith, and a firm and implicit belief in the immediate presence of the presiding deity, and the direct and positive exertion of the divine agency, in regard to the

special matter referred for the counsel or advice, the
suggestions or the commands, of the deity, and in the
divine inspiration of the ministers through whom that
counsel or advice, those suggestions or commands, were
to be communicated to the supplicant parties, but that
they should also entertain the most unlimited confidence
in the integrity and incorruptibility of these ministers.
If the veil of delusion be wholly or partially withdrawn—
if, by any means, we destroy or weaken this faith in the
superstition itself, or this confidence in the integrity of its
ministers—is it not a reasonable conclusion that the respect
and religious veneration of its votaries, and its own influence
(which stand in relation of cause and effect), should wholly
vanish, or should be diminished in the proportion of the
diminution of this faith and confidence? It is not therefore
without some surprise that we see the honest and plain-
spoken Herodotus publishing, in the face of all GREECE*,
a libel upon the ministers of the PYTHIAN god—those
important functionaries, who were supposed to receive, by
the immmediate inspiration of the deity, those awful responses, which it was their sacred province and duty
faithfully to deliver to the anxious supplicants, and which
were to regulate the conduct, and in their result, to decide.
or to declare, the fate of nations and of individuals.

* *Herodotus* recited his history to the illustrious audience assembled to
celebrate the OLYMPIC Games. *Lucian.*

He charges them, on more than one occasion, with the grossest corruption, namely, that of receiving bribes for the delivery of responses calculated to promote the political objects of the parties corrupting them.

1st. The ALCMÆONID exiles, who had been expelled from ATHENS by the superior influence of the *Pisistradidæ*, and who, during their exile, had contracted with the AM- PHICTYONS for the construction of a new temple at DELPHI, "warmed," says Herodotus, " with the generous spirit of their race," constructed a temple in splendour and beauty, far exceeding that which, according to the plan, they had engaged to build. Instead of the stone of *Porus*, which would have satisfied the terms of their contract, the vestibule was constructed of *P*ARIAN marble." This seeming liberality is not entitled to the high encomium which Herodotus has passed upon it: the sequel of the story sufficiently shews that it proceeded from interested motives : " These men," says Herodotus, " as the ATHENIANS relate, bribed the *P*YTHIANS, during their continuance at DELPHI, to suggest to every SPARTAN who should consult the oracle, either in a public or private capacity, the deliverance of ATHENS."

This corrupt scheme was successful : the LACEDÆMO- NIANS hearing the same thing incessantly repeated to them, sent an army to expel the *Pisistratidæ* from ATHENS, by which act they violated very antient ties of hospitality, thinking " it better became them to listen to the commands of Heaven than to any human consideration."

The preceding story *Herodotus* introduces on the authority of the ATHENIAN relation to it. That which follows, he states as a positive and well-authenticated fact.

Cleomenes, king of SPARTA, of the race of, and the fifteenth in descent from, *Eurysthenes*, having quarrelled with his colleague, *Demaratus*, of the race of *Procles*, availed himself of an idle story of the illegitimacy of the latter to drive him from the throne. In order the more easily to attain his object, *Cleomenes* corrupted the priestess of the DELPHIC Oracle. " He was not suspected," says Hero*dotus*, " of taking any care to influence the P*y*TH*I*AN; but it is certain that he induced *Cobon*, the son of *Aristophanes*, a man of great authority at DELPHI, to prevail on the priestess to say what *Cleomenes* desired. The name of this woman was *Perialla*, who assured those sent on this occasion that *Demaratus* was not the son of *Ariston*." This story must have been generally known in GREECE, for our curiosity informs us, that the collusion was afterwards discovered, and that *Cobon* was compelled to fly from DELPHI, and that *Perialla* was degraded from her office.

Pausanias, lib. iii. c. 4, relates the same story of *Cleo-*

menes, and adds, "that he does not know of any other person who had dared to corrupt the oracle of the god." It is rather singular that this author should have overlooked this other instance mentioned by Her*odotus*, and also the charge brought by *Demosthenes*, in one of his orations against *Philip* of MACEDON, of having bribed the oracles of GREECE.

["*Eleia and the presidency of the Olympian Festival*," p. 191.]—Although, after the destruction of *Pisa*, with the exception of the 104th Olympiad, in which the ARCADIANS violently interfered, the ELEIANS held undisturbed the presidency of that festival, while it existed; yet when they began to mingle themselves with foreign politics, and to take a part, on whatever ostensible grounds, in the wars and quarrels of their neighbours, they relinquished that sacred character, that reputation of sanctity, with which, collectively as a nation, they had, for ages, been clothed by the universal acquiescence of the Grecian people; who had thus raised around them a consecrated barrier, which afforded them the most perfect protection and security against any foreign aggressions or insults; and with them they lost those invaluable immunities and privileges, under whose fostering influence they had acquired an extent of population, and had attained to a degree of national and individual wealth, and of internal prosperity, and quiet domestic happiness, unequalled by any other Grecian state within the limits of PELOPONNESUS. Their attachment to the business and pleasures of a rural life was " chiefly nourished," says *Polybius*, " by that high regard, which, by the constitution of their government, was shewn to those that were settled in it: for justice was administered amongst them in every district; and great pains were employed that they might always be supplied with all things that were necessary to life." And he censures them, in terms of great but just severity, for not having attempted to restore to their country those sacred and invaluable immun'ties of which they had, for so many ages, been in the possession. " Certainly," says he, " they have, in this respect, been far from shewing a due regard to their own future interests: for since *peace* is that blessing which we all implore the gods to grant us—since it is that for whose sake we bear to be exposed to every danger—since, in a word, among all the things which are held in estimation by good men, there is none more generally acknowledged to deserve that name, it surely must be allowed to be a high degree of folly in the conduct of the ELEIANS to reject an acquisition of such value and importance, which they not only might obtain from the states of GREECE upon fair and honourable terms, but might hold possession of it also to all future times." From this passage, and that which follows, it is evident that *Polybius* was of opinion that these immunities might have been recovered by the ELEIANS, even in his time.

" I could wish," says he, " that these reflections might raise in the ELEIANS an attention to their proper interests ; since they never will find a time more favourable *than the present* to recover again an acknowledged confirmation of their rights from all the states of GREECE."

Polybius proceeds to observe, that " although their immunities had been long since lost, the people still retain some traces of their antient manners, and especially of their attachment to a rural life," lib. iv.

———

[" *Arcadia was early divided into many small states*," p. 192.]—We have before seen that of all the GRECIAN states in PELOPONNESUS, ARCADIA alone was uninjured and unaffected by the DORIAN conquest and its consequences, p. 128, 129, and 131 of this volume. Neither their government or their population underwent any change.

Pausanias relates that this country was originally called PELASGIA, from *Pelasgus*, the real or the fabulous founder of the ARCADIAN dynasty of kings, which continued till the end of the second MESSENIAN war.

In the reign of *Arcas*, who was the third in descent from *Pelasgus*, it is said that this country dropped its original appellation of PELASGIA, and, in honour of its reigning sovereign, assumed the name. of ARCADIA. From *Arcas*, a succession, lineal and collateral, of six kings, leads us through regions of fable, or of vague conjecture, to *Echĕmus*, in whose reign we may consider ourselves as beginning to tread on HISTORIC ground. He distinguished himself by the defeat of the army of the HERACLIDÆ on their first attempt at the invasion of PELOPONNESUS, and by his personal victory over *Hyllus*, the son of *Hercules*, who led that expedition, and who fell by the hand of *Echĕmus*, in single combat, in the year B. C. 924. Herod. lib. ix. c. 26; *Pausan.* lib. viii. c. 5; *Diod. Sic.* lib. iv. To *Echĕmus* succeeded, collaterally, *Agapenor*, who led the ARCADIAN quota to the siege of TROY, in vessels furnished by *Agamemnon*, " the king of many islands, and of all ARGOS." *Pausan.* lib. viii. c. 1; *Thucydides*, lib. i. ·*Agapenor*, on his return from TROY, was driven by a tempest to CYPRUS, where he founded a colony, and never revisited his native country; and the sovereignty of ARCADIA, in consequence, devolved again, collaterally, on *Hippothous*, a descendant of *Arcas*, the father of *Æpytus*, and grandfather of *Cypselus*, who was the reigning sovereign at the time of the return of the HERACLIDÆ. *Pausan.* ib.

That ARCADIA might have owed its happy exemption from DORIAN conquest, and the miseries of DORIAN spolia-

K

tion, in a great degree, to the rugged mountainous features of the country (which would, undoubtedly, have rendered its conquest a work of more difficult achievement), and to the uninviting character of its soil and climate, is very pro- bable. But *Pausanias* ascribes it to a prudent and politic alliance, formed by *Cypselus*, in the marriage of his daughter with *Cresphontes*, one of the HERACLIDÆ, " by which alliance," says this author, " he placed both himself and the ARCADIANS beyond the dread of war," lib. viii. c. 5. This alliance was, in all probability, the occasion of the good disposition which the same author states the ARCA- DIANS to have entertained towards the MESSENIANS from a very antient period. Ih.

We have before deduced the dynasty of the ARCADIAN kings from *Cypselus* to its extinction in the person of *Aristocrates II.*, at the close of the second MESSENIAN War.

Polybius has furnished us with a very singular and peculiar trait in the history and character of this people. The discipline and exercise of music was so interwoven with their political institutions that it formed an essential and important principle in their constitution and government. Speaking of the ARCADIANS, he says, that " they had, in general, been always celebrated for their virtue throughout all GREECE; and had obtained the highest fame, as well by their humane and hospitable disposition, as for their piety also towards the gods, and their veneration for all things sacred." It happened that, in a late period of ARCADIAN history, the inhabitants of CYNÆTHA, an ARCADIAN city, had displayed a disposition very opposite to that ascribed to the ARCADIANS in general by *Polybius :* they, on the contrary, had been noted for the savage roughness of their lives and manners, and had been distinguished by their wickedness and cruelty above all the GREEKS. He proceeds to inquire into the cause of this difference in the dispositions of the CYNÆTHANS and their countrymen; and the inquiry, in its result, leads him to ascribe it to this singular cause: " The CYNÆTHANS," says he, " were the first and only people among the ARCADIANS who threw away that institution, which their ancestors had established with the greatest wisdom, and with a nice regard to the *natural genius* and *peculia*r *disposition* of the people of the country; namely, the *discipline and exercise of music*—of that genuine and perfect music, which is useful in every state, but absolutely necessary to the people of ARCADIA." " Let it not be supposed," says he, " that the first ARCADIANS acted without strong necessity, who, though their lives and manners in all other points were rigid and austere, incorporated this act into the very *essence* of their *government;* and obliged not their children only, but the

K 2

young men likewise, until they had attained the age of thirty years, to persist in the constant study and practice of it.

He proceeds to inform us that, in ARCADIA, children from their most tender age are taught to sing, in measure, songs and hymns in honour of their gods and heroes; that, at a more advanced age, they assemble and dance with emulation to the sound of flutes, and celebrate, according to their proper age—the *children*, the *puerile*,—the *young men*, the *manly* games. " Although they may, without shame or censure," says our author, " disown all knowledge of *every other science*, they dare not, on the one hand, dissemble or deny that they are skilled in music, since the laws require that every one should be instructed in it; nor, on the other hand, can they refuse to give some proofs of their skill when asked, because such refusal would be esteemed dishonourable."

" These customs," he observes, " were not introduced as instruments of luxury and idle pleasure, but from a consideration of the painful and laborious course of life to which the ARCADIANS were accustomed, and the natural austerity of their manners, occasioned by their cold and dense atmosphere." Adverting to the influence of climate on the habits and customs of mankind, he proceeds to observe, that, " in order to smooth and soften that disposition

which was by nature so rough and stubborn," the ARCA-
DIANS " established every institution that could serve to
render their rugged minds more gentle and compliant, and
tame the fierceness of their manners."

The people of CYNÆTHA slighted all these arts, though
both their atmosphere and situation, the most inclement
and unfavourable of any in ARCADIA, rendered their attention to them the more requisite; and, in consequence,
they were continually engaged in intestine tumults and
contentions, till they became at last, says our author, " so
fierce and savage that, among all the cities of GREECE
there was none in which so many and so great enormities
were ever known to be committed."

[" *Eurysthenes and Procles,*" p. 192.]—There are various accounts of the period and mode of the death of
Aristodemus the HERACLID. By some it was reported
that he died at DELPHI, before the DORIANS returned to
PELOPONNESUS. *Pausanias,* however, does not credit this
story, but asserts that he was slain by the sons of *Pylades*
and *Electra,* lib. iii. c. 1. But·Herodotus informs us, that
the LACEDÆMONIANS affirmed that they were first introduced into LACONIA by *Aristodemus* himself, and not by
his sons, and that he died of *disease* immediately after
their birth.

According to this author, the LACEDÆMONIANS, in con-
formity with their laws, elected the elder for their king;
but which was the elder could not be ascertained. In this
dilemma the mother was applied to, but, from a desire
equally to aggrandize both her children, she professed ignorance, and declared her inability to decide. The oracle at
DELPHI was next consulted. The LACEDÆMONIANS were
commanded by the god to acknowledge both the sons as
their kings, but to honour the first born the most : but
which was the *first born* remained still to be ascertained.
The following expedient was suggested, and successfully
resorted to. The mother was carefully watched, for the
purpose of noticing which of the children she daily washed
and fed the first. *P*erceiving that she, who was uncon-
scious of the design, regularly preferred the same child,
both in washing and feeding it, the LACEDÆMONIANS
respected, says *Herodotus,* and acted upon this silent testimony of the mother. The child thus preferred by its
parent they treated as the elder, calling him *Eurysthenes,*
and his brother, *Procles.*

Herodotus expressly describes the race of *Procles* as " *an
inferior branch.*" Both had the same origin, says he, but
the family of *Eurysthenes,* as being the elder, was most
esteemed.

The brothers were of very different dispositions. They

were, throughout life, at variance, and in a state of great enmity with each other; and *Herodotus* observes, that their enmity was perpetuated by their posterity. *Pausan.* lib. iii. c. 1. But the latter author informs us, that their mutual animosities did not prevent them from concurring in all the measures of their maternal uncle and guardian *Theras,* the son of *Autesion,* of the race of *Cadmus.*

The kings of the race of *Eurysthenes* acquired the denomination of the "*Agidæ,*" from *Agis,* his son and successor; and those of the race of *Procles* acquired that of the *Eurypontidæ,* from *Eurypon,* his grandson. *Pausan.* lib. iii. c. 2, 7.

["*Little, however, of importance occurs among the traditions concerning the Lacedæmonian state till Lycurgus, &c.*" p. 193.]—Herodotus observes, that, prior to the establishment of the code of *Lycurgus,* the LACEDÆMONIANS had the worst laws of all the GRECIAN states—bad with regard to their own internal government, and intolerable to strangers.

[" *Till Lycurgus of the race of Procles, &c.*" p. 193.]—
The caution which our author has observed in this passage,
as to the age and contemporaries of *Lycurgus,* and the
judicious observation which follows it, do credit to his
judgment and good sense. I cannot say as much of his
fellow-labourer in the same vineyard*. I entirely acquiesce
also in the just and well-merited reproof which Mr. *Mitford*
has given to the chronologers in his note to this passage.
It would be well if some of our modern chronologers
would profit by it, and abate a little of that contemptible,
but disgusting and reprehensible, self-sufficiency and confidence with which they take upon themselves to decide
upon points in history and chronology,—respecting which
the greatest and wisest men of all ages have doubted or
disagreed,—and substitute in its place a portion of that
modesty and diffidence which would better become them,
and which would gain for their opinions, from their *thinking*
and *judicious* readers, a higher degree of attention and
respect. I shall here quote an expression of our historian
(p. 167 of this volume), which goes to the point. Speaking
of the evidences as to the age in which *Homer* lived, he
observes that, " but for the *respect* due to those who have
thought differently, and STILL MORE perhaps to those who
have DOUBTED, I should scarcely hesitate, &c. &c." Thus
our chronologers may learn that their opinions would be
better received, and have *greater weight,* if they were

* Dr. *Gillies.*

delivered in that style of diffidence, and courteous respect for the opinions of those who may differ from them, which it behoves and becomes every writer upon controversial subjects to adopt, instead of that tone of arrogant self-sufficiency and dogmatism which distinguishes and disgraces them. Our judicious historian has another observation, (p. 160 of this volume,) which is no less just than apposite to the subject of this article. Speaking of chronologers, he says, " it seems as if *doubts* had *decreased* in modern times in proportion, not to the *acquisition* of means for *discovering truth*, but to the loss of means for *detecting falsehood*."

The aforegoing remarks have been suggested by the perusal of the chronological antiquities of the *deep*-read and learned Mr. *Jackson*, and the more recent elaborate work of Dr. *Hales* on sacred and profane chronology ; but *more especially* by the perusal of the dissertation of the former on the institution of the OLYMPIC games and the age and date of the promulgation of the laws of *Lycurgus*.

Having shewn the opinions of *Socrates* and *Plato* to be in direct *opposition* to those of *Thucydides* and *Diodorus Siculus*—having opposed *Strabo* and *Polybius* to each other—having shewn that *Herodotus* was mistaken ; that *Pausanias* was so puzzled and perplexed by the multitude and *discordance,* no doubt, of the authorities to which he referred in the course of his inquiries for information, that he was inconsistent with himself—having, in short, by deep research, collected from all the learned authorities of antiquity, a mass of data, from whence *sober* judgment, *sound* reason, and common sense could not possibly draw any other *rational* conclusion than this, viz., that the problems of the *first* institution of the OLYMPIADS—the age of *Lycurgus* —and who were his contemporaries, have ever been, and probably will for ever remain, involved in doubt and uncertainty, our chronologer, with that self-sufficiency and confidence which appears in almost every page of his work, advances, boldly and unhesitatingly, to the most *positive* conclusions upon them all. " *There can be no doubt*," says he, " that the OLYMPIAN games had been celebrated many ages before *Chorœbus* was victor." " It is NOT TO BE DOUBTED that *Lycurgus* and *Iphitus* were contemporaries, and above a century before the OLYMPIAD of *Chorœbus;*" and " that the former assisted the latter in the institution of the OLYMPIADS;" and this historical fact having been assumed as proved, the age and date of the promulgation of the laws of *Lycurgus* is carried, as a matter of course, " to the year B. C. 884, when those games were restored." Chronol. Antiq. vol. iii. p. 333, 348.

Our more recent chronologer, Dr. *Hales*, is scarcely less self-sufficient or less confident than his predecessor, Mr. *Jackson*, vol. i. p. 31.

Sir *Isaac Newton* fixes the date when *Lycurgus* became tutor to *Charilaus*, the young king of SPARTA, in the year B. c. 708, which is sixty-eight years later than the date of the restoration of the OLYMPIADS, in the year 776, when *Chorœbus* was the victor in the race ; for which he assigns the following reasons : " *Socrates* died three years after the end of the PELOPONNESIAN war ; and *Plato* introduceth him, saying, that the institutions of *Lycurgus* were of but three hundred years standing, or not much more. And *Thucydides*, in the reading followed by *Stephanus*, saith, that the LACEDÆMONIANS had from antient times used good laws, and been free from tyranny ; and that from the time that they had used one and the same administration of their commonwealth to the end of the PELOPONNESIAN war there were three hundred years and a few more. Count three hundred years back from the end of the PELOPON-NESIAN war, and they will place the legislature of *Lycurgus* upon the 19th OLYMPIAD, and, according to *Socrates*, it might be the 22d or 23d." In this quotation from *Thucydides* our great philosopher has been led into an error, from his following the LATIN *translation* (which is erroneous) instead of the GREEK *original—humanum est errare* is a melancholy and mortifying but an universal truth, from the influence of which even the great and venerated name of *Newton* cannot be exempted. It must however be recollected, that the publication of his Chronology was a

posthumous work, and that he might possibly have corrected the error had he lived to revise it.

Our two modern chronologers appear to have caught
hold, with a malicious avidity, of the advantage which this
mistake of our great philosopher gave them in the con-
troversy.   But they have both of them used it unfairly.
Dr. *Hales* has not had the candour to admit, in a manly
and open way, the weight of the opposing authorities of
Plato and *Socrates;* and Mr. *Jackson*, with the coolest
effrontery imaginable, has got rid of them altogether, by
" concluding" that *Plato* " followed *Thucydides,* and wrote
four hundred years," although he admits that the reading
in " *all the editions* of *Plato*" is *three hundred years*.   With
as much reason and justice might the supporters of Sir *Isaac
Newton's* system conclude that *Thucydides* and *Diodorus
Siculus* wrote *three hundred years*, although the different
readings of those authors are *four hundred years*.   But,
even granting them the *four hundred years*, it would not
avail them in establishing their hypothesis of the promulgation of the laws of *Lycurgus* in the year B.C. 884; for the
PELOPONNESIAN war ended in the year B.C. 405.   Count back
from thence *four hundred years*, and it will fix *Lycurgus* in
the year B. C. 805, which is seventy-nine years later than
their assumed date of the supposed restoration of the OLYM-
PIAN games by their imaginary *Iphitus*, viz. B. C. 884.

With the conflicting opinions of so many of the most respectable authors of antiquity before him, what *judicious* historian would venture to affirm that the age or the contemporaries of the great SPARTAN lawgiver have been ascertained with *any degree of certainty ?*

[" *All the evils, &c. were daily experienced in Sparta,*" p. 198.]—Herodotus thus enumerates the many honourable privileges with which, he says, " the SPARTANS distinguished their princes."

The priesthoods of the LACEDÆMONIAN and the celestial *Jupiter* were appropriated to them. They were invested with the power of engaging in hostile expeditions whenever they pleased, and any SPARTAN who obstructed them incurred the curses of their religion. On the field of battle their post was in the front; during a retreat in the rear. They had a body-guard of a hundred chosen men*. When upon the march they might take for their use as many sheep as they thought proper; and they had the chines and the skins of all that were sacrificed. Such were their privileges during *war.*

In *peace* also they had many distinctions. In the so-

* *Thucydides* describes *Agis* as being attended by a body-guard of three hundred horse, lib. v.

lemnity of any public sacrifice the first place was always reserved for the kings, to whom not only the choicest things were presented, but twice as much as to any other person. They had, moreover, the first of every libation, and the skins of the sacrificed victims. On the first and seventh of every month there was given to each of them a perfect animal, which was sacrificed in the temple of APOLLO : to this was added a medimnus of meal, and a LACEDÆMONIAN quart of wine. In the public games they sat in the most distinguished places. They appointed whomsoever they pleased to the dignity of *Proxeni**, and each of them chose two *Pythii,* who were the persons sent to consult the oracle at DELPHI, and were maintained at the public expense as well as the kings. If the kings did not think proper to take their repast in public, two chœnices of meal, with a cotyla of wine, were sent to their respective houses; but if they were present they received a double portion. If any private person invited them to an entertainment, a similar respect was shewn to them. The oracular declarations were preserved by them, although they could not but be known to the *Pythii* also. The kings alone had the power of deciding on the following matters, viz.—

1. They chose a husband for an heiress, if her father had not previously betrothed her.

---

* It was the business of the Proxeni to entertain the ambassadors from foreign states, and introduce them at the public assemblies.

2. They had the care of the highways.

3. Whoever chose to adopt a child must do it in the presence of the kings.

4. They assisted at the deliberations of the senate, which was composed of twenty-eight persons.

Such were the honours paid by the SPARTANS to their princes whilst alive. Honours of the following description were paid to them after their decease :—

Messengers were sent to every part of SPARTA to relate the event, whilst the women beat on a cauldron through the city. At this signal one free-born person of each sex in every family was compelled, under very heavy penalties, to disfigure themselves. When a king of LACEDÆMON died, a certain number of the LACEDÆMONIANS, independent of the SPARTANS, were obliged, from all parts of LACEDÆMON, to attend the funeral. When these, together with the HELOTS and SPARTANS, to the amount of several thousands, were assembled in one place, they began, men and women, to beat their breasts, to make loud and dismal lamentations, always exclaiming, of their last prince, that he was the best. If one of their kings died in battle, they made a representation of his person, and carried it to the place of interment upon a bier richly adorned. After the burial there was an interval of ten days from all business and amusement, with every public testimony of sorrow.

The LACEDÆMONIANS had another custom in common with the PERSIANS. When a king died his successor remitted every debt due either to the king or the public.

———————

[" *Cresphontes, the Heracleid, and his descendants,*" p. 218.]—*Pausanias* has given us a pedigree of the MESSENIAN kings, from *Cresphontes* downwards to the time of their quarrels with LACEDÆMON.

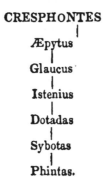

CRESPHONTES
|
Æpytus
|
Glaucus
|
Istenius
|
Dotadas
|
Sybotas
|
Phintas.

In the reign of *Phintas* the first disagreement took place between the MESSENIANS and LACEDÆMONIANS, which is related in p. 219. To *Phintas* the sovereignty descended in lineal succession. After him follow two kings who appear to have reigned jointly; but whether they were the sons of *Phintas*, or related to him in any or what other degree, does not appear from *Pausanias*.

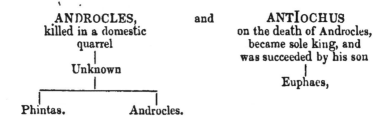

ANDROCLES,
killed in a domestic
quarrel
|
Unknown
|

Phintas.   Androcles.

and

ANTIOCHUS
on the death of Androcles,
became sole king, and
was succeeded by his son
|
Euphaes,

whose reign commenced about the time of the capture of AMPHIA by the LACEDÆMONIANS. *Pausan.* lib. iv. c. 4.

———

[" *The Lacedæmonian and Messenian stories, as to the occasion of the first quarrel between them*," p. 219.]— Trying the truth of these two stories by the only test which now remains to us (which, however, is by no means an unsafe or an unsatisfactory one), the subsequent conduct of the parties concerned in the transaction, I think we should almost necessarily be led to the inference, that truth and justice lay on the side of the MESSENIANS—treacherous aggression and the falsification of truth on the side of the LACEDÆMONIANS. The considerations (founded upon this test) by which we are led to this inference are cogent and forcible.

Let us first consult history for the purpose of ascertaining whether any and what consequences immediately resulted

from the transaction, as represented in the LACEDÆMONIAN
story.   We find history totally silent in regard to any
consequences or events as resulting or flowing from it.   We
find, to our great surprise, the LACEDÆMONIANS, that
proud, domineering people, patiently submitting to these
grievous injuries, which their story paints as of so atrocious
a character.   We find them long passive and acquiescent
under them: for we are told, by *Pausanias*, lib. iv. c. 4, that
" *one generation had passed away*" before the occurrence
of the next event, which blew up into a flame the national
animosities between the two people.   This next event, which
was the immediate cause of the first MESSENIAN war,
could not have been less than twenty years after the
transaction which is the subject of our present consideration, *one generation having passed away.*   For *so long* a
period, therefore, did this proud people remain tamely
acquiescent under the most injurious provocation which one
nation could receive from another.   If the LACEDÆMONIAN
relation of this transaction be really true, the history of
GREECE, from its earliest commencement, throughout its
most barbarous and uncivilized periods, and down to the
very time of this transaction, does not afford an example of
any thing so atrocious as the conduct of the MESSENIANS
upon this occasion.

If this story were really true, is it possible to believe that
the LACEDÆMONIANS, that proud, haughty, and high-

minded people, would have remained for so many years
tamely and ignobly acquiescent under so grievous an out-
rage, in which their sovereign lost his life, and their virgins
were driven by desperation to seek, in suicide, a refuge
from the shame of their brutal violation?

If this story had really been true, and the LACEDÆMO-
NIANS could have substantiated its truth, would not their
injuries have resounded throughout all GREECE? For the
act and its consequences did not concern LACEDÆMON
alone. It was a manifest and direct violation of that law
of nations, which had long before been established amongst
the states of GREECE for their common protection against
acts of aggression and violence from each other, similar to
those which this LACEDÆMONIAN story presents to our
view. It was equally an insult to their common religion.
Could any insult to that religion be greater than the violation of GRECIAN virgins assembled for the celebration of
festivals in honour of one of the most popular deities of
GREECE, the chaste DIANA? So gross a violation of their
international law, so flagrant an insult to their common
religion, could not fail to have attracted the notice of the
AMPHICTYONIC council (whose peculiar and special duty it
was to guard and protect that religion), and to have drawn
down upon the MESSENIANS the just vengeance of all the
GRECIAN states combined, for the purpose of punishing so
heinous an offence against their commonweal.

How are we to reconcile the LACEDÆMONIAN story with the LACEDÆMONIAN conduct upon this occasion? If their *story* be true, their tame and pusillanimous ·conduct, in quietly submitting, for so many years, to the outrageous injuries and insults which they received from the MESSE-NIANS—in not avenging the death of their king, and the cause of their violated and self-slaughtered virgins—would deserve to be stigmatized as more base, more vile, and more abject, than any that has ever disgraced the annals of an independent nation.

But such a conduct, on such an occasion, and under such provocations, would be utterly irreconcileable with the un-varied tenour of the national character, and of the public conduct of this proud, haughty, and domineering people, throughout every period of the history of their independent political existence.

On the other hand, if the LACEDÆMONIANS were in reality the offenders in this transaction—if they had me-ditated to achieve, through stratagem or treachery, the destruction of the MESSENIAN chiefs—or, in short, if they had contemplated or done any unwarrantable act towards the MESSENIANS, which they were conscious they could not justify to the world—we then should find at once a clue· to unravel and explain their otherwise mysterious conduct subsequent to this transaction. They had planned an unjustifiable attack on their neighbours; but they had failed in it, and their failure had been attended with the loss of their king, and of those who were concerned with him in the unjustifiable attempt. But as they were in the wrong, as they were in reality the aggressors, it would be prudent in them to take no further public notice of the transaction.

I must confess that the above is the only rational solution which has presented itself to me of the conduct of the LACEDÆMONIANS upon this occasion. But it is a solution which goes to the utter discredit of their story, and to attach upon them the imputation of being the aggressors in this transaction.

There are other grounds, however, which might reasonably induce a suspicion that the LACEDÆMONIANS were in reality the aggressors on the first occasion of quarrel which arose between the two nations. On the second, which immediately led to the first MESSENIAN war, a subject of LACEDÆMON was unquestionably the aggressor—his offence was one of the deepest die—robbery followed up by the murder of the son of the injured party. The distracted MESSENIAN parent applied to the SPARTAN government for redress in the punishment of the daring perpetrator of these heinous crimes; but he applied in vain. In a fit of desperation bordering on madness, he took vengeance into

his own hands, and assassinated every LACEDÆMONIAN
whom he met with on his return to his own country. The
SPARTAN demanded from the MESSENIAN government that
reparation which they had just before refused to the just
complaints of the injured MESSENIAN. The MESSENIANS
appear to have done every thing which a nation could do
consistently with its honour to avoid a rupture. It is
asserted on their behalf that they offered to refer the de-
cision of the affair to the ARGIVES, the common allies of
both people, or to the council of the AMPHICTYONS, or
even to the judgment of the AREOPAGITES. *Pausan.* lib. iv.
c. 5. To the equitable propositions of the MESSENIANS the
LACEDÆMONIANS did not condescend to return any answer.
Their whole conduct upon this occasion, which was the
very reverse of every thing manly, open, and honourable,
would seem to justify the assertion of the MESSENIANS, that
the LACEDÆMONIANS did not engage in this war, on
account either of the former or the more recent injuries
which they put forth as the ostensible grounds for it; but
that it was to gratify " their inordinate desire of dominion,—
their wish to oppress other GRECIAN cities, as they had
done those under the immediate rule of SPARTA." Id. ib.

The high authority of *Polybius* would seem to confirm
and justify the MESSENIAN assertion, as to the real motives
of the LACEDÆMONIANS for engaging in the first MESSE-

NIAN war; for the second war was wholly MESSENIAN: it originated in their patriotic determination to die with their arms in their hands, or to regain their lost freedom.

Having observed, in his encomium on the laws of *Lycurgus*, that the principles upon which he had framed his republic secured all LACONIA against any apprehension of hostile attempts, and established the liberty of SPARTA upon such strong foundation that it subsisted for many ages, he proceeds to remark, that this legislator had overlooked one great precaution, namely, that which was necessary to restrain his people from invading the territory of their neighbours, from aspiring to an extended sovereignty, or raising themselves to be the arbiters of all affairs. But while *Lycurgus* freed his citizens from jealousy and envious competition in their private manners, and in the administration of their own particular government, he at the same time allowed full scope to their ambitious projects against the rest of GREECE, and suffered them to become most eager and aspiring in the pursuits both of wealth and power; " For who is ignorant," says he, " that the LACEDÆMONIANS, the first almost of all the Greeks, were led by a desire of gain to invade the territory of their neighbours, and declared war against the MESSENIANS, *with* design to reduce them into slavery ?"

Upon the whole, therefore, I am of opinion, notwithstanding the high authority of *Strabo* (lib. vi. p. 257, 279,) on the opposite side of the question, that the LACEDÆMO-NIAN relation of the circumstances of the first quarrel between the MESSENIANS and themselves is not entitled to credit; that in this, as well as all other transactions between those two people, the brave but unfortunate MESSE-NIANS were far more " sinned against than sinning ;" and that history has not done them justice in the relation of the circumstances of this transaction.

["*Recourse was had to arms*," p. 220.]—But recourse was not had to arms by the MESSENIANS until every endeavour to avoid a rupture, which was consistent with national honour and independence, had been exerted and wholly failed. *Pausan.* lib. iv. c. 5.

["*The gates open, and no guard kept, as no hostilities were apprehended,*" p. 221.]—The LACEDÆMONIANS commenced the war with the MESSENIANS by a treacherous and dishonourable act. What a striking contrast does this dark and treacherous policy of the LACEDÆMONIANS (so unworthy of a great nation) exhibit to that manly, open, and honourable policy, which, at all times, as *Polybius* informs us, characterized the ACHAIANS, lib. xiii.; see also Annotation, under title "ACHAIA."

["*The brave and worthy Euphaes received a mortal wound*," p. 224.]—The interesting and animated account given by *Pausanias* of the contest which took place on the field of battle, between the LACEDÆMONIANS and the loyal MESSENIANS, for the body of their wounded and nearly-expiring king, deserves to be more particularly mentioned.

"*Euphaes* himself," says *Pausanias*, "was more ardent in battle than was proper for a king—rushing, with an ungovernable fury, on *Theopompus*, he received several wounds, some of which were mortal. As he lay extended on the ground, still breathing a little, yet almost ready to expire, the LACEDÆMONIANS attempted to possess themselves of his body. But the benevolence which *Euphaes* had ever shewn to his subjects, and the disgrace which would attach to them if they suffered his body to be taken by the enemy, roused the MESSENIANS to the most vigorous exertions: they felt that it would redound more to their honour to lose their lives than to survive the loss of their king."

N

Pausanias proceeds to state, that the fall of *Euphaes* both lengthened the battle and increased the courage of each army; and that *Euphaes*, having recovered a little, had the gratification to perceive that his troops were not inferior to the enemy in courage or in conduct. He died not many days afterwards, having reigned over the MESSE-NIANS thirteen years, during the whole of which period they had been engaged in war with the LACEDÆMONIANS. *Pausan.* lib. iv. c. 16.

["*Some of the Messenians emigrate,*" p. 225.]—Some of the principal MESSENIANS, who had escaped from *Ithome*, repaired to DELPHI to consult the oracle, and ask the advice of the god as to their future proceedings. It happened that the CHALCIDEANS of EUBŒA were at the same time at DELPHI, for the purpose of consulting the oracle how they were to relieve themselves from the inconveniences of a redundant population. They were directed by the oracle to decimate their whole people, and send a tenth to found a colony.

In answer to their application, the MESSENIANS were commanded by the oracle to join the CHALCIDEAN colony. The decrees of the oracle were obeyed by all the applicants. The united colonists landed on the southern coasts of ITALY, and founded RHEGIUM, which in process of time became a flourishing state. *Strabo*, lib. vi. p. 257. *Strabo* informs us, that the kings or leaders of the people of RHEGIUM were always chosen from the MESSENIAN race until the time of *Anaxilas*. Id. ib.

[*The conditions imposed by the Lacedæmonians on the Messenians*," p. 225.]—Besides the exaction of this tribute, the MESSENIANS were required, both men and women, to attend the funerals of kings and nobles, clad in a black garment, and such as did not comply were punished. *Pausan.* lib. iv. c. 14. We are informed by *Herodotus*, that upon the death of a king of LACEDÆMON a certain number of LACEDÆMONIANS, independent of the SPARTANS, were obliged, from all parts of LACEDÆMON, to attend his funeral; and that when these, together with the HELOTS and SPARTANS, to the amount of several thousands, were assembled in one place, they began, men and women, to beat their breasts, and to make loud and dismal lamentations.

Ælian, in his curious History, adverts to this condition imposed upon the MESSENIANS, whose free-born women

N 2

were compelled to walk in the funeral processions, and to lament at the deaths of those with whom they were not at all connected.

If this were so, the performance of this condition must unquestionably have been considered by the MESSENIANS as a galling badge, if not of slavery, at least of their ignominious dependence upon SPARTA. I think it must be inferred, however, from the account given by *Herodotus,* that at the funeral of a king the attendance and lamentation was of a *more general* description, and included *free-born* persons, as well the HELOTS, or slaves. At the funerals of the nobles, and other inferior persons, it might have been otherwise.

["*A leader thereof was only wanting, &c.*" p. 227.]—
Pausanias eulogizes the ardent patriotism and the spirit of independence and freedom with which the MESSENIAN youths were animated. After describing the universal feelings of discontent with which the MESSENIANS endured the harsh treatment of the LACEDÆMONIANS, and which had sown the seeds of new plans of revolt, he observes, that " the younger part of the community incited them to this revolt in no trifling degree ; and although these youths were as

yet unskilled in war, their elevation of soul was very conspicuous, and they preferred dying for the freedom of their
country to felicity in a state of subjection." " The MES-
SENIAN youth," says he, " were educated in several places,
but the best and most numerous resided about ANDANIA,"
lib. iv. c. 14.

["*Romantic Messenian adventure,*" p. 223.]—*Pausanias*
relates another romantic MESSENIAN adventure, not of our
hero indeed, but of two MESSENIAN youths of ANDANIA,
which must have happened nearly about this time, as he
states it to have been prior to the battle of STENYCLERUS.

Panormus and *Gonippus*, who had been accustomed to
make excursions into LACONIA, for the purpose of committing depredations in the SPARTAN dominions, clothed
themselves in white garments and purple cloaks, and riding
on most beautiful horses, with hats on their heads, and
spears in their hands, presented themselves unexpectedly
to a party of LACEDÆMONIANS, who were celebrating a
festival in honour of their heroes, *Castor* and *Pollux*, and
were amusing themselves in their camp after the feast
with drinking and sports. The LACEDÆMONIANS, supposing
them to be really the deified heroes, whose festivals they

were celebrating, paid them adoration as such. The youths, as soon as they were in the midst of the LACEDÆMONIANS, attacked them with their spears, made a great slaughter amongst them, treated their sacrifice with contempt, and returned to ANDANIA. *Pausan.* lib. iv. c. 27. In reading the romantic adventures of *Aristomenes* and his companions, into whom he appears to have infused a portion of his enterprising spirit, we may almost fancy ourselves in the midst of the ages of chivalry of still more *olden* times, than those in which our more modern age of chivalry existed.

———————

[" *The exertions of Aristomenes,*" p. 229.]—*Pausanias* relates that *Aristomenes* was attended in this battle by a body of eighty chosen MESSENIANS of the same age with himself, each of whom deemed himself honoured by being thought worthy to fight by the side of such a man as *Aristomenes.* They were all of them skilful in perceiving, from trifling circumstances, the assistance which they eventually stood in need of, and particularly in observing the actions of their leader, while he was actually engaged in battle, and was preparing to engage. These young men were the first that opposed the flower of the SPARTAN army, led by their king *Anaxander,* and routed it, lib. iv. c. 16.

The grandsons of *Androcles* (who, jointly with *Antiochus*, reigned over MESSENIA before the commencement of the first war, and who was killed in a domestic quarrel with his colleague), *Phintas* and *Androcles*, are represented to have distinguished themselves in this engagement. Id. ib. They were both of them killed in the battle of MEGALETAPHRUS. See *Pausan.* lib. iv. c. 17.

["*Aristocrates, leader of the Arcadian allies*," p. 231.]— *Pausanias* says that the LACEDÆMONIANS corrupted *Aristocrates* with *money;* and he speaks in terms of strong reprobation of their conduct upon this occasion, to which he applies the epithets "*unlawful*" and "fraudulent." "The LACEDÆMONIANS," says he, "are the first we are acquainted with who made presents to an enemy, and gave to the events of war a venal character." "Before the LACEDÆMONIANS acted in this *unlawful* manner towards the MESSENIANS, and *Aristocrates* was corrupted by them, those who were engaged in battle trusted to their virtue and the providence of the gods;" and he charges the LACEDÆMONIANS with having pursued the same corrupt practice at the battle of ÆGOSPOTAMOS, bribing with money the ATHENIAN commanders. "But," says he, "this fraudulent conduct of the LACEDÆMONIANS towards the MESSE-

NIANS, the *Dæmon**, in after times, turned to their destruction." The instance in LACEDÆMONIAN history to which
he alludes, was their war with the PERSIANS, in which,
under their able and gallant king and general *Agesilaus,*
they had nearly subverted the PERSIAN empire. " But the
barbarian," says *Pausanias,* " circumvented them with their
own arts by sending money to CORINTH, ARGOS, ATHENS,
and THEBES. Hence the war called CORINTHIAN originated from this bribery ; and *Agesilaus* was obliged to
abandon his possessions in ASIA," lib. iv. c. 17.

[" *The chosen band of Aristomenes,*" p. 231.]—This
chosen band consisted of 300 men. *Pausan.* lib. iv. c. 18.

[" *Escape of Aristomenes,*" p. 234.]—*Pausanias* concludes his story with an anecdote, which strikingly shews
that *Aristomenes* was not deficient in gratitude. At his
desire his son *Gorgus,* then about eighteen years of age,
married the virgin who had been the means of preserving
his father's life, lib. iv. c. 19.

* By the power called the " *Dæmon,*" which so often occurs in *Pausanias,*
we must understand *Jupiter.*

[" *The capture of Eira,*" p. 235.]—*Theocles* the prophet, the principal friend and constant companion of *Aristomenes,* was determined not to survive the ruin of his country. " The gods impelled him," he said, addressing his friend *Aristomenes,* " to fall with his country; but do you, to the utmost of your ability, exert yourself to preserve the MES-SENIANS, and to save yourself." He then rushed on the enemy, exclaiming aloud to the LACEDÆMONIANS, that " they would not perpetually rejoice in their victory over the MESSENIANS." He made a great slaughter amongst them; and at length, satiated with the destruction of his enemies, he fell, covered with honourable wounds. *Pausan.* lib. iv. c. 21.

[" *They stoned Aristocrates to death,*" p. 236.]—*Pausanias* informs us, that the ARCADIANS exhorted the MESSENIANS to join with them in the execution of this act of summary justice. " They looked, however, at *Aristo-menes,* who, fixing his eyes on the ground, wept." *Pausan.* lib. iv. c. 22. His mind was more occupied by the now irremediable *misfortunes* of his country, than the punish- ment of the criminal by whose treachery all his schemes and efforts for the preservation of its liberties and inde- pendence had been rendered abortive. It was for this

O

unjust conduct of *Aristocrates* that the government of the ARCADIANS was taken from the house of *Cypselus*. *Pausan.* lib. viii. c. 5.

[*Aristomenes excused himself from leading this expedition,*" p. 236.] — *Pausanias* has given us the reasons which induced *Aristomenes* to decline the honour of leading the MESSENIAN colony. " He declared that as long as he lived he would make war upon the LACEDÆMONIANS, and that he knew perfectly well that some new evil would always befal SPARTA through his means." It will appear in the sequel that our hero was too sanguine in this expectation. He did, however, all that man could do—he consulted the oracle at DELPHI. The gods do not appear to have held out any encouragement to his further exertions in the cause of his country, and he yielded in pious and prudent acquiescence to their will, lib. iv. c. 23.

[" *The Messenian colony, under Gorgus and Manticlus,*" p. 236.]—*Pausanias* says, that all acceded to the proposal " except such as were prevented by old age, or the want of things necessary for their settlement," lib. iv. c. 23.

[" *The Messenians and Zanclæans,*" p. 237.]—In justice
to the brave but unfortunate MESSENIANS, the historian
should not have omitted to record the circumstances which
led to this accommodation, or have withheld the meed of
praise to which their humane, honourable, and meritorious
conduct has given them so just a claim. The MESSE-
NIANS were urged by *Anaxilas* to cut off the suppliant
ZANCLÆANS, and to make slaves of those who survived,
together with their wives and children. But the MESSE-
NIANS were themselves the children of adversity : " they
had suffered persecution and had learnt mercy *;" they
revolted at the cruel proposition of *Anaxilas.* Their chiefs,
Gorgus and *Manticlus,* entreated of *Anaxilas* that they
might not be compelled to act in the same harsh and
unfeeling manner towards the GREEKS, as their own kin-
dred, the PELOPONNESIAN DORIANS, had acted towards
them. The feelings of humanity prevailed; the result
was the accommodation recorded by our historian. See
Pausan. lib. iv. c. 23.

[" *Anaxilas,*" p. 237.]—*Anaxilas* was the great grandson of *Alcidamidas,* who with other MESSENIANS had
emigrated from MESSENE to RHEGIUM, after the death of
Aristodemus, and the capture of ITHOME, in the first
MESSENIAN war. *Pausan.* lib. iv. c. 23.

* Sterne.

[*Conclusion of the second Messenian war,*" p. 238.]—It
is a circumstance not unworthy of observation, although
little redounding to the honour or credit of the LACE-
DÆMONIANS, that they commenced the first MESSENIAN
war, and gained their first success, the capture of AM-
PHEIA, by means of a dishonourable act; and they closed
the second MESSENIAN war, and gained their last success,
the capture of EIRA (which decided the fate of MESSENIA,
and made the LACEDÆMONIANS the masters and the
tyrants of that desolated country), by means of an act of
treachery. Their secret preparations for hostilities, and
their sudden attack upon AMPHEIA, without any previous
formal declaration of hostilities, were contrary to the law
of nations as then existing, " even amongst the Greeks
themselves," which required that these formalities should
be observed, " as the forerunners of honourable war;"
and the intrigue of a MESSENIAN woman, and the baseness
of a LACEDÆMONIAN slave, produced the capture of EIRA,
which closed the scene of MESSENIAN glory, and, with the
extinction for a time of its national existence, filled up the
measure of MESSENIAN misfortune. See p. 221 and 234
of this volume. How different this conduct of the LACE-
DÆMONIANS from that of the ACHAIANS, as described by
Polybius, lib. xiii.

We are now to take a melancholy leave for a time of

this brave but singularly unfortunate people, whose ardent patriotism, whose manly, honourable, and persevering struggles to rescue themselves from an oppressive tyranny, and to maintain the liberty and independence of their country—and the romantic heroism of whose chiefs cannot fail to have excited in the breast of every reader, with the deepest feelings of commiseration for their unmerited misfortunes, the liveliest sentiments of admiration of their noble and heroic conduct.

With such feelings and sentiments excited in us by the recital of the past events in MESSENIAN story—and with the intimation held out to us, beyond all hope, by our historian, that we shall, in process of time, renew our MESSENIAN acquaintance—I cannot resist the desire which I feel, before we take our present leave of them, to outrun the regular but tardy course and progression of time and history, and to indulge an impatient, and irregular, and, perhaps, an unpardonable curiosity, in regard to the future fortunes of this interesting people. I shall therefore exercise the privilege with which, as a being of the nineteenth century, I am invested, and venture, in defiance of all critical proprieties of time and circumstance, to overstep the " page prescribed"—the MESSENIAN "*present* state"—and take an insight into the " book of fate " (whose voluminous pages, in which are recorded the future events of MESSENIAN story, lay open before me), for the purpose of ascertaining by what singular and unexpected concatenation of circumstances and events, a people whose national existence appeared to have been blotted out for ever from the page of history—who would seem to have sunk under their last misfortunes never to rise again—should (after a lapse of several centuries) be restored, collectively, as a *people* to their original country—should there resume and connect their antient name and their national existence, and with them reassume their national independence, and no inconsiderable share of relative political consideration amongst the then existing republics of expiring GREECE.

Three hundred years after this extinction, for so long a period, of the national existence of MESSENIA in the PELOPONNESUS, the wasteful but transient invasion of LACONIA by *Epaminondas* was fatal at the time to the power of LACEDÆMON. The conquering THEBANS invited from all parts the relics of the MESSENIAN race to return to their former country, and to take their independent station once more amongst the people of GREECE. This long unfortunate race, although dispersed, and inhabiting RHEGIUM in ITALY, MESSENIA in SICILY, and AFRICA, now eagerly obeyed the call of the THEBANS to return to the country of their forefathers, the fairest acquisition of the HERACLIDÆ — the most desirable territory in PELOPONNESUS, or perhaps in all GREECE. *Epaminondas* was patron of the new city of MESSENIA, built at the foot of

Mount ITHOME, famous in the antient wars with LACEDÆ-
MON, on whose summit was raised the citadel. The returned MESSENIANS did not disdain an association with re-
belling HELOTS and other slaves, all or mostly of GRECIAN
origin, and many of MESSENIAN blood.

["*Unquestionably Cyprus was very early settled by
Greeks*," p. 251.]—The first GRECIAN settlement in CY-
PRUS would seem to have been that under *Agapenor*, king
of ARCADIA, who led the ARCADIANS to the siege of TROY.
On his return home he was driven by a tempest on the
coast of CYPRUS. He never revisited his native country, but
established a colony in the city of *Paphos* in that island,
and built in it a temple to the goddess *Venus*. *Pausan.*
lib. viii. c. 5.

["*Amongst the most southern, &c. is Thera, a colony from
Lacedæmon*," p. 251.]—The GRECIAN colony, in the island
of THERA, was settled by *Theras* the THEBAN, descended from
Œdipus, who was the maternal uncle and guardian of *Eurysthenes* and *Procles*, the two sons of *Aristodemus*, and, during
their minoritỹ, regent of LACEDÆMON. *Pausan.* lib. iv. c. 3.
When his regency terminated in consequence of his nephews

attaining their majority, he emigrated with a select body of Spartans from Lacedæmon, and established a colony in the little island of Calliste, which afterwards took the name of Thera, from its founder. *Pausan.* lib. iii. c. 1 ; lib. viii. c. 2 ; Herod. lib. iv. c. 147.

[" *Locri Epizephyrii,*" p. 253.]—We are informed by *Strabo* (lib. vi. p. 259) that this Locri-Crissean colony emigrated under the conduct of *Evanthes*, not long after the foundation of Crotona and Syracuse, which latter city was founded about the year b. c. 719. See *Newton's* Short Chronicle, p. 35.

[" *Sicily prior to Grecian colonization,*" p. 254.]—The Sicanians, after their defeat by the Siculi or Sicels, retired into the southern and western parts of the island, the latter of which, *Thucydides* informs us, they continued to inhabit in his time, lib. vi. c. 2.

The same author informs us that the passage of the Siculi from Italy into this island was nearly three hundred years earlier than the landing of any Grecian colony there.

Now the first GRECIAN colony, which was that from CHALCIS in EUBŒA, under the conduct of THUCLES, settled in SICILY and founded NAXUS in the year 720 B.C., according to Sir *Isaac Newton's* Chronology. That under *Archias* of CORINTH, by whom SYRACUSE was founded, and which was in the following year, being fixed by *Newton* in the year B.C. 719. Short Chron. p. 35.

Supposing, with our great philosopher (Chronol. p. 118), this invasion of SICILY by the SICULI to have taken place two hundred and eighty years before the earliest GRECIAN colonization in that island, which may correspond with the expression of *Thucydides* of nearly three hundred years, we should fix the date of this invasion in the year 1000 B.C., or ninety-six years before the date of the taking of Troy, which, according to the same chronology, was in the year before Christ 904. Short Chron. p. 29.

Thucydides observes that the SICULI continued to possess the midland and northerly parts of the island even in his days, lib. vi. c. 2.

The date of the TROJAN and PHOCIAN settlements is clearly defined by reference to that of the TROJAN war, and would therefore be about ninety-seven years after the invasion of the SICULI.

[*" Sicily, Grecian colonizations in that island,"* p.255.]—
The date in the margin, of the emigration of *Archias,* according to the *Newtonian* Chronology is evidently a mistake. *Newton* (Short Chron. p. 35) places this emigration in the year B. C. 719.

Although *Thucydides* ascribes the foundation of CATANA to *Thucles* and his CHALCIDIANS, yet he informs us that the CATANEANS themselves laid claim to *Evarchus* as their founder.

Lamis, according to *Thucydides,* planted his colony in a spot called TROTILUS, upon the river PANTACIAS. But, removing from thence to LEONTIUM, he formed an association with the CATANEANS for the protection of his colony; which, however, was of short duration. Being driven by the CATANEANS from LEONTIUM, he founded THAPSUS, and died. Upon his death his colony quitted THAPSUS, and under the conduct and protection of *Hyblon*, a SICILIAN king, they founded that settlement of MEGAREANS, which was denominated HYBLÆAN, of which they and their posterity continued in the possession for two hundred and forty-five years, when they were expelled from their city and territory by *Gelon*, the tyrant of SYRACUSE. About one hundred years after the settlement of the HYBLÆAN MEGARA, its population had so far increased as to enable it to send forth a colony.   It was led by *Pammilus*, (who had lately arrived from MEGARA, the parent city,) and who established the new settlement of SELINUS, lib. vi.

The *PE*LOPONNESIAN war ended in the year B. C. 405 ; and *Gelo* flourished about seventy-eight years before the end of the *PE*LOPONNESIAN war.   " Count backwards," says our great philosopher, whose chronology we follow, " the seventy-eight, and the two hundred and forty-five years, and about twelve years more for the reign of LAMIS in SICILY, and the reckoning will place the building of SYRACUSE about three hundred and thirty-five years before the end of the *PE*LO-PONNESIAN war, or in the 10th *Olympiad;* and about that time *Eusebius* and others place it; but it might be twenty or thirty years later, the antiquities of those days having been more or less raised by the GREEKS," p. 117.

Add to four hundred and five the three hundred and thirty-five years, and we shall fix the building of SYRACUSE in the year 740 B. C.   Twenty years later would bring it down to the year 720 B. C., which is within one year of that in which *Newton* has placed it in his Short Chronicle, p. 35, viz. 719 B. C.

Thucydides states that GELA was built " in the forty-fifth year after the foundation of SYRACUSE," which would answer to the year 675 B. C.

ACRAGAS, the Roman AGRIGENTUM, was built by a colony from GELA, whose civil institutions it adopted, one
hundred and eight years after the foundation of its parent
city, which answers to the year 567 B.C. *Thucydides,*
lib. vi.

We have seen (p. 236 of this volume) that ZANCLE was
originally founded by a band of pirates, who were afterwards
joined by a considerable reinforcement from CHALCIS and
other parts of EUBŒA; that it was attacked by the con-
federated forces of *Anaxilas,* king of RHEGIUM, and of the
unfortunate band of MESSENIANS, who, under *Gorgus* and
Manticlus, emigrated from PELOPONNESUS after the ruin of
their country, and was reduced to great extremities; and
that the humanity of the MESSENIANS led to an accomoda-
tion under which the ZANCLÆANS and themselves became
one people, the city and territory of ZANCLE relinquishing
its antient name, and assuming that of MESSENE, in honour
of its humane conquerors. This event took place in the
year B.C. 588.

HERNERA was a colony from ZANCLE, whose numbers
were increased by a numerous reinforcement of CHAL-
CIDIANS, and some exiles from SYRACUSE. *Thucyd.*
lib. vi.

ACRÆ, CASMENÆ, and CAMARINÆ, were all of them

colonies from SYRACUSE, and were respectively founded at the following periods, viz. ACRÆ, seventy years after the foundation of SYRACUSE, the year B. C. 649; CASMENÆ, twenty years after the foundation of ACRÆ, the year B. C. 629; CAMARINÆ, one hundred and thirty-five years after the foundation of SYRACUSE, the year B. C. 584.

Thucydides states that before these GRECIAN colonizations of SICILY, the PHŒNICIANS had settlements all round the coast of SICILY. But when the GRECIANS, in considerable numbers, began to cross over and fix their residence there, the PHŒNICIANS abandoned their other settlements, and, uniting together, seated themselves at MOTYA, SoLŒIS, and *P*ANORMUS, near to the ELYMI, secure of their own continuance in these quarters from their friendship with that people, and because, from this part of SICILY, the passage to CARTHAGE is exceedingly short, lib. vi. c. 2.

———————————

[" *The Epizephyrian Locrians, and their system of laws framed by Zaleucus,*" p. 256.]—*Zaleucus* was an ITALIAN, born at LOCRIS, of a noble family. He was a man of great learning, and held in high estimation by his countrymen, and was therefore chosen by them to be their lawgiver.

Diodorus Siculus informs us, that *Zaleucus* commenced his code of laws by enjoining, above all things, a firm and steadfast belief in the existence of the gods, from whom all that is good descends upon man, and by inculcating the adoration and worship of the SUPREME BEING with minds pure and unspotted; the gods being better pleased with the just and honest actions of righteous men, than with all their costly sacrifices.

Amongst his other precepts he enjoins that none should be implacable one against another, but that all should so temper and regulate their animosities, as to leave open a path to a speedy reconciliation, and to a full and cordial friendship with their adversaries, lib. xii. c. 20, 21.

These precepts are unquestionably admirable and excellent: they embrace the main and fundamental points of the doctrines inculcated by our own blessed religion—the love of GOD, and the love of man. " Thou shalt love the LORD thy GOD with all thy heart, and with all thy soul, and with all thy strength, and thou shalt love thy neighbour as thyself *."

* This, says our great philosopher, was the religion enjoined by *Moses* to the uncircumcised stranger within the gates of ISRAEL, as well as to the ISRAELITES; and this is the primitive religion both of JEWS and CHRISTIANS, and ought to be the standing religion of all nations, it being for the honour of GOD and good of mankind. Chron. p. 189.

But however wise the political institutions, however admirable and excellent the religious and moral precepts of the EPIZEPHYRIAN lawgiver, if we may credit *Polybius*, I fear we must infer that they had not that salutary influence on the conduct of the EPIZEPHYRIAN LOCRIANS, which the framer of them undoubtedly contemplated and expected.

This author informs us, that having often visited the LOCRIANS, and having performed for them some considerable services, they had always treated him with singular respect and honour, and that he should be therefore inclined rather to speak favourably of them than otherwise; yet he does not hesitate to declare that *Aristotle's* account of this colony is nearer the truth than that of *Timæus*. He is confirmed in this assertion by the admission of the LOCRIANS themselves. He then relates a story, on their own authority, which a common regard to their national honour and character should have led them rather to endeavour to conceal and to consign to oblivion, than to confirm and to promulgate, inasmuch as it displays a total want of every proper religious feeling as to the solemnity and sacred obligation of an oath, and a total absence of every moral and honourable feeling, which should equally govern and regulate the conduct of nations and of individuals in their transactions with each other.

When they first came into the country, says their tradition, they circulated the purport of a convention with the
Siculi in the following terms, viz. " that they would live
together as friends, and possess the country in common, as
long as they should tread upon this earth, and carry their
heads upon their shoulders." The Locrians, at the time
of taking this oath, had put some earth within the soles of
their shoes, and some heads of garlic, which appeared not
in sight, upon their shoulders; and having afterwards
shaken the earth out of their shoes, and thrown away the
heads of garlic, they seized the first favourable opportunity,
and in a short time drove the Siculi out of the country.

Among other singular customs of the Epizephyrian
Locrians, *Polybius* relates, that all nobility of ancestry
amongst them is derived from women, and not from men,
lib. xii.

In justice to the Locrians, or rather to the laws and
institutions of *Zaleucus*, it should be kept in mind that
the above dishonourable transaction with the Siculi took
place before the promulgation of the laws of *Zaleucus*. At
the same time it must be inferred, from the expression of
Polybius, that the conduct of the Locrians was such, that
he could not be justified in speaking of them in favourable
terms.

Strabo has so just an observation in regard to legislation, that I cannot dismiss the subject of this article without inserting it.

Those cannot be said to be governed by a good system of laws, he observes, who would seek by minute, and multiplied acts of legislation, to prevent every occasion of offence or scandal, but rather those who, having laws simply and plainly written, religiously, and with every care, endeavour to preserve them, and to ensure their due observance, lib. vi. p. 260. Nor less just is the observation of *Plato*, quoted by *Strabo*, that the existence of a multitude of laws is a certain indication of bad morals, depraved habits, and litigious dispositions in a people, as a multitude of physicians indicates an extraordinary prevalence of disease.

It were to be wished that our BRITISH legislators would keep in mind, and observe as a rule of conduct, these wise and wholesome maxims of the sages of antiquity.

————

[" *The interval between the death of Codrus and that of Alcmæon, the thirteenth and last archon*," p. 259.] — It appears to me that, in allowing an interval of only one

Q

hundred and fifty-seven years between the death of *Codrus*
(B.C. 804) and that of *Alcmæon*, which Sir *Isaac Newton*
places in the year B.C. 647, our great philosopher is not
consistent with himself (see Short Chron. p. 34 and 37);
for if we divide one hundred and fifty-seven years between
thirteen *archons*, we shall have only TWELVE years for the
administration of each. Now in his Chronology, p. 127,
after enumerating the kings of ATHENS from *Theseus* to
Codrus, he goes on to say, " there reigned *twelve* (this is
a mistake, it should have been *thirteen*) *archons* for life,
which at FOURTEEN or FIFTEEN years apiece, the state
being unstable, might take up about one hundred and
seventy-four years," which is the exact mean between fourteen and fifteen years multiplied by twelve.

Now supposing each *archon* to have reigned fourteen
years and a half, which is the mean of Sir *Isaac Newton's*
allowed duration of the reign of each, the interval should
have been one hundred and eighty-eight years and a half
between the death of *Codrus* and that of *Alcmæon*, instead
of one hundred and fifty-seven.

[" *Cylon's attempt to acquire the sovereignty of Athens*,"
p. 260.]—Many a wiser man than *Cylon* might have been

deceived and misled by the response of the oracle. · It was by no means dubious as to the main object which *Cylon* had in view. As to that, it was clear, distinct, and positive. It was dubious only as to season, or occasion of action. *Cylon* was directed by the DELPHIC deity " to seize the citadel of ATHENS upon the greatest festival of *Jupiter*." *Cylon* interpreted the meaning of the oracle as applicable to the OLYMPIC festival of *Jupiter* in PELOPONNESUS, imagining that to be the greatest festival of *Jupiter*, and to bear a particular relation to himself as a victor, which he had been at the OLYMPIC games. *Thucyd.* lib. i. c. 126.

This author observes, that whether the greatest festival meant was to be held in ATTICA, or any other place, neither *Cylon* had considered, nor had the oracle declared; and that there was a festival of *Jove*, observed by the ATHENIANS, which was called " the greatest festival of *Jupiter* the propitious."

Thucydides and *Herodotus* differ in their relation of this transaction. The former tells us, that " *Cylon* and his brother privately made their escape ;" whereas it must be inferred from the relation of *Herodotus*, that *Cylon*, as well as his companions, was traitorously put to death. When disappointed in their hopes of success, *Cylon* " with his companions placed themselves," says *Herodotus*, " before

Q 2

the shrine of *Minerva* as suppliants." " They were persuaded to leave their sanctuary, under a promise that
their lives should not be forfeited." Their being soon
afterwards put to death was generally imputed to the
Alcmæonidæ." Such is the account given by *Herodotus* of
this transaction.

Thucydides does not assert that the followers of *Cylon*
quitted the altars under any promise of personal security.
He says, that some of them had already perished by
famine, and the rest sat themselves down as suppliants by
the altar in the citadel; that the ATHENIAN guard having
ordered them to arise, as they saw them just ready to
expire in the temple, to avoid the guilt of profanation,
led them out and slew them. Some of the number, who
had seated themselves at the very altars of the venerable
goddess, they murdered in the act of removal. For this
action, says this author, not only the persons concerned in
it, but their descendants also, were called " the sacrilegious, and the accursed of the goddess."

Plutarch's relation of this transaction, in his life of *Solon,*
is still somewhat different from either of the preceding.

Megacles the archon, says he, persuaded the conspira-
tors, who had taken sanctuary in *Minerva's* temple, to quit
their sanctuary and abide a trial; but when they had tied

a thread to the image of the goddess, and kept hold of one end of it in token of their being still under sanctuary, just as they came down by the temple of the Furies the thread happened to break, upon which *Megacles* and his followers rushed upon and seized them, as if the goddess had withdrawn from them her protection. As many as were without the temple were stoned; those who fled to the altars for sanctuary were murdered there; and only those escaped who made their application to the wives of the magistrates. From that time, says *Plutarch*, these magistrates were called " *execrable,*" and held in great detestation.

It may be proper here to observe with regard to the variances above noticed between the relations of these three authors, that in all ATHENIAN affairs more especially, the authority of *Thucydides* would seem to be preferable to that of the other two. It is due in justice, however, to *Herodotus*, to refer to Mr. *Mitford's* note, in p. 302 of this volume, wherein he bears testimony to the general accuracy of that author in regard to the domestic politics of ATHENS, and his coincidence with *Thucydides*.

The transaction which has been thus described by these three authors, was denominated " the pollution of the goddess;" and we shall see hereafter that the LACEDÆMO-NIANS, previously to the commencement of the PELOPON-NESIAN war, required of the ATHENIANS, by their ambassadors, that they should " drive away the pollution of the goddess," by which was meant that they should expel from ATHENS the descendants of those who were concerned in the transaction. For we are informed by *Thucydides*, that although the ATHENIANS banished these sacrilegious persons out of the city—that although *Cleomenes*, the LACEDÆ-MONIAN, drove them out again when he was at ATHENS, and even dug up the bones of the dead, and cast them out—yet, in process of time they returned, and some of their posterity were still in ATHENS in his time. In making this requisition of the ATHENIANS, says the same author, the LACEDÆMONIANS aimed indirectly at *Pericles*, who was maternally descended from the ALCMÆONIDÆ.

It appears from *Pausanias* that a statue of brass was erected to *Cylon;* and he is perplexed to find a reason for it. He conjectures, however, that it arose from the beauty of his person, and a reputation by no means obscure ; for he was victor in the second course at the OLYMPIC Games, lib. i. c. 28.

["*Amongst those families, the Alcmæonid, &c.*" p. 260.]—We have seen that the *first Alcmæon,* from whom, in all probability, this antient family derived its denomination, was the great grandson of the venerable *Nestor*.

NESTOR
|
Thrasymedes
|
Syllus
|
Alcmæon.

(*Pausan.* lib. ii. c. 18).

[" *The Athenians recovered the island with little loss,*"
p. 263.]—The relation given by *Plutarch* (in Vit. Solon.)
of the manner in which *Salamis* was taken should satisfy us
that nothing certain was known upon the subject. *Pausanias* states that the people of MEGARA asserted that
certain exiles, whom they called DORYCLEII, mixing with
the inhabitants of SALAMIS, betrayed the island to the
ATHENIANS, lib. i. c. 40.

[" *The republic was unable to compel them,*" p. 263.]—
It would seem from *Plutarch* that a special tribunal, consisting of three hundred persons chosen from amongst the
chief men of the city, was appointed for this occasion.

[" *Epimenides, &c.*"]—*Plutarch* says of him that he was
accounted the seventh wise man by those who would not
admit *Periander* into the number.

[" *Each seems to have been born for his own age and country,*" p. 268.]—*Plutarch* adverts to the different circumstances in which the SPARTAN and the ATHENIAN lawgivers were placed, as vesting in the *one* a greater power and ability to effect the objects which he had in view than in the other. *Lycurgus*—from his illustrious descent—from his having been himself, though for a short period, the reigning sovereign of LACEDÆMON, and afterwards guardian of his nephew and successor—had acquired reputation, power and friends, and a great personal influence, which he could use in modelling the state. *Solon*, on the other hand, was only a common member of the state and of moderate fortune, and had nothing but his own prudence and the good opinion of his fellow-subjects to rely on. (In Vit. Solon.)

[" *Taking from the creditor all power over the persons of the debtor,*" p. 268.]—*Plutarch* says, that in making this regulation the lawgiver pleased neither party. For he disobliged the *rich* in cancelling their bonds, and the *poor* still more in not making a division of land as they expected, and in not making all equal in estate after the example of *Lycurgus*. (In Vit. Solon.) He goes on, however, to observe, that being in a little time sensible of the advantages which they derived from this regulation,

they desisted from their complaints, and joined in the
public sacrifice mentioned by our historian. Id. ib.

[" *Solon not contented with giving his country a constitution, &c.*" p. 285.]—In answer to an inquiry which was
afterwards made of *Solon*, " whether he had left to the
ATHENIANS the best laws that could be given;" he is reported by *Plutarch* to have replied, " I have established
the best that they were *capable* of receiving." In Vit.
Solon.

[" *The character of* Herodotus *as an historian,*" p. 293.]
—I do not dissent from the character which Mr. *Mitford*
has here given us of *Herodotus* as an historian ; and,
generally speaking, I believe him to be as free from prejudices as most historians. But I cannot help thinking
that, from some cause or other with which we are unacquainted, his mind had imbibed a prejudice against the
family and government of the *Pisistratidæ,* and a strong
bias of an opposite description in favour of the *Alcmæonidæ.*

In describing the government of the *Pisistratidæ,* he
speaks of it not as a tyranny merely, according to the

R

GREEK signification of the term, (by which he might have meant nothing opprobrious, but simply the government of one person,) but as a tyranny, according to its modern acceptation; that is, as a government of oppression, by which the ATHENIANS were kept under a grievous restraint and subjection, which paralyzed all their energies, and rendered them incapable of any spirited exertions as a nation.

The general tenor of his expressions in regard to the government of the *Pisistratidæ* is often contradicted by the facts which he himself relates.

The following extracts from this author will shew the grounds upon which I have formed this opinion, and whether it be well founded or not :—

1st. He first introduces the family of the *Pisistratidæ* to our notice by telling us, that " *Crœsus* had received information that ATHENs suffered much from the oppression of *Pisistratus,* the son of *Hippocrates,* who at this time possessed the supreme authority." But after describing the artifice by which he obtained the supreme power, Her*odotus* informs us in the very same chapter that " he neither changed the magistrates or altered the laws; he suffered every thing to be conducted in its ordinary course, and his government was alike honourable to himself, and useful to the city" (lib. i. c. 59; see also p. 289 of this volume). Such an account of the administration of *Pisis. tratus* is utterly inconsistent with the idea of the sufferings of ATHENS from an oppressive government.

2d. When *Pisistratus,* after his second expulsion, re. turned with an armed force to recover his influence at ATHENS, he encamped in the vicinity of MARATHON. " He was soon visited," says *Herodotus,* " by a great number of factious citizens from ATHENS, and by all those who pre. ferred tyranny to freedom."

Mr. *Mitford* considers this last expression as unintelli. gible, unless we put upon it the forced acceptation which he suggests in p. 294. Now it is perfectly intelligible if we consider it with reference to the prejudice which I have supposed to exist in the mind of *Herodotus* against the family and government of the *Pisistratidæ*, and is quite consistent with that prejudice. The expression is used by *Herodotus* ironically and contemptuously of those who could prefer a real tyranny, that is, slavery and oppression, to freedom. It is worthy of observation, as confirmatory of my supposition, that *Herodotus* terms those friends and partizans of *Pisistratus,* who remained in ATHENS, and who flocked to his standard at MARATHON, " *factious citizens,*" lib. i. c. 62. And that striking act of humanity, which our historian, Mr. *Mitford,* justly considers as " the more ad-

mirable, as it was then uncommon," by which *Pisistratus*
stopped the slaughter of the flying votaries of freedom (as
Herodotus would probably have termed them), and ordered
his sons to overtake them, to remove their apprehensions, to
assure them of personal safety, and to desire them to pursue
their usual employments. This distinguished act of humanity *Herodotus* chooses to consider and to designate as
a mere *sagacious stratagem* of war. He will allow no
praise to *Pisistratus*, his family, or his government, unless
it is extorted from him, Herodot. lib. i. c. 62, 63 ; see also
p. 294 and 295 of this volume as to the conduct of *Pisistratus* after his resumption of the supreme authority, which
Mr. *Mitford* observes was *singularly mild*, if compared
with what we shall hereafter find " usual in revolutions of
GRECIAN cities." Compare it, especially, with the conduct
of the head of the *Alcmæonid* faction, after the expulsion
of the family of *Pisistratus*.

3d. " The *Alcmæonidæ*,' says Herodotus, " had been
driven from their country by the *Pisistratidæ*." He describes their attempt to recover their former situations in
ATHENS, as " an effort to deliver their country from its
oppressors," lib. v. c. 62.

4th. Speaking of the death of *Hipparchus*, he says,
that for four years after his death, the ATHENIANS suffered
greater *oppression* than before. This expression necessarily

implies that the ATHENIANS suffered *oppression* under the preceding administration of the *Pisistratidæ,* although not in so great a degree as after the death of H*ipparchus,* lib. v. c. 55.

5th. After relating the final expulsion of H*ippias* and the *Pisistratidæ* from ATHENS, he observes that " the ATHENIANS were thus delivered from *oppression,*" and he proceeds to commemorate the prosperous or calamitous events which they experienced after " they had thus re-covered their liberties." " ATHENS," says he, " was con-siderable before, but its liberty being restored, it became greater than ever" (lib. v. c. 65, 66); for the word " *liberty,*" we might probably more properly read " *factious,*" which immediately revived, when the administration of the *Pi-sistratidæ* ceased.   That of the *Alcmæonidæ* succeeded to the supreme authority; and from H*erodotus's* own ac-count we may infer that *Clisthenes,* the head of that party, was not less the tyrant of ATHENS than *Pisistratus* had been.   There is a striking contrast between the conduct of these two persons under circumstances not very dissimilar. We have adverted, in a former part of this article, to the humane and " *admirable*" conduct of *Pisistratus* upon the occasion of his return to ATHENS after his second expulsion. Let us see what was the conduct of CLISTHENES upon the occasion of his triumph over the faction of *Isagoras.*   The ATHENIANS who had joined the party of the latter were put

in irons, and condemned to die; and amongst them was
Timesitheus of DELPHI, of whose gallantry and spirit, *Herodotus* says, he was able to produce many testimonies.
These ATHENIANS were put to death in prison. H*er*od.
lib. v. c. 72, and p. 303 of this volume.

6th. After relating the retreat of the army of LACE-
DÆMON under *Cleomenes,* and the defeat of the BŒOTIAN
and CHALCIDIAN forces, H*er*odotus observes, that " the
ATHENIANS continued to increase in numbers and importance.   Not from their example alone, but from various
instances, it may be made to appear that an equal form of
government is the best.   While the ATHENIANS were in
subjection to *tyrants* they were superior in war to none of
their neighbours, but when delivered from their *oppressors*
they far surpassed them all; from whence it is evident,"
says he, " that whilst under the restraint of a master they
were incapable of any spirited exertions, but as soon as
they obtained their liberty, each man zealously exercised
his talents on his own account," lib. v. c. 78.

Of the individuals thus stigmatized by Her*od*otus with
the appellation of *tyrants*—(in the most opprobrious sense
of the word), of oppressors, the *first* (*Pisistratus*) was by
every account " a man singularly formed for empire," of
whom *Solon* is reported to have said, that, saving his ambition, " there was not a man more naturally disposed to

every virtue, nor a better citizen;" a man, " the excellence
of whose character, and whose unblamable conduct in the
administration of the affairs of ATHENS, is established by
the concurrent testimony of all antiquity;" " whose mild-
ness, patience, and forbearance were not less remarkable
than his ability, activity, and intrepidity;" "whose kind-
ness to the poor and distressed was not a dissembled
virtue, assumed for the advancement of his ambitious views,
but was conspicuous; and who, after having, during life,
directed the administration of ATHENS with great wisdom,
and with the esteem of all men, died, at an advanced age,
in peace." Of the *second* (*Hippias*) we are informed, on
the authority of *Thucydides*, that he was courteous and
affable to all men; that under him the administration was
still conducted according to the established laws. The
power which he and his brother *Hipparchus* possessed,
appears to have been exercised very beneficially for the
public (until the assassination of the latter), and without
severity towards their opponents; he was laudably active in
public business, he improved the public revenue, and he
prosecuted the improvements in the city which his father
Pisistratus had commenced. Of the *third* (*Hipparchus*)
we are told, on no less authority than that of *Plato*, that
his character was one of the most perfect in history. Such
were his virtues, his abilities, and his diligence, that this
great philosopher does not hesitate to assimilate the period
of his administration, jointly with his brother *Hippias*, to

that of another *golden age.* He was the friend of learning
and learned men. *Thucydides* says of H*ipp*ar*chus,* that the
power which he had was never exerted so as to draw upon
him the popular hatred, and his deportment was neither
invidious nor distasteful (lib. vi. c. 54). Of the three collectively, as a dynasty (if we may be allowed the expression)
of persons holding the sovereign rule in a state, we are
told, on the same high authority, that they " singularly cultivated wisdom and virtue." They did not oppress the
people over whom they ruled with a heavy, rigorous taxa-
tion; on the contrary, they exacted only a twentieth part
of their revenue; they beautified and adorned the city;
they made no fundamental changes in the constitution of
the state, but made the laws existing before their assumption of the government the rule of their conduct. They
gave the most ample encouragement to learning and learned
men of every description, so that the rise of ATTIC taste in
every branch of the arts and sciences is referred to the period of their administration ; and, in short, throughout the
whole period of it, the affairs of the commonwealth were
conducted, in peace and in war, " happily at home, and
honourably abroad." *Plutarch,* in Vit. Sol.; *Plato ; Thucydides,* lib. vi. c. 54, *et seq.;* and this vol. p. 287—299.

Such were the persons whom H*er*o*dotus* invariably (but
with what justice the reader must decide) styles the
tyrants—the *oppressors* of their country.

The reader must decide whether there are not sufficient grounds to justify the charge which I have brought against *Herodotus* of entertaining a prejudice against this illustrious family, and whether he has not unfairly imputed to their administration and government a character which it does not merit.

The wise, firm, and able conduct of the *Pisistratidæ* in the administration of the government of their country secured for it respect, and, with it, peace from abroad;— it repressed turbulence and faction, and by those means secured for it internal peace, and prosperity at home. The increased energies and spirit of enterprise which the ATHENIANS displayed, the superiority over their neighbours in war, to which they attained after the disastrous fate of this family, are ascribed by *Herodotus* to their deliverance from its *tyranny* and *oppressions*, and from the restraints which it imposed upon them. It is not always in our power satisfactorily to trace the immediate causes which may give rise to, and lead the march of an intelligent, high-spirited, and ambitious people (which we so often meet with in the history of the world) towards the attainment of increased national power and importance. But I should be disposed to assign the domestic factions which followed the expulsion of the *Pisistratidæ,* and which led to foreign quarrels, as the immediate causes of *this march* of the ATHENIANS to which *Herodotus* alludes.

Whether the ATHENIANS really gained either national prosperity or individual happiness by the expulsion of the *Pisistratidæ* is much to be doubted. If the government had continued in that family, and had been administered with as much wisdom and ability as characterized the administration of it by *Pisistratus* and his two sons, they might not have been crowned with the immortal glories of MARATHON and SALAMIS, but they might have avoided the disgrace and ruin which followed the fatal day at ÆGOS-POTAMOS. Their history might have been less brilliant and less interesting; but they might have enjoyed a greater share of true and solid prosperity as a nation, and of real and substantial happiness as a people.

The proofs which I shall adduce in support of my position that *Herodotus* was partial to the family of the *Alcmæonidæ* are the following, viz.—

1st. Speaking of the contract which the *Alcmæonidæ*, while in exile, entered into with the AMPHICTYONS, to construct a new temple at DELPHI, he says, that they were not deficient in point of wealth, and, " warmed with the generous spirit of their race," they erected a temple far exceeding the model which had been given in splendour and in beauty. They built of PARIAN marble the vestibule, which, by the terms of their contract, they might have constructed of PORINE *stone*. But we find from the relation of *Herodotus* himself, that instead of this "generous spirit," which he so much extols, they were actuated in what they did by the most interested motives. To excite the LACEDÆMONIANS to make war upon their country, and by those means to effect their restoration, they bribed the PYTHIAN to propose to every SPARTAN who should consult her, in a private or public capacity, the deliverance of ATHENS. The exertion of this "*generous spirit*" was no doubt a part of the bribe to the *Pythoness* to induce her to violate her sacred duties. Herod. lib. v. c. 72, 73. This mean and dishonourable act of the *Alcmæonidæ*, he seems, in another place, to applaud rather than condemn, as having been the cause of the liberation of ATHENS from the tyranny of the *Pisistratidæ*, lib. vi. c. 123.

2d. The murder of the followers of *Cylon*, by the *Alcmæonid* party, *Herodotus* states, as if it were not a well known and authenticated fact. It " was generally imputed to the *Alcmæonidæ*," says he.

3d. He mentions a rumour, merely for the purpose of discrediting it, that the *Alcmæonidæ* acted the part of traitors at the battle of MARATHON, and held up a shield by way of a signal to the PERSIANS. He speaks in terms of extravagant praise of one *Callias* of this family, whose

principal merit in the eyes of our author seems to be " his
hatred against all tyrants ;" but more especially his having
been " ever distinguished by his implacable animosity
against *Pisistratus*." He thus eulogizes the whole family
for being, as well as *Callias,* remarkable for their enmity
to tyrants. He had forgotten that *Clisthenes,* the son of
Megacles, and the head of the family, was, on his own
shewing, as great a tyrant as *Pisistratus.* "While a system
of tyranny prevailed in their country," says our author,
" they lived in voluntary exile." Here he is inconsistent
with himself; that their exile was an involuntary one, he
has himself, in another part of his history, assured us. For
in book v. c. 62, he says, "they had, in conjunction with
some other exiles, made an effort to recover their former
situations, and to deliver their country from its oppressors,
but were defeated with considerable loss. They retired to
LIPSYDINOM, beyond PÆONIA, which they fortified, still
meditating vengeance against the *Pisistratidæ*." " And it
was by their contrivance" (a base and dishonourable one it
was) "that the *Pisistratidæ* resigned their power." He
considers them as having more assisted the cause of freedom
than either *Harmodius* or *Aristogeiton.* " They were
avowedly," says he, " the deliverers of ATHENS. The
Alcmæonidæ were always amongst the most distinguished
characters of ATHENS ; but *Alcmæon* himself, and *Megacles,*
his immediate descendant," (mark! the latter was the rival

and political opponent of *Pisistratus*,) " were more partieu-
larly illustrious."

It seems to me that these proofs very sufficiently establish
the truth of both the aforegoing propositions, viz.—

1st. That H*erodotus* had imbibed a prejudice against
the family and government of *Pisistratus*, which led him,
at the expense of justice—at the expense of truth,—in
opposition to the concurrent testimony of all antiquity—in
opposition to the evidence of facts which he himself relates—to brand the illustrious individuals who composed
this family with the name, and to impute to them the
character of *tyrants*, in the modern opprobrious sense of
that term ; and to brand their wise, able, mild, and pater-
nal administration with the odious name, and to impute to
it the disgraceful and unjust character of a harsh, severe,
and *oppressive tyranny*. His " ardour in the cause of
liberty" may have perverted his sense of justice, distorted
his views of the truth, blinded his reason, and impelled him
to follow and prefer the name and shadow of freedom to
its substance.   Under the administration of the *Pisistratidæ*, the ATHENIANS enjoyed a well-regulated and rational
freedom, as much probably as it is good for man in a state
of society to possess.   The boasted freedom of ATHENS,
after the extinction of this family of tyrants, was the most

grievous and intolerable of all tyrannies—the tyranny of a turbulent and unruly democracy.

2d. That *Herodotus* had a strong bias of an opposite description in favour of the *Alcmæonidæ*.

The forced and extravagant encomiums which he heaps upon this family, are as little justified by the facts which he himself relates of them, as the opprobrious epithets which he applies to the family and government of *Pisistratus*.

———————

[" *Hipparchus*," p. 298.]—It cannot but excite in us sensations of deep regret, when we find such a man as *Hipparchus* (whom the " godlike *Plato*" has handed down to us as one of the most perfect characters in history) recorded, by an eminent historian, as the slave of a detestable vice, forbidden by the laws of nature, and therefore directly contrary to the dictates of reason ; and when we find such a man as *Thucydides*, speaking of it in no other terms than as if it had really been one of those venial and pardonable weaknesses and infirmities of our imperfect natures, from which we are none of us exempt, and which we are therefore apt to consider rather as necessary incidents to our imperfect and unfortunate condition, instead of its being characterized in its true colours, as a crime of the deepest die and of the foulest and blackest complexion.

[" *Defeat of Anchimolius*," p. 300.]—It does not appear that the ATHENIANS were themselves engaged in this action. *Anchimolius*, who came by sea, was driven by stress of weather to PHALERUS, where he disembarked his little army. The ATHENIANS were then in alliance with the THESSALIANS, who at their request sent a body of one thousand horse to their assistance. The ATHENIANS levelled the country about PHALERUS, by which the cavalry would be enabled to act with more effect, and sent them against the SPARTANS. H*erod.* lib. v. c. 63.

The THESSALIANS were not so successful in an attack which they made upon *Cleomenes* on his first entrance into ATTICA. They were defeated with the loss of forty men ; upon which they made no further efforts, but abandoned their allies, and retired into THESSALY. Id. c. 64.

[" *Cleomenes*," p. 300.]—He was the son of *Anaxandrides*, of the race of the *Agidæ*, and was the fifteenth in descent from *Eurysthenes*. The circumstances of his family and his birth are rather singular. His father, *Anaxandrides*, had been for some years married, but his wife had not produced him any children. The *Ephori*, anxious that the race of *Eurysthenes* should not become extinct, called upon him to repudiate his barren wife, and to marry another. Fondly attached to his wife, who, saving her infirmity of barrenness, was " in all other respects," says *Pausanias*, " the best of women," he refused to comply with their request. Having consulted with the senate, they, having regard to his conjugal affection, retracted their requisition for the repudiation of his wife, but urged him in the strongest terms to marry another, by whom he might have offspring. To this proposition *Anaxandrides* assented, and married a second wife, by whom he had *Cleomenes*. " He *alone* of all the LACEDÆMONIANS," says *Pausanias*, " had two wives at the same time, and in consequence of this a twofold progeny " (lib. iii. c. 3); for about the same time his former wife, after so many years of barrenness, proved also with child, and not long after the birth of *Cleomenes* produced a son who was named *Dorieus*. She had afterwards two other sons—*Leonidas*, who *lost* his *life*, and *gained* immortal *fame* at the straits of THERMOPYLÆ, and *Cleombrotus*. The second wife of *Anaxandrides* had no other child but *Cleomenes*.

On the death of *Anaxandrides*, the LACEDÆMONIANS conceived themselves bound by the laws and customs of their country to prefer *Cleomenes*, as the first born, who in consequence succeeded to the vacant throne; but, according to *Pausanias,* this preference was given with great reluctance, *Dorieus* being distinguished by his accomplishments, and very much superior to *Cleomenes* * in those qualifications which fit a man alike to shine in the council and in the field.

The lot of *Dorieus* seems to have been peculiarly hard. Despoiled, as it were, of his birthright, by a marriage unsanctioned by the usages of his country, he had the mortification to see the offspring of that, to him injurious, marriage ascend a throne, which but for the precipitancy of the *Ephori* and the senate of SPARTA, and its consequences, would have been his inheritance. His proud and independent spirit could not brook the mortification of remaining in a subordinate station in that country, of which, in all probability, he deemed himself the rightful sovereign, and his brother an usurper : he determined therefore to abandon his native country. With a number of his countrymen who chose to follow his fortunes, he sailed for LYBIA, and settled his colony there in a delightful situation

* From the manner in which *Herodotus* contrasts the qualifications of *Cleomenes* and *Dorieus,* it might almost be inferred that the former had a tendency to insanity, *even at the time* of his *accession* to the *sovereignty.* " Of *Cleomenes,*" says he, " it is reported that he had not the proper use of his faculties, but was insane; *Dorieus,* on the contrary," &c. &c. It is universally agreed that *Cleomenes* killed himself in a fit of insanity (see p. 358 of this volume). The precipitancy and hasty passion which marked the conduct of *Cleomenes,* might seem to justify this inference.

T

on the banks of a beautiful river; but in the third year of
his residence he was expelled from thence, and returned
to PELOPONNESUS. From thence, under an approving
response from the oracle at DELPHI, he went to found a
colony in SICILY. *Herodotus* furnishes us with two accounts
of the future fortunes of *Dorieus*, both of which are very
confused, but they both agree in the circumstance of his
death; and concludes with this remark, " that if he could
have submitted to the authority of his brother *Cleomenes*,
and had remained at LACEDÆMON, he would have succeeded to the throne of SPARTA."

[" *Hippias retired to Sigeium*," p. 300.]—*Pisistratus*
assumed the chief power in ATHENS, according to Sir
Isaac Newton's Chronology in the year B. C. 550. This
family, therefore, would have enjoyed the supreme authority
about forty years. According to Her*odotus* only thirty-
six. Of the three sons of *Pisistratus* — *Hippias*, *Hipparchus*, and *Thessalus* — *Hippias* alone had sons. *Thucydides* informs us, that the column which was erected in the
citadel of ATHENS, to commemorate the abolition of the
tyranny, and " for a perpetual brand of the injustice of the
tyrants," enumerated five sons of *Hippias*, by *Myrrhine*, the
daughter of *Callias*, and that one of them, *Pisistratus*, had
enjoyed the annual office of *archon* at ATHENS; and in his
archonship, he dedicated the altar of the twelve gods in the
public forum, and that of *Apollo* in the temple of the
Pythian.

SIGEIUM, the place of *Hippias's* retirement, had been taken by force by his father, *Pisistratus*, from the people of MITYLENE, in the island of LESBOS. *Pisistratus* appointed his natural son, *Hegesistratus*, governor of the place, who had much difficulty in retaining his situation. SIGEIUM was the occasion of frequent and long hostilities between the people of MITYLENE and ATHENS. In one of these encounters, the LESBIAN poet, *Alcæus*, disgraced himself by running away from the field of battle. These disputes were at last settled by the arbitration of *Periander*, the son of *Cypselus*, and SIGEIUM devolved from thenceforth to the ATHENIANS.

[" *Isagoras*," p. 301.]—Herodotus informs us that *Isagoras*, the son of *Tisander*, was certainly of illustrious descent, but that his particular ancestry he was unable to specify. The same author insinuates that an improper connexion subsisted between the wife of *Isagoras* and *Cleomenes*, which circumstance may possibly have added weight to the political or other motives which induced *Cleomenes* to enter with such alacrity, as he appears to have done, into the interests of *Isagoras*.

[" *Banished seven hundred families*," p. 302.]—" As polluted," says Herodotus. *Thucydides* says, " that *Cleomenes*

T 2

not only drove away the living (ALCMÆONIDS), but even dug up the bones of the dead, and cast them out."

[" *The ambassadors consented to those humiliating terms.*"]—For which, however, says Herodotus, " they were severely reprimanded on their return."

[" *Demaratus, king of Sparta, retreated with them,*" p. 341.]—This dissension between their princes gave rise (as Herodotus informs us) to a law of SPARTA, by which *both* their kings were forbidden to march with their armies at the same time, lib. v. c. 75.

[" *The ransom of the prisoners,*" p. 341.]—Whom they at first kept in irons and close confinement. Herod. lib. v. c. 77.

[" *Six guineas a-head,*" p. 341.]—After this ransom the chains were suspended on the walls of the citadel, and were remaining there in the time of Herodotus. The ATHE-NIANS consecrated one-tenth of the money produced by the ransom, and with it purchased a chariot of brass, which was placed at the entrance of the citadel with an appropriate inscription. It was still there in the time of *Pausanias*. From this period "the ATHENIANS," says Hero*dotus*, "con. tinued to increase in numbers and importance."

[" *The barren island of Ægina*," p. 341.]—The original name of ÆGINA was ŒNONE. For the fable as to the change of name, and the first peopling of this island, see *Pausanias*. The same author informs us, that of all the GRECIAN islands ÆGINA is the most difficult of access by sea, being surrounded on all sides by latent rocks, and dangerous prominences.

The old causes of enmity subsisting between ÆGINA and ATHENS, to which our historian refers, are thus related by Hero*dotus* :—*Epidaurus* being afflicted with a severe famine, consulted the DELPHIC oracle, which enjoined them to erect statues, made of the wood of the garden olive, to *Damia* and *Auxesia* (who were the same as *Ceres* and *Proserpine*). The EPIDAURIANS applied in consequence to the ATHENIANS for permission to take one of their olives, which were esteemed the most sacred, for this object. The request was granted on condition that the EPIDAURIANS should furnish an annual sacrifice to *Minerva Pobias*, and to *Erectheus*. The statues were accordingly made of the sacred olive; the lands of the EPIDAURIANS, says Hero*dotus*, became immediately fruitful, and they punctually fulfilled their engagements with the ATHENIANS.

The ÆGINETÆ made use of the naval superiority which they in process of time acquired, to plunder their former masters, the EPIDAURIANS, and, amongst other things, carried away the statues of *Damia* and *Auxesia,* which they placed in the centre of their own territories, and instituted sacrifices and ceremonies in honour of them.

With the loss of these sacred images, the EPIDAURIANS ceased to observe their engagements with the ATHENIANS, alleging that their obligations with the latter had in consequence become void, and had been transferred from them to the ÆGINETÆ. The ATHENIANS appear to have acquiesced in the reasons alleged by the EPIDAURIANS, and demanded the images of the ÆGINETÆ, who refused to restore them, denying that the ATHENIANS had any business with them. The ATHENIANS attempted hostility to possess themselves of them. Her*odotus* tells us a marvellous story (which he admits to be incredible) of this attempt. But the result seems clear. The ATHENIANS completely failed in this, with the loss of the whole of the town employed in it.

Strabo informs us, that this island was peopled by AR-GIVES, CRETANS, EPIDAURIANS, and DORIANS; and that money was first coined here by *Pheidon*, for the purposes of commerce.

Pausanias adopted the story related by *Herodotus*, as to the old causes of enmity between the ÆGINETÆ and the ATHENIANS, and informs us, that he had seen the images of *Auxesia* and *Damia*, and had himself sacrificed to them.

CÆTERA DESUNT.

London: Printed by WILLIAM CLOWES, 14, Charing Cross.

Lightning Source UK Ltd.
Milton Keynes UK
UKHW052036191218
334261UK00017B/838/P